Daniel A. Helminiak, PhD, PhD, L

Sex and the Sac___
Gay Identity
and Spiritual Growth

Pre-publication
REVIEWS,
COMMENTARIES,
EVALUATIONS . . .

"In engaging, easy-to-read prose, Helminiak addresses the central work of spirituality today: to tease out the rich meaning behind religious myths and doctrines so that they make sense to the lesbians and gay men who have been so influential in creating religion yet are so victimized by it. As theologian, Scripture scholar, psychologist, and gay spiritual apologist, Helminiak shows that spiritual commitment is not at all inimical to modern LGBTI consciousness. The essays on heaven as everlasting orgasm and on the homosexual modeling of relations within the Blessed Trinity are delightfully provocative and downright queerly brilliant."

Toby Johnson
Author, *Gay Perspective:*
Things Our Homosexuality Tells Us
About the Nature of God and the Universe
and numerous other books;
Former Editor, *White Crane:*
A Journal of Gay Men's Spirituality

"In his study on the Bible, Helminiak diffused 'the holy texts of terror' used to condemn homosexuality. Now in *Sex and the Sacred,* he presents an equally illuminating study of the queer spiritual experience. Indeed, this book should serve as a beacon for lesbian, gay, bi, and trans people, whether religious or not, who have lost their spiritual way."

Christian de la Huerta
Author, *Coming Out Spiritually*;
Founder and President of Q-Spirit

"This book is a sane and reasonable approach to sexuality and spirituality—well worth the cost, if only for the commonsense chapter on 'The Right and Wrong of Sex, Queer and Otherwise.' Something everyone needs to hear!"

Sister Jeannine Gramick, SL
Co-founder of New Ways Ministry;
prolific author on gay spirituality;
censured by the Vatican for her
educational ministry

More pre-publication
REVIEWS, COMMENTARIES, EVALUATIONS . . .

"Daniel Helminiak's *Sex and the Sacred* is a long-needed book in the fields of sexual ethics, religious studies, and pastoral counseling and for the LGBT communities. The book reclaims the word 'spirituality' for all people who are seeking wholeness and holiness. This book will be a must-read in my World Religions and Sexual Ethics course. But I am most excited about all the good this book will do for families, brothers and sisters, and partners, so all can once again begin their spiritual journey to wholeness and holiness."

Reverend David O'Leary, STL, DPhil
University Chaplain
and Adjunct Professor in Comparative
Religions and Medical Ethics,
Tufts University, Massachusetts

"This is an extraordinary book for which all lesbian, gay, bisexual, and transgendered people should be grateful. Daniel Helminiak—a polymath in the many connected fields of theology, biblical scholarship, psychotherapy, and spiritual direction—brings his erudition, insight, and wisdom to bear on neuralgic issues facing the gay community. Whatever he touches he illuminates with prose that is easy to read and understand. I especially commend Chapter 10, 'The Trinitarian Vocation of the Gay Community.'"

Father John McNeill
Author, *The Church and the Homosexual*
and numerous other books on gay
spirituality; ousted from the Jesuits
by the Vatican for his ministry to gay
and lesbian Catholics

HPP

Harrington Park Press®
An Imprint of The Haworth Press, Inc.
New York • London • Oxford

Sex and the Sacred
Gay Identity and Spiritual Growth

HARRINGTON PARK PRESS®
Titles of Related Interest

Sex and the Sacred
Gay Identity
and Spiritual Growth

Daniel A. Helminiak, PhD, PhD, LPC

HPP

Harrington Park Press®
An Imprint of The Haworth Press, Inc.
New York • London • Oxford

For more information on this book or to order, visit
http://www.haworthpress.com/store/product.asp?sku=5480

or call 1-800-HAWORTH (800-429-6784) in the United States and Canada
or (607) 722-5857 outside the United States and Canada

or contact orders@HaworthPress.com

Published by

Harrington Park Press®, an imprint of The Haworth Press, Inc., 10 Alice Street, Binghamton, NY 13904-1580.

PUBLISHER'S NOTE
The development, preparation, and publication of this work has been undertaken with great care. However, the Publisher, employees, editors, and agents of The Haworth Press are not responsible for any errors contained herein or for consequences that may ensue from use of materials or information contained in this work. The Haworth Press is committed to the dissemination of ideas and information according to the highest standards of intellectual freedom and the free exchange of ideas. Statements made and opinions expressed in this publication do not necessarily reflect the views of the Publisher, Directors, management, or staff of The Haworth Press, Inc., or an endorsement by them.

Cover design by Jennifer M. Gaska.

Stained glass piece that appears on cover by Heather L. Marrs.

Library of Congress Cataloging-in-Publication Data

Helminiak, Daniel A.
    Sex and the sacred : gay identity and spiritual growth / Daniel A. Helminiak.
        p. cm.
    Includes index.
    ISBN-13: 978-1-56023-341-1 (hc. : alk. paper)
    ISBN-10: 1-56023-341-9 (hc. : alk. paper)
    ISBN-13: 978-1-56023-342-8 (pbk. : alk. paper)
    ISBN-10: 1-56023-342-7 (pbk. : alk. paper)
    1. Homosexuality—Religious aspects. I. Title.

BL65.H64H45 2005
200'.86'64—dc22

                                                                2005010640

To John McNeill

pioneer and living martyr
for the cause of gay liberation
in the face of religious oppression

ABOUT THE AUTHOR

Daniel A. Helminiak, PhD, PhD, LPC, teaches sexuality and spirituality as Associate Professor in the Department of Psychology at the University of West Georgia. A former Catholic priest ordained in Rome, he is also a psychotherapist and theologian and was teaching assistant to the Jesuit philosopher, theologian, and methodologist Bernard Lonergan, whom *Time* magazine called the Thomas Aquinas of the twentieth century.

Dr. Helminiak is author of *The Same Jesus: A Contemporary Christology*; *Spiritual Development: An Interdisciplinary Study*; *The Human Core of Spirituality: Mind as Psyche and Spirit*; *Religion and the Human Sciences: An Approach via Spirituality*; the best-selling *What the Bible Really Says About Homosexuality*; and most recently *Meditation Without Myth: What I Wish They'd Taught Me in Church About Prayer, Meditation, and the Quest for Peace.*

CONTENTS

THE COVER ART:
A GAY SPIRITUAL JOURNEY

This stained glass piece features a Celtic symbol. With no beginning and no end, it represents a continuous journey. I offer this piece, "A Gay Spiritual Journey," as a new symbol of gay liberation, one that speaks of our spirituality as well as our sexuality.

Every element of this piece is symbolic: the Celtic knot, the outer triangles, the circle of clear, swirled glass, the colors, and the placement of the colors. The blue of the central knot represents our past—filled with sadness, struggle, and bravery. The green represents our present—filled with new understandings and growth. And the purple represents our future—alive with magical possibilities, dreams, goals, and hope. Green and purple result from mixing a second color with blue (blue and yellow make green, blue and red make purple). Let us always remember that where we are and where we are going depend on and are colored by where we have been.

The three outer triangles are warm colors—red, orange, and yellow. None of these triangles is next to its opposite color, but each points to it. Opposite colors intensify each other. This placement is symbolic of the possibility of disharmony and chaos and of our ongoing efforts to create a space in which genuine love, in any configuration, is recognized as a sacred and beautiful blessing.

Both the Celtic knot and the triangles are encircled in clear, swirled glass. The clearness of the glass reminds us of our search for clarity of understanding, honesty, and goodwill. The swirls of the glass remind us that no matter how well we think we see through things, emotional and unconscious processes always add texture to our experience and sometimes distort our view.

The Celtic knot is inverted to suggest a downward-pointing triangle. Like the outer triangles, it is an ancient cultural and spiritual symbol for the feminine energy. The triangle also reminds us of the pink triangles worn in the Nazi concentration camps to indicate homosexual men and the black triangles worn to indicate lesbians and "unde-sirable" women. Let us reclaim this ancient symbol as one of pride and beauty. The spectrum of six colors is used to remind us of our "rainbow flag," a symbol that we have long fought for and flown with pride.

This stained-glass piece, which was given to my partner Lisa, now hangs in our home as a constant reminder of how fortunate we are to be able to live fully and peacefully in our love for one another. It also reminds us that love overflows and its power transforms our world.

Heather L. Marrs, MA
Artist

Foreword

For thirty-five years I have been involved in the spiritual growth of the LGBT (lesbian, gay, bisexual, and transgender) community. One of the first lessons I learned in the early days in my own denomination (The Universal Fellowship of Metropolitan Community Churches) was the number of people to whom I talked who did not believe they could be gay and Christian. In the early years of my ministry, I watched people throw the baby out with the bathwater. One of the greatest difficulties was getting people to reconcile their spirituality with their homosexuality. One of my maxims that I used to tell groups of people was this: if you don't hear anything else I say, remember this: God didn't create you so God could have someone to hate. I thank God people heard what I had to say, and today religious groups all over the world are debating whether to include gays and lesbians in the spiritual communities that make up their churches.

The book you hold in your hand, *Sex and the Sacred: Gay Identity and Spiritual Growth,* is the work of Daniel A. Helminiak, a wonderful Roman Catholic writer who explores the vast topic of spirituality for LGBT people.

Daniel writes in the book that the core of the lesbian and gay experience is spiritual and that many gay and lesbian people pass through that door precisely because of their homosexuality.

He proposes a newer, truer understanding of spirituality, one that remains in accord with former understandings but, by downplaying differing religious connotations and by emphasizing our wondrous, common humanity, includes all who seek the meaning of life in openness, honesty, and goodwill.

This book comes at a time when the entire world is debating the continued roles of religion in our cultures, whether it be in marriage, salvation, or biblical translations, as it affects the gay community. Dr. Helminiak has done an incredible job. He speaks to the issue of spirituality in a way that I haven't encountered in a long time.

This book reminds me of a fascinating discovery that I made when I came out of the closet: Accepting that I was gay was not enough.

Don't misunderstand me. I believe coming to accept our homosexuality is a vital and indispensable step in growing into wholeness and emotional health, but for me, a powerful, life-giving component was still missing from my life. I had not addressed the God-given hunger for spirituality that is found in every human being in every culture around the world. Dr. Helminiak addresses this issue and so much more. I only wish that this book had been available for me when I first started my search for spirituality as a gay man.

Reverend Troy D. Perry
Founder, The Universal Fellowship
of Metropolitan Community Churches

Preface and Acknowledgments

Same-sex relationships are nothing new. They have been a part of every culture and every era, but they were usually kept on the sidelines of a heterosexual marriage or in the shadows of unspoken secrecy. Contemporary gay liberation is new in that it claims legitimacy for gay relationships up front and unapologetically.

Since World War II, the gay liberation movement has been working to secure that claim. Much effort has been spent to defend homosexuality on many fronts. My book, *What the Bible Really Says About Homosexuality,* was part of that defensive maneuver. It shows that the Bible, understood in its own historical context, had no concern whatsoever for what we call "homosexuality" today. On the religious front, the argument has been that homosexuality is *not* a sin. The medical argument has been that it is *not* a sickness. The psychological argument has been that it is *not* a mental disorder. And the sociological argument has been that it is *not* a deviancy even as the historical argument has been that it is *not* an anomaly.

This book presumes that the verdict is in and the defense has won the case. On the basis of massive evidence, this book presumes that nothing is unhealthy or unethical about homosexuality and same-sex relationships per se. Homosexuality is merely a natural variation. Thus, this book takes the next step and develops a positive agenda. Accepting the legitimacy of homosexuality, what are we going to make of it?

To be accurate, of course, the debate about homosexuality is hardly over. In many places, antigay oppression is stronger than it was before gay liberation. The level of paranoia over changing sexual mores is astonishing. Many religious folk, whole churches, and entire religions have dug in their heels, ignored the research evidence, and refused to legitimate gay relationships. Fortunately, these conservatives, vocal as they are, are becoming a minority. At this point in history, the evidence on every front is so overwhelming that it is outrageous for an educated person to demean lesbian and gay people and their intimate relationships. At this point in history, only personal discomfort, religious myth, collective prejudice, or inexcusable ignorance support antigay attitudes. While not neglecting the ongoing debate, the gay community needs to move on.

In many ways the gay community had moved on long ago, but the result was not always happy. I can't count the number of times that a gay person has come to talk privately with me as I sit in a coffeehouse or finish a lecture or, sometimes, just walk down a street. The topic is always that Bible-and-homosexuality thing—and religion. For better and sometimes for worse, these people are as out as out can be: dressing "gay," clubbing, cruising, drinking and drugging, tricking, dating, coupling, sometimes even raising children. They are committed lesbians and gays. So you would think they were completely at ease about being homosexual. But often, it is not so. Far from it. Their gay life is a facade. Beneath a colorful front they harbor gnawing concerns of conscience: Are they really going to go to hell? Should they be having gay or lesbian sex? Should they break off their relationship? Is homosexuality really okay? Spiritual doubts hang on and eat away at their souls. Perhaps for this reason, vacillating in their consciences, some find respite in unwholesome and even self-destructive behaviors.

Ousted by religion, many lesbians and gays have just chucked the whole spiritual enterprise. To gain their freedom, they sold their souls. Often they knew no other option. Most spokespersons for religion were certainly of little help. As a result, secretly, many gays and lesbians still believe that they are, indeed, condemned to hell. Painfully, many still struggle against religion's emotional bonds that entangle our rational minds. Sadly, many just gave up concern about spiritual matters and, following the lead of our spiritually bankrupt culture, threw themselves into the gay sex scene: They were "liberated."

Over the years I have pondered these matters, and often I addressed them. I have frequently written on the spiritual dimension of the gay experience. My articles appeared in journals and magazines, which are now collecting dust in libraries. Those papers are still relevant, perhaps more so today than when I first wrote them. So I took them out and dusted them off. I updated and refurbished them, and I present them in this book. Except for Chapter 9 on Jesus and gay liberation, all these essays have been published elsewhere. I am grateful to the publishers for their gracious permission to reprint these essays in this collection. As noted in the introductory footnote of each chapter, the original publications provide documentation for anyone seeking to know my sources. Editing my articles to read as simply as possible and crafting them to fit this popular collection, I avoided cluttering this book with references and other technical apparatus. I did, however, provide an index. Quotations from the Bible are from the New Revised Standard Version.

The title of this book says what it's about: the sacred dimension of sexuality, the integration of spirituality and sexuality. The subtitle reads *Gay Identity and Spiritual Growth* and, thus, suggests a specific focus: nonheterosexual sexuality. However, the word *gay* is not completely accurate, for here it stands for a broader category than the word usually encompasses. I use *gay* in this instance in the same way many today use the word *queer*. It has come to refer to all nonstandard sexuality and to the LGBTI communities: lesbian, gay, bisexual, transgender, and intersex people, all those who are developing nonheterosexist ways of expressing sexuality in our day. But the term *queer* is jarring to many people. Also jarring are the juxtapositions in my title and subtitle. Spirituality is not usually the first idea that comes to mind when people think of homosexuality.

Talk of gay spirituality may seem odd, peculiar—queer. However, as sociological and anthropological studies have shown, queer people have regularly been the spiritual leaders of societies across time and around the globe. The psychologist Carl G. Jung noted that homosexual people tend to possess an intense spiritual sensitivity. The shamans of indigenous religions often engaged in nonstandard sexual practices. Many Native American tribes revered their masculine-feminine or feminine-masculine members as "two-spirited," doubly blessed, able to share the worlds of both women and men. Politically and spiritually these two-spirited people often served as tribal leaders. Nothing is unusual about the notion of gay and lesbian spirituality, and our homophobic society would do well to ponder this fact. Thus, this book reclaims for queer people the status of priest and priestess, prophet, shaman, guru, or spiritual leader, which they have, in fact, held throughout history.

Although my emphasis is gay spirituality, I want to address a broad audience. I believe that spirituality is common to all human beings. I do not believe it is particular to religion. I don't even think it is necessarily linked with belief in God. On my understanding, the order is the exact opposite: Religion and belief in God grow out of spirituality. Spirituality comes first; the infinite longings of the human heart are the starting point. Discovery of God and belief in God are a natural outworking of spiritual sensitivity; they are a projection and an elaboration of core human spirituality.

Accordingly, the early essays in this book address spirituality in a generic way. I speak of the spiritual apart from any connection with specific religions. I present spirituality as a completely human, fully psychological, enterprise. I believe that this humanistic emphasis is my contribution. I show how, with or without religion, with or without belief in God, every person has a spiritual dimension to his or her being. I show how this spiritual dimension needs to be integrated with one's sexuality. I show how this core spirituality can naturally flow into organized religion, for those who want it.

The value of this emphasis is twofold. First, it allows gays and lesbians, condemned to hell by religion, to reclaim their spirituality—despite the religions, if need be. Second, it presents an approach to spirituality that fits the present times, for on the basis of our common humanity, this approach embraces all peoples and cultures. Surely, what our world sorely needs is a way to bring the religions of the world together in peace, and focus on a common spirituality provides that way.

Later essays in the book come from a Christian perspective. They connect core spirituality with Western religion. I think it is fair to assume that most people reading this book will have been raised in some Christian church or will at least be familiar with Christian beliefs. Besides, the lessons I derive from Christian themes apply to that core human spirituality, which is ever my focus. So, in one way or another, from cover to cover, this book should be useful to anyone concerned about the spiritual growth of LGBTI people.

This book will also be of interest to anyone, gay or straight, who is concerned about what sexuality has to do with spirituality. Their relationship has become a popular topic. But really, it is difficult to find an approach to this topic that does not involve a particular religion, a belief in God, or an ethical agenda. This is to say, most approaches to sexuality and spirituality turn into expositions of some religion and its morality. I offer something different. I interrelate sexuality and spirituality on a completely human level, and I also show how this humanisitc level opens onto a religious and theological level, for those who want it. Applying the research of Bernard Lonergan (1904-1984)—the philosopher-theologian-methodologist for whom I was a teaching assistant at Boston College—I offer a unique approach to sexuality and spirituality. I suggest a novel way of relating the social sciences and religion. I believe this approach should enrich the thinking of anyone pondering the relationship of sexuality and spirituality, and should be particularly useful for professionals such as physicians, nurses, psychotherapists, educators, business executives, and legislators and politicians—who need to address spiritual issues in a nonsectarian way.

I treated this understanding of spirituality in technical detail in my books *The Human Core of Spirituality* and *Religion and the Human Sciences,* and I offered a popular presentation in *Meditation Without Myth.* In this book I provide another popular application of the same approach.

I write as a religious scholar and a social scientist. I hold PhDs in both theology and psychology and am well published and respected in these fields. With this book I would share the fruits of much of my professional life, including decades of priestly ministry and pastoral counseling. In 1995, for reasons of personal integrity, I submitted to the Vatican an official resignation from the Catholic priesthood. The Vatican has never responded. I take this refusal to accept my resignation to mean that the Vatican is allowing me to continue to represent them. Besides, according to Catholic teaching, once a priest, always a priest: Ordination effects an ontological change in the soul that is irreversible. Thus, sincerely exercising my priestly ministry in my own way, I also write as a Catholic priest, and I hope that this religious credential will provide added reassurance to you, my readers, about my treatment of the controversial topic of this book.

I am grateful to many people who contributed to the creation of this book. I thank Sylvia Chavez Longnecker. She co-authored the original article that is now Chapter 3. I am grateful not only for her graciously allowing me to include our article in this book but also for her introducing me to this field of research. Through her instigation and co-authorship of the article, I first thought about and began to write and teach about the relationship of sexuality and spirituality.

I am grateful to the Reverend Troy D. Perry, who kindly wrote the foreword to this book. From the humble and farsighted beginnings of a house church in Los Angeles in 1968, he founded the Universal Fellowship of Metropolitan Community Churches, which is dedicated to Christian ministry to lesbian and gay people. As its moderator, he continued his leadership of UFMCC until his retirement in 2005.

I also thank my friends and colleagues who graciously endorsed this book. I thank them not only for their endorsement but also for their generous pioneering work in spiritual gay liberation.

- Father John McNeill wrote the groundbreaking 1976 book *The Church and the Homosexual* and numerous other books on gay spirituality. In 1986, after the Vatican called homosexuality an "objective disorder" geared toward an "intrinsic evil," McNeill broke his nine years of Vatican-imposed silence, and the Vatican ousted him from the Jesuits. However, through counseling, lecturing, and writing, he bravely and generously continued his ministry to gay and lesbian people. In retirement, he celebrated his 80th birthday in 2005.

- In 1977, with Father Robert Nugent, SDS, Sister Jeannine Gramick, SL, founded New Ways Ministry "to promote justice and reconciliation between lesbian and gay Catholics and the wider Catholic community." She has authored and edited many important books and articles on gay spirituality. Censured by the Vatican in 1999 and again in 2000, she, too, would not be silenced, saying, "I refuse to collaborate in my own oppression." She has found creative ways within Catholic circles to continue her educational ministry.

- Toby Johnson is the author of *Gay Perspective* and a list of other important books, including delightful novels, about the gay spiritual experience. He has served tirelessly as editor of *White Crane: A Journal of Gay Men's Spirituality* and is involved in founding White Crane Institute for gay spirituality. He worked with the core group that organized and sponsored the May 2004 Gay Spirit Culture Summit at Garrison Institute, Garrison, New York. The "Statement of Spirituality" that emerged from this summit is included as the Appendix to this book.

- Christian de la Huerta is author of *Coming Out Spiritually* and founder and president of Q-Spirit. Through Q-Spirit and a grueling schedule of travel, lectures, and workshops, he fosters gay spirituality internationally.

Five chapters in this collection were published over the years as articles in *Pastoral Psychology,* and Professor Lewis Rambo of San Francisco Theological Seminary, San Anselmo, California, has been editor of this journal throughout that time. I salute him for his openness to new ideas and thank him for his constant support for my work in spirituality. In this professional journal for Christian ministry, he published what I could not get published in gay periodicals (Go figure!)—arguments about topics such as AIDS, the Trinity, the future of Christianity, and sexual ethics. Tellingly, I never received one formal comment from colleagues about these provocative articles, but by word of mouth in pastoral-theology circles, I know that people were reading and thinking about them. I am deeply grateful to Professor Rambo for originally publishing these articles and for supporting their republication in this book.

I thank Dennis Weakland, my research assistant at the University of West Georgia, for his help in preparing this manuscript, and I thank my colleagues there for their firm and constant professional support. I also thank my sister Celia and my brother Allan and my friends—especially John Adamski, Cami Delgado, Marcus Fleischhacker, Bruce Jarstfer, Paul Drew Johnson, Raymond Marchesney, and Lee Smith—for the personal support that allows me to continue my work of research, teaching, and writing.

May the confluence of contributions of so many people to this book make it a blessing to the queer community and to spiritual seekers everywhere.

Chapter 1

The Spiritual Dimension of the Lesbian and Gay Experience

I met Richard about three years ago. A new bar was opening in town. It was the place to be that evening. So after the Dignity Mass, I stopped by to join in the celebration.

He's a young man. I'm not even sure how he got into the place. Maybe he really was nineteen—but just barely, at best. Tall, slim, blond, attractive, he was soft-spoken, well mannered, and thoughtful. He'd just recently come out. He was making a living by hustling and was obviously successful at it.

THE SENSELESS BURDEN OF A BAD CONSCIENCE

When the question of my occupation came up and Richard learned I was a priest, the conversation turned to religion. Again I was confronted with that phenomenon I never could and perhaps never will understand.

Here was this fine young man who thought he was doomed to hell because he was homosexual and who had decided that that was the way it would have to be. He did not think himself particularly guilty of anything. He was just being himself. There wasn't much he could do to change things. He had already tried denying and avoiding his homosexuality, but it would not go away. He simply had to accept it.

This chapter was originally published under the pseudonym David Davidson in *Christopher Street*, December 1986, issue 106, volume 9, number 10, pages 29-33, as "The Spiritual Dimension of the Gay Experience" and republished in *Dignity/USA Journal*, 1992, volume 24, number 2, pages 14-19, as "The Spiritual Dimension of the Gay and Lesbian Experience."

But his religion had taught him that homosexual people could not be saved. He also accepted that! Then he threw himself into the gay sex scene with abandon.

I just do not understand how anyone could live with such a contradiction: to know that being homosexual was none of your doing and still to believe that you are already hopelessly condemned for it. This contradiction seems to bother Richard, too, when he lets himself think about it. To this day, whenever we meet, the same topic comes up and there's that same promise to get together and work through this whole question once and for all someday. Yet he continues to live with this impossible burden.

Here's the damnable part: He goes on like this because he's a good person! With childlike faith he believes what his religion teaches, and with confidence that comes from a loving upbringing he also believes in himself. He's too honest to just blow off the whole question, and he's too religiously naive to resolve it.

He's not the only one. Many gay people feel they have moved beyond religion and even beyond all salvation. They feel they've thrown themselves up against the whole of society and even against the cosmos in a willful protest of freedom: "I have come out, and I will not be repressed. I'll be damned, if I must, but I will be myself!" Fist-raised-to-heaven rebels, they have committed the ultimate crime.

Richard was not quite like that. He is too gentle a soul for such aggressive feelings, although he did consider himself among those who have moved beyond the pale of all religion.

THE MEANING OF "SPIRITUAL"

Yet I believe that at the core of the lesbian and gay experience is a spiritual experience. I believe that Richard stands at the door of a profound spiritual transformation. Many gay and lesbian people have passed through that door—precisely because of their homosexuality.

Does this sound crazy? Obviously, it depends on what you mean by "spiritual." If the very institutions that condemn homosexuality are also allowed to define the term *spiritual*, nothing that has to do with homosexuality will be seen as spiritual. However, the same historical forces that provide a new understanding of homosexuality today also provide a renewed understanding of spirituality. Within the new perspective—and it is not in contradiction to the old—the gay and lesbian experience and the spiritual experience may coincide.

When I say *spiritual,* I do not necessarily suggest any reference to religious faith, to God, or to Christ. I refer to something that is simply human, something in human experience that goes beyond the here and now. We have in us an opening to a beyond. That something is spiritual.

Different people might experience their spiritual nature in different ways—watching the stars at night, listening to a symphony, working through an intellectual problem, seeing a child at play, walking through a forest, jogging down a road, dancing to a disco beat, gazing out at the ocean, making love. A dimension to human experience exists that pulls us out of ourselves and lets us know that we, our very selves, are caught up in something that is vast and marvelous. We are bigger than ourselves. We are naturally self-transcending.

Sometimes this experience is intense, but it need not be. In a less dramatic way this same kind of experience is a part of our everyday lives. It happens whenever we use our minds. Every time we become aware of something new, we have been pulled out of ourselves. Every time we understand something and have an idea, we have broken out of our former world. Every time we learn a new fact, we have moved in reality beyond ourselves. And every time we make a decision, we change ourselves and the world.

All these experiences move us beyond ourselves. All are self-transcending experiences. All open us up to reality that is clearly not limited to the sensible, the concrete, the physical, the here and now. These experiences open us up to what is potentially universal and eternal. Through such experiences we move beyond ourselves, and more and more we ourselves become that beyond toward which we move. These are spiritual experiences.

Yet this opening up in unending self-transcendence is a wholly human phenomenon. It is precisely what makes humans different from other animals. Apart from any consideration of God or religion or any such thing, at the core of the human is the spiritual.

Here is a legitimate understanding of the term *spiritual.* In fact, this understanding is the most fundamental meaning of the term. It is the basis for any possible talk about God.

THE INNER PUSH TOWARD SPIRITUAL GROWTH

Built into human beings is an urge toward self-transcendence, a spiritual drive. We even sing about it. In the disco era, the words were "I'm gonna live forever, I'm gonna learn how to fly!" And more recently: "I believe I can fly. I believe I can touch the sky." If we give this urge the lead, we will find ourselves becoming ever more attentive and alert to all that exist within and around us. We will find ourselves delighting in understanding whatever we experience. We will find ourselves knowing more and more about more and more. We will find ourselves deciding and acting in accord with what we know, acting responsibly on every occasion, keeping this open-ended dynamism flowing. Perhaps on some occasion or other, all these everyday experiences of self-transcendence will fuse and we will find ourselves caught up in one of those intense, ineffable experiences, in a mystical moment.

Deliberately following our inner spiritual urge, we will be refashioning ourselves to be more and more in accord with this urge toward self-transcendence that is our very nature. We will be engaging ourselves in snowballing growth whose ideal goal is nothing less than to become one with all that exists. We will be on a spiritual quest. We will be involved in spiritual growth.

Does being gay or lesbian provoke such a quest? Is such an experience at the core of the gay experience? I think the answer is yes. In fact, I think the answer is so strikingly yes that I say homosexuality demands spiritual growth.

Certainly, in comparison with the heterosexual experience, growing up lesbian or gay forces you to contend with issues that are essentially spiritual. No gay or lesbian person can complacently move along the standard path of life: school, marriage, children, grandchildren, respectable death. The path runs out all too soon for gay and lesbian people, and they must search out the meaning of life. Carl Jung wrote that one of the particular gifts of homosexual people is a heightened sense for the religious. Perhaps here is an explanation of what he meant.

COMING OUT AS A SPIRITUAL EXERCISE

Consider the experience of coming out. Whether you come out early or later, the process begins with a dawning. You become aware that something is different about you. Something is unusual. It's a given. It just keeps presenting itself. And just by having that awareness, you are already in a new place.

Then comes the uncertainty, the questioning. What is going on in me? Why do I feel the way I do? What's wrong with me? Are these feelings going to stop? The spontaneous desire to understand, which makes us human, asserts itself. But now you are questioning about your own self. The stakes are very high. The very experience of homosexual feelings makes you begin to look at yourself and wonder about yourself. This sort of introspection is central in most spiritual traditions, and it is an inevitable part of being gay.

After some time, you conclude that you are homosexual. It's a fact. There is no denying it. All the evidence confirms it. Here again, you have to move beyond yourself. You have made another step forward in self-transcendence. You have moved from what you—and your family and friends and all of society—might expect or want or hope; and you have moved to what you really are. You have given up fantasy for reality. You are homosexual. This acknowledgment of truth, any acknowledgment of truth, is a spiritual act.

Still, knowing that you're gay or lesbian is only the beginning of coming out. You still have to decide what you're going to do about it. This is where Richard is still hung up. He's not yet at peace with himself.

Our inner drive toward self-transcendence moves us to decide and act according to what we know. That is, it calls us to be responsible. So the appropriate response to knowing you're gay or lesbian is to accept it and begin doing something positive with it. You need to put this piece together with all the rest that you know and are.

To deny or repress or ignore the truth is dishonest. Such behavior opposes our fundamental need for what is real. On the other hand, to acknowledge the truth is to be real, and to act according to the truth, to integrate each new truth with all else that you know and are, is already to grow spiritually. It is to become a unified self, consistent, through and through. It is to become a spiritually committed and mature person. In the language of the spiritual traditions: it is to be single-minded, to become crystal clear, to walk the razor's edge. To neglect such integration is to enter a spiritual dead end.

The very process of coming out is spiritual. Just being homosexual impels you to pursue the central spiritual task of knowing and accepting and "re-forming" yourself.

But there is more to coming out than that. Accepting your homosexuality is no easy task. Of course, anyone who is creative, sensitive, disabled, talented—anyone who is different in any way—faces a challenge in self-acceptance. Everyone pays a price who dares to be himself or herself. The stigma attached to homosexuality is particularly cruel. The name-calling, the rejection, the bashings and murders, the quiet pain and silent tears, the suicides, all resulting—for no good reason—from being gay or lesbian do not need to be rehearsed. You accept your homosexuality only in the face of opposition. Even decades after the beginning of gay liberation you risk great loss: family and friends, job and housing, respectability and influence, and you suffer the loss of that proposed heterosexual fulfillment: licit romance and wedding, children, and home. You lose your share in the great, and very narrow, American dream with which all of us as children, gay and straight, were entranced.

Coming out is a challenging, difficult, and painful process. In spiritual terms, coming out is a kind of conversion. This conversion takes courage, conviction, and profound dedication to truth and to responsible behavior.

Coming out also takes a faith, a belief that you can move beyond the mores of stereotypical, heterosexual society and still find valid meaning and purpose in life. Coming out requires faith that you can be yourself, an affront to your society, and still achieve the fulfillment demanded by the very urging that requires you to risk losing all fulfillment.

Responsible coming out is a heroic act. It is a noble and lofty act. In spiritual terms, it is a saintly act.

LOVE AS A SPIRITUAL EXERCISE

Consider the gay experience of falling in love. Loving someone of the same sex has far-reaching implications.

Of course, any deep love opens people up to rich and disturbing inner experiences. Somehow the caverns of the psyche are unlocked and out flow dreams and hopes, memories and fears. You may be overwhelmed by them. Meanwhile, you are required to relate with another person—whose memories may differ, dreams may conflict, fears may provoke, values may challenge, opinions may confront, and habits may irritate.

If it is to grow beyond the stage of infatuation, any love demands extensive self-knowledge and continued personal growth. Two people who wish to relate profoundly and lastingly must be willing to share their minds, to express their feelings, to expose their doubts, to change their opinions, to compromise their plans, and to purify their values. Love engages that spiritual principle that lies in the core of us. The very experience of loving is a spiritual exercise. Love fosters spiritual growth as surely as any fasting or vigil or meditation or retreat. Similar to these traditional spiritual practices, love honestly lived is also a form of asceticism, a spiritual discipline.

But once again, the issue is complicated in same-sex relationships. Little boys are programmed to relate to little girls, and little girls are programmed to relate to little boys. The strengths of the one are generally the weaknesses of the other. The two are made to complement each other. This arrangement holds whether the little girls and boys are homosexual or heterosexual. Socialization is no respecter of persons.

Then, once grown, though lesbian and gay, homosexuals are still men and women, and they respond as such. Put two women together, who are trained to be sensitive, supportive, self-giving, and nurturing, and you get a relationship that is loving and stable and profoundly affectionate but that is also liable to become ingrown and die of suffocation. Put two men together, who are trained to be competitive, outgoing, independent, and tough, and you get magnificent and exotic fireworks that are likely to burn down quickly, grow dull, and sputter out.

These descriptions are stereotypical. However, in allowing for a certain range of variation, they do express how society would have us all be. If actual lesbian and gay relationships are not as I just described it is because the people in question have grown beyond the narrow sex stereotypes. And that is my point. They have grown precisely *because* they are homosexual.

In any lasting homosexual relationship, the couple must expand their personalities. They must find in themselves the complementary qualities that society regularly programs only into the opposite sex. Lesbians also become rugged and independent, and gay men also become nurturing and sensitive.

GAY STRENGTH, VIRTUE, WISDOM, AND SPIRITUAL GROWTH

The personal growth in question here is another facet of spiritual growth. This expansion of the personality, this integration of psychological opposites—masculinity and feminity—is nothing other than an unfolding and an enhancing of one's own spiritual nature. This process entails an opening to broader experience, a delight in deeper insight, a movement toward surer acceptance of reality, and an embrace of more responsible, more realistic behavior.

This is a process of self-transcendence. It moves you beyond your own narrow self, beyond your fantasies and illusions, and into touch with reality, into a universe of challenge, wonder, and marvel. This process is the actualization of the human spirit's drive to embrace all that is. It is part of a cosmic movement. And it occurs directly as a result of the couple's being homosexual.

I have suggested that spiritual experience is at the core of homosexual experience. Considerations of coming out and of homosexual love suggest what I mean. Other facets of the homosexual experience could elaborate the point as well: the frequent development of deep, opposite-sex friendships in the gay and lesbian community; acceptance of all people despite social stereotypes; the homosexual experience of loneliness and rejection from earliest childhood; the need to express generativity apart from having children. And let us not forget the compassion, service, sense of humor, and heroic commitment that are so characteristic of the gay community and that are being publicly demonstrated in the face of the AIDS epidemic.

How many aspects of the gay experience demand delving into yourself and finding inner strength! Religions call this virtue. How much being gay demands personal integration and self-found wisdom! Religions call this spiritual growth.

DETOURS FROM THE SPIRITUAL PATH

Of course, I have been presenting an optimistic picture. If budding spirituality lies at the core of the gay experience, that spiritual dimension is often obscured and lost. Remember Richard and others similar to him. What could be a profoundly spiritual experience often turns out to be defensive, angry, and desperate, or stylish, superficial, and cynical, or else sheepish, obsequious, and self-effacing. The reasons are many.

Organized religion simplistically and consistently misdefines the spiritual. Understandably, then, gay people often fail to recognize the spiritual dimension of their experience, so they often abort the spiritual dimension of their gay experience. The profoundly holy experience of coming out in painful honesty and responsible self-esteem gets sidetracked. Spirituality gets lost in a secret and murky subculture, in the blare of pounding rhythms, in the stupor of alcohol and drugs, in the fantasy of seductive bodies and irresponsible sex acts. The sacred longings for deep love and honest sharing get channeled into superficial and sham amusements.

What a crime! For survival's sake spiritually sensitive and gentle people must deaden themselves to the music of their souls because the religions are blind to the very essence of the spiritual that they are supposed to foster.

Nonetheless and despite it all, the fact remains: Spiritual experience lies at the heart of the gay and lesbian experience. We need only to recognize and name it as such.

THE TUG-OF-WAR BETWEEN RELIGION AND SPIRITUALITY

This understanding of spirituality is free from the domination and distortion of religious institutions. The key to the spiritual lies in the human heart. Buried there is a passion for honesty and love, for wholeness and integrity, for the lofty, the noble, and the worthwhile. Buried in the human heart is a passion to encompass the universe.

Being gay makes you grapple with your heart and touch its spiritual core. When you give that core the lead, the whole of your gay experience becomes a genuine spiritual experience. You walk on a path of open-ended growth, a path of constant self-transcendence.

This spiritual growth results regardless of what religions or society or any others may say. If they oppose this understanding of spirituality, they cannot be of open mind, reasonable judgment, and responsible decision. They offend against the very requirements of the self-transcending human spirit within us. Thus, they discredit the basis of their own, or any, argument. While claiming to have the truth, they shut down the very process by which humans come to know the truth. While claiming to be acting in love, they forbid pursuit of what is obviously to the good of everybody involved. They reject the very basis of truth and love. They can hardly be advocating genuine spirituality. They disqualify the spiritual itself.

Yet the understanding of spirituality presented here is not opposed to traditional religions. I did not talk about God or Jesus Christ in this account of the gay spiritual experience, but if God is supposed to be the Fullness of Truth and Love, then what I did talk about points Godward. If Jesus Christ is supposed to be the instance of full union of humanity and divinity and the human attainment of all that is, then the risen Jesus might appear to exemplify the fulfillment of the longings of the human heart. The Holy Spirit might appear to be behind those longings.

This notion of gay and lesbian spirituality is not opposed to theist or Christian religion. (By *Christian* I do not mean Fundamentalist.) Such human spirituality is their basis. Those who believe in God or those who believe in Jesus Christ may still remain faithful to their beliefs while pursuing the gay spiritual experience. However, I lay down this challenge: Can you really believe in God or really believe in Jesus if you do not also believe in yourself? Your own self is the basis for any understanding, belief, or love. If you reject your own self, you reject the possibility of any worthwhile achievement, including genuine religious faith.

SPIRITUALITY WITHOUT GOD OR RELIGION

On the other hand, you need not believe in God to be a spiritual person. Nontheist Buddhism and Chinese Taoism stand as incontrovertible evidence of this fact. Therefore, if some homosexual people have understandably rejected all established religion, they need not reject their own souls, their own selves, as well. At this point in history, the driving power behind the gay and lesbian experience is precisely acceptance of one's self. This acceptance is a spiritual act. It has spiritual implications. It starts you on a spiritual path—if you understand what the word really means. I wonder if Richard will ever understand this—and act on it.

Chapter 2

A Spiritual Lesson
from the AIDS Epidemic

"What's it all about? Why are we here? What's worth living for?"

These are the kinds of questions that gays and lesbians face when they decide to buck the tide and accept their homosexuality. These are the questions that also arise in any crisis of life. These are the questions that have shaken the gay community in the wake of the AIDS epidemic.

Spread of the human immunodeficiency virus (HIV) has provoked a medical crisis, but it has also provoked a spiritual crisis. Such was John Fortunato's argument in his important 1987 book, *AIDS: The Spiritual Dilemma.*

Why a spiritual crisis? For a number of reasons. HIV most frequently affects people in the prime of life. Unlike any other disease, HIV/AIDS has three frightening characteristics: it is transmissible, terminal, and stigmatized. Even in the era of more hopeful medications, HIV infection results in ongoing uncertainty that can produce stress, depression, guilt, withdrawal, and hopelessness. Living with HIV/AIDS provokes the big questions: What is my life all about? What am I going to do now? How can my life be worth living? What does all this mean? Why me? Why this? Why anything? These are spiritual questions.

These questions are spiritual because they concern human meaning and purpose; they touch on the ultimates of life. They are spiritual also because they are the questions at the heart of all religion. What is more, people have explicitly related AIDS to religion and called it the

This chapter was originally published with documentation in *Pastoral Psychology,* 1995, volume 43, number 5, pages 301-318, under the title "Non-Religious Lesbians and Gays Facing AIDS: A Fully Psychological Approach to Spirituality." Reprinted with permission.

scourge of God, especially when it is associated with homosexuality. From every perspective, then, HIV/AIDS has spiritual ramifications.

Consideration of those ramifications is important—not only for lesbians and gays living with AIDS but also for all gay and lesbian people and for anyone facing death or struggling with life. In times of crisis we must dig deeply into ourselves to regain a solid spiritual base. An exploration of the spiritual dimension of the HIV/AIDS crisis will uncover the profound spiritual treasure lodged in the gay experience. Such exploration is important for anyone questioning the meaning of life and weighing its value. That is to say, such exploration is important for us all. Whether we ourselves are living with HIV/AIDS or not, we are all living, and inevitably life brings on big questions.

Another angle must be considered when we speak of a spiritual crisis. Those who address the spiritual crisis of HIV/AIDS usually interpret it in religious terms, and in Western civilization religion includes God. Of course, many insist that spirituality and religion are not the same thing and that religion's task is to foster spirituality. Some even allow that spirituality need not include belief in God. Nonetheless, for most people, spirituality has to do with a "relationship with God," and they address the spiritual challenge of HIV/AIDS in these same terms. Then, as John Fortunato concluded, a ready-made answer to the big questions exists: God lovingly guides our world, so everything happens for the best although it may be difficult at times to understand this; and after death God will receive us into an unending heavenly fulfillment, blissful beyond all imagination. Such is the standard religious answer. It rests on trust in God.

In fact, some 90 percent of Americans profess belief in God, so that religious answer speaks to most of us. But some still get left out. That answer fails to address the spiritual concerns of people who are agnostic or atheist.

Some members of the lesbian and gay community are among the agnostics or atheists. Religion has failed in ministering to the gay community, and religion has often outright rejected lesbian and gay people. As a result, many lesbians and gay men do not adhere to established religion, and in all honesty some cannot even affirm the existence of God. Nonetheless, these nonbelievers also face the spiritual crisis that shows itself in the AIDS epidemic, because questions about the meaning of life touch us all.

This chapter addresses the neglected aspect of the spiritual crisis of AIDS. This chapter focuses on *nonreligious* gay and lesbian people affected by HIV/AIDS. In so doing, this chapter proposes an approach to spirituality that anyone can embrace.

The first section of this chapter outlines a spirituality conceived apart from, though not in opposition to, belief in God. The second section shows how such spirituality is relevant to the gay experience. The final section relates this spirituality specifically to gay men and lesbians living and dying with AIDS or facing other terminal diseases. In this way, this chapter presents a fully humanistic spirituality—that is, a nonreligious and nontheological spirituality. Thus, this chapter is relevant for anyone asking questions about spirituality and especially for lesbians and gays facing life's big questions.

A HUMANIST SPIRITUALITY

The Possibility of Nontheist Spirituality

Tibetan and Zen Buddhism stand as incontrovertible evidence of the possibility of nontheist spirituality. These venerable traditions teach a profound spirituality based on an inherent aspect of humanity, Buddha nature, whose flowering results in enlightenment. Focus is not on God, a Supreme Being, or anything nonhuman. Unlike Hinduism wherein atman is Brahman—that is, the soul is Divinity, God, within us—Buddhism does not even speculate about God, the soul, or other metaphysical issues. For Buddhism, theorizing about God only distracts us from the task of mindful living. Buddhism is fully nontheist: it brackets the question of God and deliberately ignores the question altogether. Similar to agnosticism, which also leaves the question open, Buddhism is not atheistic; it does not deny God. To do so would be to express an opinion, but Buddhism has no opinion. Buddhism is not concerned with God. Focus in Buddhism is on the self, on the human mind and its capacities. Here, then, is a clue to the essential feature of spirituality.

The standard Western picture of the human being is body and mind or, in the parallel religious version, body and soul. The difference between mind and soul is not important in this discussion because both notions are too fuzzy to allow real comparison. Besides, in either case the picture is inadequate—not because the mind or soul is not actually a dimension different from body, but because *mind* and *soul* are umbrella terms that include numerous differing facets of inner experience. According to Bernard Lonergan, at least two different aspects of the human mind exist: psyche and spirit. When these two are added to *body,* the result is a three-part (or tripartite) model of the human: body, psyche, and spirit. If spirit really is an aspect of the human mind, spirituality has its foundation in humanity, and, thus, God need not necessarily be brought into the discussion. This focus on the human spirit allows for a Western version of the nontheist spirituality of Buddhism: the human spirit is the Buddha nature.

The Human As Tripartite: Body, Psyche, and Spirit

This three-part model of the human can be elaborated. Body is simply the physiological system of systems that is the object of study in physics, chemistry, biology, and medicine. This first part of the matter needs little explanation. We all understand what the body is.

Psyche and spirit are aspects of the human mind. Psyche includes emotions, imagery, and memory, which together make up personality, a person's built-in and standard way of responding and behaving. Humans share this aspect of mind with other animals. We commonly allow that different breeds of dogs and even different dogs, for example, have different personalities.

In contrast, spirit is an aspect of mind that is distinctive to humans. Spirit is, essentially, self-awareness. This peculiarly human self-awareness results in wonder, marvel, awe. Questions and the desire to understand follow. This desire is not disappointed, because our human spirit also allows us to have insights, to ponder, and then to judge, and eventually to make decisions. Because of our human spirits, then, we carry the burden of determining our own life and constructing our own world. Our spirit leads us ever beyond ourselves into new interests, commitments, ways of living. The human spirit is the source of the self-transcendence of which I spoke in Chapter 1.

The hallmarks of spirit are meaning and value. We build our lives around meanings and values—or, said otherwise, visions and virtues, or ideas and ideals, or understandings and commitments, or knowledge and love, or cognition and choice, or dreams and promises. These are what we need to rethink when we come out. These are our answers to life's big questions. These are spiritual matters.

In *Man for Himself* and *The Anatomy of Human Destructiveness,* Erich Fromm also wrote about two aspects of the mind. He spoke of the human need for orientation and devotion. His point was this: we humans need some understanding, a cognitive road map of life, to guide our living; and to get through life we also need commitment to that living as we understand it. Orientation and devotion may be a poetic way of speaking about the meanings and values that we need to structure our lives.

However, to be more precise, talk of orientation and devotion seems to intermingle meanings and values, psyche and spirit. Devotion, for example, is a matter of a value commitment, of something proper to the spirit, yet devotion is always tinged with emotions, memories, and images, things proper to the psyche. In talk of human devotion, psyche and spirit seem to flow together. Are they really two different things?

The distinction between psyche and spirit is subtle, but it is real. Although you cannot have devotion without emotion, just feeling emotion is not the same as making the commitment to someone or something that devotion requires. Though the two go together, emotion is not the same thing as choice.

Similarly, although you might not have an idea (a matter of the spirit) without the help of an image (a matter of the psyche), simply to have an image is not the same thing as to achieve insight and have an idea. Although you will not understand what I mean apart from reading the words that I write, simply to take in my words and even to repeat them from memory is not the same thing as to understand them.

As aspects of the human mind, psyche and spirit are distinct although they are inseparable—just as the body is another distinct yet inseparable aspect of the human being. Simply because some things always go together does not mean that they are the same thing. The human mind includes both psyche and spirit.

The Nature of Human Spirit

The Four-Level Structure of the Spirit

It is difficult to say outright what *spirit* is. In this regard, I have found the analysis of Bernard Lonergan, the late Canadian philosopher-theologian, very helpful. Lonergan provided a detailed account of human consciousness. For Lonergan *consciousness* and *spirit* are two words for the same thing, so here I follow his analysis of human consciousness to explain in more detail what spirit is.

Consciousness is awareness, and it is a dynamic affair. As conscious, we are always beyond ourselves, so to speak. We are always one step ahead of what we have already expressed. We are aware of more than we know. This gap between awareness and knowledge makes for marvel, wonder, awe, question.

But no sooner are we aware than we are asking, What is it? And no sooner do we have an idea than we are asking, Is it so? Am I correct? And no sooner are we sure of our correctness than we are asking, What am I going to do about it?

Four levels (or applications or expressions or functions or facets) characterize human consciousness or spirit: (1) awareness, (2) understanding, and (3) judgment of fact; these three relate to knowing. Knowledge then leads to (4) decision or judgment of value, which relates to doing. Moreover, the fourth, decision or choice, changes things in the real world, so decision results in new experience, and new experience provokes another round of marvel, wonder, awe, and question, understanding and judgment and choice, and so on, incessantly.

By engaging our human spirit, we engage and shape our world. In the process we also form and re-form ourselves. As we and all that is become more and more attuned, we move ever more deeply into reality. I am saying here in more detail what I said poetically about coming out in Chapter 1.

An Open-Ended Dynamism

This unfolding of spirit in us is open-ended. In the ideal, it will never stop until it encompasses the universe.

We would want to understand everything about everything. We would like to embrace all that is. We would somehow become one with everything. All that there is to be known and loved—being it-self—is the ideal goal of our spiritual urge.

Our emotional longing, our yearning, our incessant aching for more, is the psychic footprint of that spiritual urge at work within us. Emotions accompany our understandings.

Spirit and psyche work together to lead us ever onward. Open-ended, ever self-transcending dynamism is our very nature as conscious or spiritual beings.

The Requirements of Spiritual Unfolding

The open-ended dynamism that we are as partially spiritual beings contains its own requirements of unfolding. Become aware of data, and the very structure of our being wants to know, What is it? Have an idea about it, and the very structure of our being wants to know, Is it so? Determine that it is so, and the very structure of our being pushes the further question, What am I going to do about it? This "what to do about it" carries the requirement to "do the right thing." We need to be correct or, at least, to honestly believe we are. We need to do what is right or, at least, to keep ourselves from realizing we have acted wrongly.

Only what is actually true and only what is actually good provide the solid basis for the continued unfolding of our open-ended spirits. We cannot build a life on lies. Falsehood and evil eventually self-destruct; this is their very nature. Aware of more than we know and wanting to have it all, the open-ended dynamism that is our spirit fears such a negative outcome. Its built-in homing device, geared to the fullness of reality, already anticipates what alone will bring ultimate fulfillment. Thus, our very spiritual nature—the "voice of conscience"—urges us to be open, honest, and loving. For only if we are so can the open-ended desire of our spirit hope to attain all that is.

A Humanist Basis for Spirituality

Hopefully, the brief account of the human spirit just given resonates with your sense of spirituality—even though the topic is simply an everyday aspect of what it means to be human. The matter is as everyday-ordinary as asking an honest question or deciding where to spend the weekend and with whom. Yet the matter opens onto experiences as profound as being lost in wonder at the stars or the ocean, reassessing the meaning of your life, or dedicating yourself to the service of humanity as if a hero or a saint. The everyday heart of authentic human living is the task of finding meaning and purpose that have validity beyond the mere here and now. The down-to-earth challenge of spirituality is to create a life worth living.

That ordinary but wondrous core of human living is rightly called *spiritual*. Its expression shows all the characteristics of spirituality, as people generally conceive it. That core is a built-in self-transcendence that pushes toward a broader and deeper grasp of life. At stake is something intuitive and illusive: at one and the same time, it bespeaks both what is already somehow grasped and what somehow still lies beyond us. Spirituality tends toward all that there is, so its scope is infinite, boundless, limitless. As such, it is also somehow already beyond space and time, ubiquitous and eternal. It anticipates the unity of all things wherein I would become one with all that is. Thus, mystery is also at stake, and even mysticism: living in reverence, awe, and wonder, being ever caught up in something bigger than oneself. Referring to spontaneous and unexpected giftedness, even the religious word *grace* could accurately apply to the workings of the human spirit.

This account retains all the standard characteristics of spirituality, although talk of God has never once entered the discussion. Here is an understanding of the essential feature of all human spirituality. Here is the grounding that spirituality has in the human being. Here is the heart of religion that gets elaborated in different eras and in various cultures.

However, this nontheist understanding of spirituality is also open to theist interpretation: you could name as "God" the unity, the eternal, the infinite, the ubiquitous, the all, toward which the human spirit strives. In the process, you might also recognize that much of our talk about God is really talk about core aspects of merely human experience. Even more, you would certainly be correct in holding that, if God-talk is to be anything more than childish fantasy about some omnipotent Santa Claus in the sky, any responsible practice of belief in God points right back to the essential human features of spirituality that I highlight, for even belief in God does not excuse us from the challenge of open, honest, and loving living in this world. Thus, although this treatment of a humanistic spirituality does not include reference to God, it is certainly open to God for anyone who wants to take that additional step.

For those interested in exploring this topic further, I have presented this understanding of spirituality in more detail in a number of other books. *Spirituality for a Secular Society* and *Meditation Without Myth* are popular presentations. *The Human Core of Spirituality* and *Religion and the Human Sciences* are more technical presentations. These books cover all the far-reaching religious and philosophical questions that are involved in the discussion of spirituality.

Summary of a Nontheist Spirituality

The human is a complex of body, psyche, and spirit. The spiritual component bespeaks a built-in self-transcendence that is wondrously open to the universe. This inherent self-transcendence is the essential feature of all spirituality and is prior to all religion and belief in God. Indeed, it is what religion and much of theism at their best are about. The human spirit itself grounds an absolutely legitimate spirituality.

Apart from all organized religion and belief in God, we must acknowledge an essential spiritual component in the human being. This spiritual component provides a solid base for living that is open to the wonder of the cosmos and that is noble, laudatory, virtuous, and ultimately fulfilling.

We could also add *spiritual* to that list of adjectives—noble, laudatory, virtuous, fulfilling—and speak also of spiritual living. But what difference would this addition make? Once the essential human meaning of spirituality is made clear, all facets of life naturally appear to be spiritual. The spiritual is part and parcel of being a human being. It is the human spirit that makes humans human, and this same human spirit is the basis of spirituality.

Lived with an eye to wholesome growth, to honest personal integration, to responsible interrelationship with others and with one's world—that is, lived with an eye to the inherent and relentless unfolding of the human spirit, *every aspect of living is a step on the spiritual path*. This realization is key to the legitimate treatment of spirituality within the human sciences, the human services, and secular society. This realization is also key to a nonreligious understanding of the spiritual issues at stake in the gay and lesbian experience.

THE SPIRITUAL DIMENSION
OF THE GAY AND LESBIAN EXPERIENCE

The Spiritual Significance of Coming Out

The nontheist understanding of spirituality just outlined is particularly well suited to the needs of the gay and lesbian community, even in the face of AIDS and other mortal issues. Too often, standard religious versions of spirituality cannot apply. Not only does much religion continue to reject the gay community, but some gays and lesbians themselves have also rejected religion and belief in its "God." However, the weight of the evidence tips the spiritual scales in favor of the gays and lesbians. If all spirituality is grounded in what is part and parcel of being a human being, if the essence of spirituality is basic human integrity, then pivotal to all spiritual growth is the option to affirm oneself rather than submit to societal and religious expectations. Lesbians and gays have made that option.

Accepting their homosexuality in all soul-searching, honesty, and anguish, in the face of misunderstanding, opposition, and rejection from family, friends, religion, and society at large, homosexual people take the giant step of self-acceptance that hurls them naked into the universe. There they face the uncertainty, mystery, and marvel that is our human allotment in the raw. In their teens and twenties and thirties, they take into their own hands the ultimate questions that others tend not to have to face until middle and old age. They grapple with the meaning of life, with the purpose of their existence. They struggle with their own individuality, with who they are and what they can pretend to be. They weigh the cost of honesty, the price of being one's unwelcome self. Breaking the supreme taboo of men loving men or women loving women, they are freed to question all else: family, friends, religion, and even God. They seek and create purpose in living without many of the raw materials society routinely provides as handouts to the young. In the process, they recognize as sham the rewards that society often holds out as a carrot.

Deciding to trust their own experience, understanding, and judgment, lesbians and gays are in fact engaging their spiritual capacity. They affirm the validity of their own selves, and without a road map they launch out in individuality on life's course. Trusting in themselves and in the mixed wisdom of their companions, they live by faith. Only the longings of their hearts and souls provide a compass for the journey. With few exceptions, even at this late date, the spiritual leaders of a homophobic society have abandoned them.

In light of the nontheist spirituality I have outlined, coming out as gay or lesbian is, indeed, a spiritual quest. In the symbolic language of the spiritual traditions, it is a search for the Holy Grail. It is the adventure of a hero or heroine. It is the pilgrimage of a saint.

A Response to the Religionists

Religious folk might scoff at such analogies: How can pursuit of homosexuality be anything holy? However, homosexual sex acts are not the issue. Rather, honesty, goodwill, courage, and personal integrity are the issues. Approve or not of the direction these characteristics take, they remain noble and virtuous traits, and they need to be honored. Besides, that the choice of one's homosexuality is misguided and wicked is a less and less tenable claim. The evidence of biblical scholarship, the conclusions of historical research, the overwhelming majority of the findings of the social sciences, and the ongoing discoveries of biology and medicine more and more solidly discredit condemnation of gay and lesbian love.

What is more, it may be easy to make a gay-positive argument today as the evidence continues to mount. But forty, thirty, or even twenty years ago, when the gay men and lesbians living today with AIDS were first grappling with their sexuality, the option was much harder. The choice, as it often still remains, was between self and respectability, pure and simple. The gay men and lesbians chose self. They chose to act honestly. They chose to trust things as they really are. They chose to live life without illusion. If in the process, for whatever complex reasons, their choice meant rejection of God, they had the courage and wisdom to opt for what is the more basic: personal integrity—a choice that even God must approve of.

Other notions of spirituality—such as those that appeal to magic and miracle or rely on tradition and supposed revelation—may be in opposition to such assertions about personal integrity. But in no longstanding religious tradition are naive pieties credited as valid. The Great Religions all respect and value the poignant human struggle with personal freedom, responsibility, meaning, and death. Noble, courageous, heroic, even holy and saintly—these words certainly fit the coming-out process. At the heart of the gay experience is a spiritual challenge.

NONTHEIST GAY SPIRITUALITY
IN THE FACE OF DEATH

In its defining experience, coming out, and in the challenge of living as lesbian or gay, the gay community has a treasure of spiritual richness. This treasure may serve it well in the face of the AIDS epidemic and other challenges. Only to recognize this treasure for what it is and to draw on it in the present need remains.

The heart of the spiritual crisis surrounding AIDS is the torture of slow debilitation, painful decline, and inevitable death. Although new medications may stave off these consequences, they continue to loom as a threatening specter for all and remain a gruesome, present reality for many. They come much too soon for people in their supposed prime of life. They strip away former boasts and joys, they undermine the reasons for living, and they erode whatever hope one might have. What resources does the gay and lesbian community have to address this spiritual crisis?

Running Away in Life's Fast Lane

First, denial tactics and dead-end solutions are to be avoided. Unfortunately, the spiritual potential in the gay experience is often lost. The inherent sacredness of the experience is missed. As a way of life in the sexually liberated 1970s and 1980s, many—not all—lesbians and gays had taken to unbridled sex and sensuality, abuse of alcohol and drugs, and the flimsy shield of fashion, fine foods, and high living. These allowed gays and lesbians to hide from the Pandora's box of spiritual issues that their life choices opened up. Sad to say, these same denial tactics have now become commonplace in the superficial American culture of the early twenty-first century. Widespread lack of meaning in our society fosters escapism. In this situation, news of HIV infection becomes just another thing to flee, and some choose to deal with their HIV-positive status by not facing it. Especially with the help of new medications and designer drugs, some HIV-positive people hide away in the party-oriented gay subculture and bide their time.

To be sure, learning to enjoy yourself, despite HIV infection, is an important part of (spiritual) health. To get out and socialize; to spend pleasant times with a lover, friends, and family; to take a long-dreamed-of vacation; these are positive practices. They reveal the goodness that life always holds, and they elicit a reverent and saving appreciation for just being alive. They are sources of spiritual enrichment. However, pushed to the limit and out of balance, these same pursuits can become escapism. Then they prevent us from grappling with the inner issues whose resolution becomes imperative as increasing limitations and inevitable death approach.

Of course, no one is really able to tell others how to cope with their anguish and pain. All people are not equally able to look reality in the face. To some extent, the rule does hold: "whatever works" is what is needed. But for most, at some point, "whatever works" does not work anymore. Honestly facing this fact, as done when facing one's homosexuality, can be a healing and enriching endeavor. It can open up whole new realms of experience.

Fully facing this challenge is not for everyone. Some are simply running out of time. Some lack the finances or social support for such an enterprise. Some just don't have the knack or inner resources for dealing with crises. Some have no history of prior achievements on which to rely and build. As a result, for many, spiritual unfolding is unlikely at the eleventh hour. The vision presented here is an ideal. As is always the case in life, what would be the very best is seldom achievable. Accepting circumstances as they are and learning to make the best of them is a major facet of (spiritual) wisdom—just as in the case of accepting one's homosexuality. Being able to see and appreciate the good that is already here, limited though it be, is already (spiritual) depth of character. Finding the balance between striving for more and being content with the status quo is (spiritual) virtue.

Falling Back onto Religion

Another way that gay and lesbian PWAs (people with AIDS) respond to the spiritual challenge of AIDS is to return to religion—sometimes for better, sometimes for worse.

Reconciling with One's Religious Upbringing

Many of the established religions are finally addressing the spiritual crisis of gay and lesbian PWAs. These religions are providing gay-sensitive ministry and helping many HIV-positive men and women to be reconciled with their religious upbringing and to find peace with their God. When this reconciliation respects the personal integrity of the people involved, it may provide the easiest resolution of the spiritual crisis. It may also be the most beautiful resolution because it can be a homecoming. It can put all the pieces of one's life back together again. It can allow reconciliation also with family and childhood community. In the process, this reconciliation can broaden the understanding of all concerned about the true meaning of religion and God in the real world, where some people are homosexual and some people get AIDS. The clergy who provide such healing ministry are a blessing to the gay community. Lesbian and gay PWAs who can respond to such ministry meet the spiritual challenge of AIDS effectively.

Finding a New Religion

In the face of HIV infection—as in coming out—other gay men and lesbians seek out a religion different from that of their upbringing. Often some form of New Age religion meets the need. Again, when such honest conversion occurs to the benefit of the new believers, this is a welcome outcome that honestly addresses their spiritual needs.

However, one common belief in the New Age movement calls for a caveat. The belief is that in some way people actually choose every aspect of their own fate, so a person's infection must be the result of his or her own decision—a decision, which, in some versions of this belief, is supposedly even more powerful than HIV in causing the disease. This belief has led some to think that, by sheer willpower and meditative techniques, they can become immune even to the immunodeficiency virus. This magical belief makes the (spiritual) mistake of obscuring a fact of the real world: humans are not, and never can be, in total control of their lives. Understandably, wanting to feel in control, some people accept this belief, but they pay for it with guilt, recrimination, and self-doubt. Gays and lesbians are often familiar and have learned to be comfortable with such negative feelings. Acceptance of this belief may covertly rest on internalized homophobia or some other deeply seated shame. Such spirituality must be bogus. Rather than helping people achieve a sense of integrity that allows them to embrace life even if it does include death, the belief that disease is self-inflicted sabotages the very foundation of spiritual growth. This spirituality requires people to mistrust their own selves. It requires people, whose every conscious desire is to live, to believe that they really want to die.

Being Coerced into Conversion

Another spiritually destructive maneuver is eleventh-hour conversion to some traditional, antigay religion. Unfortunately, belief in revelation from God lends a totalitarian air to much institutional Western religion. Firm in their own belief, some clergy unscrupulously coerce vulnerable dying gay men and lesbians into repudiating their whole life.

Of course, some things in life do need to be repudiated; some acts do call for repentance. To admit your real guilt and to repent your culpable mistakes is an important requirement for achieving (spiritual) wholeness. Erik Erikson made this point when treating the challenge of late adulthood, Integrity versus Despair: "'A thousand little disgusts'... do not add up to one big remorse." Avoiding final despair at life's end and finding personal integrity often require bearing the anguish of conscience and remorse. So lesbians and gays do need to admit wrongdoing, irresponsibility, abuse—the religious word is "sin." People reviewing their lives do need to repent of, and not just be disgusted at, some of what they have done. Recognizing real wrong as different from mere taboo is a major requirement of (spiritual) maturity. Then, accepting yourself as fallible and somewhat even perverse, as is the entire human race, and *forgiving yourself* become further steps on this same spiritual path.

Nonetheless, repudiating your whole life just because it was homosexual—and doing so merely for fear of eternal damnation—is unlikely to be a lesbian's or gay man's step toward profound personal integration. With all due respect to religion, this maneuver violates the essence of spirituality.

Still, people cannot do more than they are able. For some, to repudiate their gay life may be the only possible way of achieving a fragile peace of conscience or may be the only means of making precious reconciliation with deeply loved—or, more pragmatically, needed—family. People must do "whatever works." Still, it is deplorable that in the name of religion people must settle for so spiritually bankrupt a resolution.

Spiritual Wealth Within the Gay and Lesbian Community

If finding religion again can be of help to some gay PWAs, the spiritual concerns of the nonreligious still need to be met. Some lesbians and gay men are opposed to all institutional religion and unable to believe in God. What avenues toward transcendent living does the gay community offer them?

Reassessing Purpose in Life

Knowledge of HIV infection changes the status quo. As the disease or fear of it worsens, a need to rethink your life emerges. You must reaffirm the old, or find new, purpose in living.

It has been said that people are lucky who know that their life is ending. They have the occasion to look back and reassess, to change the aspects of life that are really not worthy of them, to focus on what really matters, and to look forward and plan how best to use the time that is left. At the end, these people can die with their lives in the order they would want. They can die knowing that they have—at least at the end, if not all along—lived their lives well and that the very wholesomeness of their lives is a unique contribution that will remain when they are gone.

Such reassessment is a spiritual matter. It engages you explicitly in the ultimates of life. It determines the meaning and value of your life. It involves you deliberately in things that transcend the here and now.

Getting Involved Politically, Socially, and Personally

As part of this spiritual enterprise, many HIV-positive gays and lesbians get involved in service and causes, often to the explicit benefit of the gay community and of those living with HIV/AIDS. The works of ACT UP (AIDS Coalition to Unleash Power) and Queer Nation are particularly obvious examples of contributions that HIV-positive gay men and lesbians, along with others, make to the gay community and to society at large. Similar are the contributions of less-publicized groups for political activities, AIDS services, educational projects, and other social concerns.

Formation of new community is another facet of the matter. Support groups and medical circles for PWAs result in new friendships and affiliations. People's worlds broaden. New interests and concerns emerge. Facing serious issues of life and death, people share on deep levels and, thus, achieve, sometimes for the first time, real emotional intimacy. Attending seriously to health and well-being, HIV-positive gays and lesbians also find motivation to address alcohol, drug, and sex addictions. Improved or renewed physical and psychological health and increased social involvement is the (spiritually) positive result. Or again, facing HIV/AIDS and death, lesbians and gay men also often dare—or are forced—to reach out to their families of origin. When mutual understanding and reconciliation follow, personal integration and inner strength surge on all fronts.

Such political, social, and emotional involvement facilitates deep change within the psyche. Hidden levels of feelings surface; hopes, dreams, and fantasies emerge; and new patterns of response develop. The mental structures of the person shift, and new inner space is created. In this space the spirit is free to assert itself and to reach out to the cosmos that it would embrace. That is to say, all these matters are important aspects of spiritual growth.

Achieving Self-Affirmation

Consolidation of a positive sense of self is another facet of spiritual growth. Developing new friendships, sharing with others on a new level, checking your addictions, and renewing ties with your family all enhance self-esteem. They elicit a positive attitude toward life: there is good to be shared even as the shadows of life lengthen. Self-esteem is directly related to spiritual growth, as will be discussed in Chapter 4.

Other engagements can also enhance self-affirmation or self-esteem. For example, helping other PWAs, if only by honestly expressing your own experience, provides a sense of worth, value, and belonging. Sharing with others how it is to live with intense awareness of mortality—that is, how it is to accept one's humanity—is a gift beyond measure in our unbalanced culture of denial. Being the gift giver confirms your awareness of yourself as spiritually rich, gifted, blessed, in the very moment of facing your own demise. Similarly, remaining faithful to a life partner despite HIV infection and AIDS can be a source of fulfillment, pride, and self-affirmation. It is hard to imagine a more lasting satisfaction—despite overwhelming burden—than that of a committed relationship lived to death's door. Likewise, being honest with potential sex partners about your HIV status confirms your self-respect, and it matters more in the end than loss of a shared orgasm.

Those and other simple acts, all done in honesty and goodwill, lead to, express, and enhance personal integrity. Authenticity counts. By itself it can confer a new sense of purpose and meaning in life, for authenticity entails radical self-affirmation. Personal integrity is something that nothing, not even death, can take away.

Facing Death

When the final stages of AIDS or other terminal diseases arrive, involvement with others falls off, and physical activity is reduced to a minimum, people at peace with themselves and their world can surrender to the last adventure of life. They can depart with serenity and dignity. Their act of dying is their last confirmation of trust in life, which they have trusted enough to live with gusto all along. Having lived in faith—never knowing for sure where life's course would lead yet having arrived, nonetheless, at a point of centeredness, at a sense of involvement in a wonder bigger than any of us—they can trust one more time and go off serenely into the great beyond. What lies ahead no one can say. If further life exists, it must certainly be theirs, for they have lived as deeply and honestly as any could hope. If nothing is beyond, they die knowing, nonetheless, that they lived well and that their love and contributions live on after them. They have left a mark on this world in everyone whom they have let know them.

Would such a dying be really any different from that of the truly honest believer in God? Is trusting deeply in life really any different in practice from trusting in God? Is hoping that some continued life lies beyond, but being willing to live honestly and lovingly in whatever case, really any different in practice from believing in heaven? The religionist may put hallowed words on the matter—God, heaven, revelation, creed, worshiping community—but the human living, if it is honest, is still done in unknowing, trust, and hope.

Besides, putting holy words on the matter, confirmed with unwarrantable certainty, often merely fosters dishonest living. Unrealistic religious belief leads people to avoid the enigma of life. If so, those who have lived without that supposed certainty but lived honestly and lovingly, nonetheless, may well be the more deeply spiritual, the more deeply immersed in the transcendent stuff of human life. This, at least, is the thesis advanced in this chapter. This is an offer of hope to people living with and dying of AIDS, rejected by and rejecting bankrupt religion, because they will not pretend to be other than what they honestly are. This is a human-science account of spirituality that challenges even the religions to match up to the basic requirements of human worthiness.

FINAL CONSIDERATIONS

The essential feature of this nontheist spirituality is the human spirit, a principle of self-transcendence built into humanity. This spiritual principle expresses itself in honest and loving living, openness to things as they truly are, and wonder and awe at the universe. The unfolding of this principle implies acceptance of yourself and of your lofty yet humble place in the whole. Such acceptance and affirmation of your inherent self-transcendence results in trust in the universe, awareness of goodness and beauty all around, and a sense of gratitude for all that is. Such spirituality stands firm even in the face of death.

Four brief, further considerations help round out this discussion. First, some practices usually associated with religion suggest other aspects of a nontheist spirituality. One important example is the use of ritual.

Through symbols, gestures, and poetic turns of phrase, ritual gives expression to the inexpressibles of the heart. A Thanksgiving meal—as in Paul Monette's *Afterlife*—the celebration of a birthday or holiday, quiet talk over a weekly cup of tea, the soft glow of a candle lit in a moment of solitude, the warm embrace of a hello or good-bye, travel (pilgrimage) to a place of fond memory or to a grave, gifting friends and family with treasured mementos—multiple facets of life may serve ritual purpose. The spirituality in the love behind such gestures should not go unnoted.

Another example of religious practice is meditation and retreats. At stake in these practices is the basic human need for quiet time. Questions of God and religion need not be part of the matter. Time alone or time apart is healthy for people facing HIV, AIDS, and death. The practice of structured meditation reduces stress and facilitates dealing on deep levels with unresolved personal and emotional issues. Unstructured time to think, to muse, to experience the depths of the heart, time to mourn one's passing life—these are necessary for people at any point in life, and all the more so for people living with HIV/AIDS. I deal with meditation in detail in my book *Meditation Without Myth*.

Second, support groups are useful to pull individuals out of their sometimes excessive solitude. Group sharing about the big questions of life and about the trivialities that become overwhelming is really a delving into the spiritual dimension of life. For nonreligious PWAs, these groups can be valuable alternatives to weekly church, synagogue, mosque, or ashram gatherings. The regularity of the meeting provides structure and security, and structure or routine is an important aspect of spirituality. True spirituality means living at the point of growth, living on the edge or living in between, neither here nor there, so spirituality thrives only in a delicate balance between the fixed and the open-ended.

Third, individual psychotherapy may sometimes be the contemporary version of traditional "spiritual direction" or consultation with the religious leader, the holy man or woman, the guru. Still, standard psychotherapeutic attention to "merely" emotional and relational issues is also part of the spiritual picture. If the key to transcendent living is the human spirit, the key to unleashing the spirit is the restructuring of the psyche. In the mentally healthy person, body, psyche, and spirit work together to maintain an overall equilibrium wherein human needs at the various levels demand attention in ever-shifting urgency. When, for the sake of a person's sanity, ego defenses against long-repressed anxiety, anger, sadness, or hurt healthily prevent openness, the human spirit is not free to soar. Attention to such emotional issues is the road to spiritual unfolding. Only when we get our emotional houses in order can our spirits transcend. Happily, in times of physical weakness or intense stress—as in facing HIV infection,

AIDS, and death—body, psyche, and spirit often strike a new alliance. Sometimes, relatively easily, rapid restructuring of the psyche can result and spirituality can blossom. The role of psychotherapy in spiritual development must not be underestimated. Emotional health and spiritual health go hand in hand. As John McNeill is fond of saying, good psychology is good spirituality.

Finally, the question: Who is to function as minister in this non-theist spirituality for gay men and lesbians living with a terminal disease and facing the reality of death? A number of options are available.

Fortunately, some ministers of organized religion have begun to address the spiritual needs of people who do not necessarily qualify as members of their own flock. These ministers are open enough to recognize true spirituality in homosexual people. Much in line with what is written in this book, they would willingly accompany pilgrims on any valid version of the spiritual path.

Moreover, others without professional religious credentials may also be spiritual companions. Friends and associates in the gay community may meet the need admirably, particularly because they share the same basic experience of homosexuality. Caregivers, as well, can exercise the spiritual role: nurses, doctors, therapists, hospital volunteers, social workers, group leaders, buddies, hospice volunteers, receptionists in medical offices and hospitals, as well as family, friends, and neighbors—anyone who really cares. At stake is simply the challenge of honest human living, not of institutional religion. On this basis, anyone willing to engage life deeply accrues spiritual experience and can claim spiritual expertise.

This final point summarizes the main thrust of this chapter. When spirituality is understood as a core human reality, every aspect of life can be credited as spiritual. Every open, honest, and loving person can be seen as being on a spiritual quest. The gay and lesbian experience, itself, lived honestly and lovingly, in flamboyant life or in horrid death, can be acclaimed as profoundly rich, sacred, holy—and spiritual. One need only understand the meaning of this word to salute the spiritual almost anywhere.

Chapter 3

Sexuality and Spirituality:
Friends, Not Foes

In Western civilization sexuality and spirituality have commonly been at odds. However, recent developments in psychology and theology reconcile the two. This chapter explores these developments.

The argument is firm: Sexuality and spirituality are not antagonistic. On the contrary, they are complementary, interdependent, and inseparable. Both sexuality and spirituality are aspects of the total person. Different aspects of one and the same being, they enhance each other. Growth in one facilitates growth in the other as the whole person grows. A fully developed spirituality implies a fully developed sexuality, and vice versa. Obviously, then, if people are uncomfortable with their sexuality, including homosexuality, they cannot achieve spiritual insight or transforming spiritual experience.

This chapter surveys some past positive approaches to sexuality and spirituality and also briefly considers the predominantly negative attitudes that our culture holds. The chapter then explains how sexuality and spirituality are, indeed, friends, not foes.

POSITIVE ATTITUDES

Many religions have viewed sexuality as integral to spiritual pursuit. In *Transcendental Sex,* Jerry Gillines notes that the ancients considered sexual union the closest experience to divine bliss that one could achieve. P. D. Ouspensky goes further and states, "Of all ordi-

This chapter was co-authored with Sylvia Chavez-Garcia (now Sylvia Chavez Longnecker) and originally published with documentation in *The Journal of Pastoral Care,* 1985, volume 39, pages 151-163. Reprinted with permission.

nary human experiences only sex sensations approach those which we call 'mystical.'" In fact, the use of sex in religious rituals for the attainment of enlightenment has a history almost as old as the human race.

Mystics have traditionally expressed their experiences by using the language of sexual love even though they admit that such language is inadequate to convey their experience of the "divine." The Jewish prophets Isaiah, Jeremiah, and especially Hosea used the language and imagery of sexual relationship, intimacy, and intercourse to describe the union of God and God's people. Lovers often speak of being "divinized" by their love and relate experiences or illuminations that verge on the mystical.

Different people have explored ways of integrating sexuality and spirituality into their cultures and religions. For example, in the courts of medieval Europe, courtly love was the ideal. A young knight would love and idealize a married noblewoman, transforming any sexual feelings into devotional service, tenderness, and gallantries. It was believed that such restraint and devotion would spiritually elevate the knight.

Other sexual-spiritual rituals may have existed elsewhere in medieval Europe. Some believe alchemists employed sexual rites as a secret part of their work and point out that those who practiced witchcraft often used sex in spells and rituals. Medieval magicians used orgasm to create supercharged affirmations and visualizations. Within a heterosexual model, medieval kabbalism held that males and females possess "divine" energies of opposite polarities. When combined in the proper way, these energies would keep sexuality holy by drawing down the supernal light.

Much more recently, in 1866, the religious founder John Humphrey Noyes introduced karezza in America. This is a practice of prolonged, nonorgasmic copulation, and it was mandatory for members of his Oneida Community, who used it successfully until at least 1879. Although its original purpose was to avoid unwanted pregnancy, Noyes's followers soon discovered karezza induced a relaxation and mutual devotion far surpassing that of ordinary sex. In the early 1900s, Dr. Alice Stockman, an English physician and sex educator practicing in America, popularized karezza. She found it more spiritually uplifting than orgasmic intercourse and wrote that it produced "exquisite exaltation" and "a perfect satisfaction surpassing mortal understanding."

In the 1920s, Dr. Rudolf von Urban, an American physician and marriage counselor, developed an innovative tantra-like technique. Von Urban theorized that "bioelectric energies" of opposite polarities were exchanged between lovers. His technique called for thorough relaxation before sex and for prolonged intercourse in a special position. Although this technique did not produce orgasm, his patients claimed it generated ecstatic pleasure, profound contentment, and even physical healing.

Some sexologists criticize such concepts as myths strictly for "mystics" who delude themselves with fairy tales. Yet these practices and claims are similar to those of tantric ritual and sexual yoga, which are the product of five millennia of Indian culture. These same claims find confirmation in the contemporary exercises of Joseph Kramer's Body Electric workshops for gay men. In addition to rhythmic breathing and meditative exercises, these practices engage the powerful physiological force of sex, not for the propagation of the race, but for the attainment of a higher state of consciousness in which the personal ego is transcended. As Dio Urmilla Neff reports, "Couples who regularly practice Tantra claim remarkable experiences. They describe a rapture that transports them beyond their ordinary selves and an inexpressible state of timelessness. Their limits and edges seem to dissolve; they merge into one being."

In summary, sex can, indeed, be used to shift physiological and psychological functioning and, thus, induce spiritual experiences. Sexuality and spirituality can go hand in hand.

NEGATIVE ATTITUDES

In contrast, Western civilization has generally opposed the integration of sexuality and spirituality. The origins of this negative attitude lie in the interaction of the Jewish, Christian, and especially the Greek traditions, which formed our culture.

In the Judaic tradition sex is the creation of God, and it is good. One of its prime functions is to continue the family lineage and propagate Israel, God's people. On the other hand, the Canticle of Canticles (Song of Solomon or Song of Songs), a book in the Old Testament, is a blatant celebration of sex and romance, and it shows no concern whatsoever for procreation. This initial Jewish attitude toward sex was very affirming.

Negative restrictions arose when Israel encountered the supposedly orgiastic religious practices among the Canaanites and others in the "promised land." To keep Israel's religion pure, separate from that of the Gentiles, the "Holiness Code" of Leviticus, especially Chapter 18, forbade sexual practices that were perhaps associated with pagan rites. This same chapter forbade penetrative sex between two men as an "abomination" or an uncleanness. In this case, the concern was the "mixing of kinds," that is, the blurring of the idealized line between the male and the female, similar to the "unclean" mixing of two fibers in one fabric or of two different seeds in one field.

Throughout these ancient Jewish prohibitions, religious and cultural concerns, not sexual-ethical concerns, were at stake, yet the practical effect was the same. Even today Fundamentalist groups rip these passages out of their cultural context and cite them to condemn contemporary homosexuality, which is very different from what the ancient texts addressed. Overall, however, from the Jews early Christianity inherited a basically positive attitude toward sexuality. Greek thought was the primary source of the sex-negative attitudes.

The earliest Greeks held that sexual abstinence was requisite for sublime purity. This view influenced the Greek philosophers, including Plato and Aristotle, who in turn had great influence on subsequent sexual attitudes. Later Stoic philosophy prized the soul rather than the body and held that asceticism and self-denial were the only way to true perfection. Stoicism tolerated sex only for procreation. The idea was that procreation expressed the essential nature of sex and that sex for pleasure's sake was a violation of that nature and, hence, an unreasonable act. A biological emphasis carried the day.

In those ancient Greek philosophies, a dualist outlook—the supposition that spirit is good and matter is evil—reigned. These ideas prevailed in the early centuries of Christianity's development. So, following the Stoics, Neoplatonists, and Aristotelians, Christians began to insist that sexuality conform to the laws of "nature," which supposedly limited sexual activity to situations in which procreation was intended. This influence affected contemporary Western nations in which penal codes still sometimes prohibit certain sexual activities, and this influence still controls the understanding of sex in official

Roman Catholic teaching, which has co-opted the notion of "natural law" and restricted its meaning to imply that sex is for procreation only. Chapter 11 explores Catholic teaching in more detail.

Gnostic influence is also clearly evident in the Christian ascetic and mystical tradition. For example, Evagrius Ponticus, a late fourth-century Egyptian monk, understood charity to be the *love of the contemplation of God* above all else—and not the love of God and neighbor themselves, as Jesus had it.

Extreme ascetic practices, in no way taught by Jesus or the Christian Testament, continue to abound in Christianity. Saint Augustine of Hippo (354-430 CE) was a main conduit of this body-negative influence. Before he converted to Christianity, he was a devotee of Manichaeism, an explicit dualist philosophy that stressed the essential evil of matter, including sexuality. Augustine never did come to terms with his own sexuality, and Christianity carries on Augustine's personal struggle: the sins of the father visited upon the children.

As a young man, Augustine had both a male and a female lover—which was nothing unusual in his day—and a child whom he loved dearly. His concubine and son died young, and Augustine was heartbroken. Augustine agonized with guilt over his sexual exploits, but he was unable to rein in his desire for sex. His mixed feelings toward sex are obvious in the prayer he prayed as he struggled to convert to Christianity: "Lord, make me chaste—but not yet."

Augustine never did purge his sexual teaching of the dualism of Manichaeism, and sex-negativism became the Christian legacy. Augustine was the most cited ancient Christian figure in medieval Christendom. This spiritual giant's impact on Western Christianity is beyond measure.

Medieval Christianity considered sexual abstinence to be spiritually superior to marriage. At the same time, increased devotion to the humanity of Jesus—especially his passion—and the harshness of life in that era fostered an ideal of body-denying asceticism. For example, Anselm of Canterbury's theory of atonement—the explanation of how Jesus saved us—legitimated this ascetic ideal. Borrowing on a then prevalent notion of the value of suffering for others' sake, Anselm suggested that Jesus saved humanity precisely by suffering and dying, that is, by paying the price of sin and, thus, restoring the order of justice. Although English translations of the Christian scriptures, reflecting the theology of Martin Luther and John Calvin, might support such a notion, it is not biblical. It suggests that physical suffering and self-denial are somehow redemptive in themselves—as if God likes human suffering. What a perverse idea! This same notion flowed into sex-negative attitudes.

REEMERGING POSITIVE ATTITUDES

Subsequently, sexual attitudes underwent numerous fluctuations. During the nineteenth-century Victorian period, for example, the general belief was that sexual activity and even sexual impulses were a moral threat and should be held in suspicion. People thought it best to suppress sexual feelings as well as information about sex.

The twentieth century brought an explosion of technology and research affecting sexuality. This explosion greatly influenced attitudes about sex, and it helped to ease previous restrictions on sexual behavior. For the first time in human history, sex became a topic of discussion and research. Associated with this novelty are such people as Sigmund Freud, Henry Havelock Ellis, Richard von Krafft-Ebing, and Magnus Hirschfeld (the gay Jew, whose Institute for Sex Science was destroyed by the Nazis in 1933) and, later in the century, Alfred Kinsey, William Masters and Virginia Johnson, Helen Kaplan, and Edward Laumann.

The rebellious playfulness of the "roaring twenties" and the invention of the automobile—which gave young couples a place to have sex free from parental supervision—chipped away at Victorian standards. Sex became less dangerous with the discovery of vulcanized rubber—and, later, latex and polyurethane—useable for condoms and of penicillin and other antibiotics for curing sexually transmitted diseases.

World Wars I and II further loosened sexual mores by exposing hundreds of thousands of soldiers to the sexual practices of other societies. One song from the era of World War I captured this effect in these words: "How ya gonna keep 'em down on the farm after they've seen Paree?" After World War II, the gay community in San Francisco formed when military personnel returning from the Pacific never did go back to the farms.

The liberating effect of chemical birth control cannot be exaggerated. "The pill," marketed in 1960, effectively separated sex and procreation and, thus, changed the meaning of sex. Moreover, emphasis on the dignity and equality of all people within the civil rights movement gave rise as well to the women's movement and, then, to the gay liberation movement. Throughout the century, increasing psychological sophistication helped recast the meaning of sex. Now not procreation but interpersonal sharing was recognized as the distinctive essential of human sexuality. Not simply setting up a household but bonding in affectionate intimacy became the essential requisite of marriage. The divorce rate rose not because people became less responsible, but because people were now marrying for emotional intimacy, and no one is yet very good at it.

Although this interpersonal understanding of sex came as a surprise, it should not have. From prehistoric times on only humans have sex face-to-face, only humans routinely want and have sex outside of fertile periods, and among all other species only human females routinely experience orgasm. Clearly, sex between humans means something different from the merely reproductive sex between barnyard animals.

Catalyzed by the "sexual revolution" of the 1960s and 1970s, some religious bodies reexamined their positions on sexual ethics. Their teaching now tended to be less legalistic and more situational. In 1965, at the Second Vatican Council, even the Roman Catholic Church officially allowed a more affirming approach to sexuality. Whereas formerly procreation was considered the primary end of marriage, now the "unitive aspect"—bonding, interpersonal intimacy, sometimes also called the "re-creative" dimension of sex—is placed on a par with procreation. It is precisely this emphasis on interpersonal bonding that legitimates homosexual love as a normal variant alongside heterosexual love. Furthermore, humanistic psychology and the holistic health movement also influenced the contemporary view that sexuality and spirituality can be seen as two sides of the same coin. Sexuality and spirituality are complementary dimensions of human nature.

RENEWED INTEREST IN SPIRITUALITY

In recent years, spirituality has also come out of the closet. Spirituality is no longer considered the exclusive domain of religion, and it is no longer cloistered away from the mundane world. Increasingly, laity as well as clergy and other religious professionals want information about down-to-earth spirituality and wholesome sexuality, and they want credible teaching about how both contribute to human integration and growth.

This concern for human integration—or personal wholeness—is a recent phenomenon. Integration is a psychological notion. It refers to getting all the facets of your being into harmony. It is what psychologists, psychotherapists, and counselors are trained to facilitate. It refers to overcoming conflicts between your thoughts and your feelings, between your upbringing and your later experience, between your hopes and your fears, between your physical and emotional urges and your good sense. Amazingly, because of Phil Donahue, John Bradshaw, Oprah, and the like, this notion is already very well known. It even has a popular name: Getting your shit together.

In former ages, a person was to keep his or her urges in check and even to deny and suppress some of them—for example, sex. Of course, pressure-cooker-like, people found ways, often deviant, to let off steam, or one day they simply exploded. Today, the goal is to uncover the inner tugs and pulls and to find some way for them to work together for the overall good of a person and society at large. In the past *integrity* referred to ethical trustworthiness. Our current psychological understanding of integrity includes far more. Psychology has made us aware of a zoo of different forces living within ourselves. Integration means making peace among them all so that, supporting and reinforcing one another, they all flow in one wholesome direction. In the imagery of the prophet Isaiah, the wolf and the lamb, the leopard and the kid, the lion and the ox shall all lie down together, and there will be no hurt or harm on all God's holy mountain.

This shift in outlook is massive, and the challenge it raises is daunting. As we now understand ourselves, however, this challenge cannot be avoided, and it is never ending. Our potential is infinite, so our growth is ongoing. Personal growth results in a person of increasing integration.

As might already be obvious, such integration is the key to spiritual growth. In today's understanding of the matter—not always in opposition to the traditional—good psychology is good spirituality.

INTEGRATION OF BODY, PSYCHE, AND SPIRIT

How is it that sexuality and spirituality involve each other? Simply as a matter of personal integration. Sexuality is a complex reality. It has physical, psychological, and spiritual dimensions.

The physical dimension is most obvious. Sexuality entails the bodiliness of a human being as female or male. In question is the physical body with its particular sex organs and their functioning. Physical bodiliness also has a social aspect. The body is the basis of human interaction, for the body is the vehicle through which people meet the need for communication and communion. Indeed, communication, both verbal and nonverbal, requires the vehicle of the body; communion finds a primary expression and experience in physical touch.

This state of affairs characterizes the human situation overall: we exist as physical realities. We experience our physical sexual characteristics, our psychological states and emotional moods, and even our philosophical musings and most sublime longings in the body and only in the body. The very care and concern we show for ourselves is predominantly care for our bodies: good nutrition, exercise, rest, grooming, and recreation. The bodies in question are male and female (though sometimes they are mixed).

However, sexuality involves more than bodily function. It also entails the psyche—emotions, memories, images, and personality types. These play vital roles in human sexual experience. Many now agree that this psychological dimension of sexuality is paramount in human beings, even when the main concern is only to satisfy bodily needs. The largest sex organ in the human being is the brain; to an overwhelming extent, human sex is a mental thing.

Recognition of that fact allows that even when you are not having sex, your sexuality comes into play. Our psychological reality includes the awareness of ourselves as having a male or female body and as living out or rejecting masculine and feminine stereotypes. No matter what we do, we do it as men or women. Thus, I am not a self who happens also to have a body. I am an embodied self, and my body is my self-present-to-the-world. My self is a body-self. Sexuality pervades the individual.

The capacity to be deeply aroused by what we experience is part of the psychological dimension of sexuality. Because of it, our whole being—including our sex organs—is able to respond to what we feel, understand, know, or desire. Human wholeness requires a willingness to respond with as much of our totality as we are able. Human wholeness includes the strength to risk our own feeling and experiencing as we risk feeling and experiencing others. Thus, sexuality includes a psychological as well as a physical dimension, and the two are intertwined.

Yet there is more. Sex also includes a spiritual dimension. The attractions and repulsions experienced in sexuality—"I like you," "I don't like you," "I respond pleasantly to you," "I become all uptight with you"—these attractions and repulsions imply values. They involve me in choices about what I prize or abhor. They bespeak love and hate, and these are spiritual matters.

Other aspects of sexual experience—"I will be myself with you," "I cannot be myself with you," "I am fully open and honest with you," "I have to pretend with you"—involve questions about the truth. Am I honest, will I be honest—about me, about you, and about what is really going on between us? Truth is another spiritual matter.

Honesty and love—or truth and value, or ideas and ideals, or meanings and values, or understandings and commitments, or beliefs and ethics, or dreams and promises: these pairs are different formulas for the same thing—are spiritual matters. Sex leads right into them. A bodily function opens onto an emotional experience that provokes spiritual concerns: having sex seduces lovers into sharing dreams and making promises. Human sex includes a spiritual dimension.

Then how does spirituality enter the picture? In one way or another, all human behavior is an expression of the human spirit, so spirituality has been in the picture all along. As I understand it, spirituality depends first and foremost on the human spirit itself, not necessarily on religion or reference to God. I offer a fully nontheist beginning point—but it certainly opens onto theological considerations, for those who want them—in the following ways. A theist would see the human concern for truth and goodness—honesty and love, ideas and ideals, dreams and promises—as the human tendency toward the Fullness of Truth and Goodness, which Western theology names *God.* Thus, you could say that the human spirit, created by God, naturally tends Godward. Going even further, a Christian would look forward to actual entry into that fullness: union with God, oneness with divinity, human deification. Paul repeatedly speaks of our being adopted into the divine family: "God sent his Son . . . so we might receive adoption as children . . . crying 'Abba! Father!'" (Galatians 4:4-7; see also Romans 8:15, 23; 9:4; Ephesians 1:3-5). John 17:21 puts the following prayer on Jesus' lips: "As you, Father, are in me and I am in you, may they also be one in us." The First Letter of John 3:1-2 says, "See what love the Father has given us . . . we will be like him, for we will see him as he is," and 2 Peter 1:4 says that we are destined to "become participants of the divine nature." Likewise, an ancient Christian prayer, retained in the Roman Catholic Mass, reads, "May we come to share in the divinity of Christ, who humbled himself to share in our humanity." According to Christian belief, the Holy Spirit energizes the human spirit and incorporates right-living people into Christ and, with Christ, into the Eternal Father-Mother. Christian faith is trinitarian precisely to explain how humans could become divine: In Christ, through the Holy Spirit, humans are to live the very life of God. Chapters 5 and 13 treat this theme in more detail.

However, religion and theology are not my focus here. Rather, the focus is "merely" on honesty and love, and I understand these are understood to be expressions of a dynamism built into the human mind, namely, the human spirit. Honesty and love are spiritual phenomena. Although they are inseparable from the body and the psyche, they nonetheless go beyond the body because they are not merely physical, and they go beyond psyche because they are not merely emotional. Honesty and love introduce a whole other dimension to human experience, a built-in penchant toward all that is true and good, toward what holds everywhere and always. This dimension of the human mind engages us with what is timeless and ubiquitous. To this extent we are godlike, or, as Genesis 1:26 phrased the matter, we are made in the "image and likeness of God." We are in part spiritual.

Deliberate integration of this spiritual dimension of the mind is the sum and substance of spiritual growth. The term *spirituality* refers to the concerted human effort to integrate the spiritual dimension of the mind into the permanent structures of one's being. As I understand it, in the first instance, spirituality is simply a matter of healthy personal wholeness, the integration of body, psyche, and spirit. Spirituality is simply a matter of becoming a full, genuine, authentic human being. Only secondarily does spirituality involve religion and theology. Religion and theology are expressions and elaborations of this core, human spirituality.

To be sure, this understanding raises far-reaching philosophical questions, which are further and better discussed in my other books, especially *Religion and the Human Sciences* and *The Human Core of Spirituality.* Nonetheless, in passing, recall that dishonesty causes stress and is dangerous to your health and that people deprived of love die. Such evidence suggests that following one's spiritual drives toward honesty and love is essential to human integrity and health. Spirituality is a natural aspect of being a human being.

EMBODIED SPIRITUALITY

This understanding of spirituality is fully down-to-earth. It is not focused on unusual happenings such as seeing visions, hearing voices, channeling entities, and, in general, somehow floating, "blissed-out," above mortal life. Many people believe that such occurrances are what spirituality is about. Of course, intense spiritual development does often open people to certain paranormal powers—telepathy, clairvoyance, telekinesis, precognition—powers that are real but about which we still have little understanding. Completely apart from anything that might be called spiritual development or intense spirituality, some people are born gifted with these very powers. It is obvious, then, that these two—developed spirituality and psychic gifts—do not necessarily go hand in hand; they are not essentially related. I believe that fascination with psychic gifts and unusual occurrences, sometimes called "woo-woo spirituality," distracts from the core spiritual requirement of good living in this world. In fact, such otherworldly emphasis belongs to the dualistic tradition that demeans the body and physical matter and sees spirituality as some escape to another world. Such an otherworldly emphasis in spirituality has little room for sexuality. Accordingly, these extraordinary occurrences are not the concern here.

The main point of this chapter should be coming into focus: The issue of reconciling spirituality and sexuality is simply the issue of achieving human integration. Since body, psyche, and spirit are not separable parts but, rather, different aspects of the human being, human integration entails all three: bodily-sexual integration, psychological-emotional integration, and spiritual-transcendent integration. Sexual integration and spiritual integration are different sides of the same coin; they necessarily go hand in hand. The spiritual pursuit of truth and value in honesty and love does not proceed unless it is supported and sustained in a healthy, responsive, and sensitive body. Conversely, expansive and pleasurable sexual experience does not occur unless it is shared in honesty and love. Sexual experience must be honest and loving to be healthy. This realization is the key to sexual ethics, which is discussed in Chapters 6 and 7.

In different ways many others have made that same point. For example, in *Between Two Gardens* James Nelson states that "movement toward a more healed, holistic spirituality and movement toward a more healed, holistic sexuality cannot be separated. It is not that they just ought not be separated; quite literally they cannot be. One is necessary for the other."

In *Urgent Longings* Thomas J. Tyrrell insists that both sexuality and spirituality are present in the total range of human experience, which achieves its highest manifestation in interpersonal love. This type of love is the experience of a healthy integration of our sexuality through life-giving intimate relationships, a taste of the transcendent dimension of our lives.

In *The Mystery of Sexuality* Rosemary Haughton states, "The unfolding of sexuality is also the unfolding of the human spirit," and "Sexual development cannot be separated from personal spiritual development."

Finally, in a 1981 article in *Studies in Formative Spirituality,* Vincent Bilotta develops this theme: our sexual unfolding is a story of transcendence. Beneath the sexual is the search for the spiritual. The sexual lifts us out of ourselves and opens up the deeper spiritual hunger that resides in us all. We are in search of "more than." The sexual restlessness of our hearts reveals that we are thirsty to drink of the presence of the other and, ultimately, of the presence of the divine other.

Thus far I have been discussing the integration of the body, psyche, and spirit, but another aspect of integration also needs to be considered: the integration of the supposed "feminine" and "masculine" within a person's psyche. Because it pertains to the psyche, this issue is primarily a psychological one, not a physical or spiritual one. This issue arises because every society specifies stereotypical masculine and feminine roles and imposes them on its members, and we are left needing to reconcile the masculine and the feminine within ourselves.

Because of their female or male bodies, girls and boys are brought up to develop certain characteristics and to repress others. Culturally approved masculinity and femininity result, and they are designed to complement each other. For example, in our society men are not generally aware of, or responsive to, their feelings; women are not generally inclined to self-assertion and efficient productivity. This complementarity serves society well, but it leaves the individuals themselves impoverished.

Psychological sexual integration requires that a person develop the complementary aspects of his or her personality. Growth in this direction gives rise to an androgynous personality, a shifting harmonization of masculinity-femininity. Androgyny—from the Greek *andros* (male) + *gyne* (female)—implies a retrieval of the whole expanse of human "sexuality," both masculine and feminine. Such integration leaves people free to cross and combine stereotypic roles as desired: men can be gentle and nurturing, and women can be strong and assertive.

Obviously, a heterosexual relationship provides a ready means for seeking the psychological complement. As man and woman stretch to meet each other on the psychological ground where the other is more at home, they surpass the limits of their own stereotypic femininity or masculinity. Homosexual relationships demand a similar emotional stretching. Two men will not sustain a deep relationship long if they do not learn to deal with their feelings. Likewise, two women must learn to deal with the practicalities of the world if they would sustain their relationship. Indeed, gay and lesbian people may actually have a head start on straight people because homosexual people often already embody both feminine and masculine traits before they ever enter into interpersonal relationships. Thus, heterosexuality and homosexuality offer potentially equal but different avenues to psychological integration and spiritual wholeness.

One common religious argument against homosexuality is the claimed "complementarity" of the sexes—the supposition that God created woman and man especially for each other. However, as noted here, obviously any two people can complement each other on a range of psychological characteristics. So the appeal to the complementarity of the sexes is really an appeal to biological plumbing, and the unspoken presumption is that the most important aspect of sex is the physical. Such an understanding reduces sex to a barnyard-animal affair. The emphasis on sheer biology obscures the fact that in human beings biology takes on richer and broader meaning. For people, sex is not just a physical act but an interpersonal sharing; human sex includes emotional and spiritual components, and the interpersonal sharing is the most important dimension of *human* sexuality. Understood in this way, sex between two women or between two men can express as much complementarity as sex between a man and a woman. What matters is the people, not their genitals.

MEANS OF INTEGRATION

What are some ways sexuality and spirituality complement each other? First, note some familiar negative considerations. For example, because I have learned a negative response to my body, I am at odds with myself as a body-self. Partially cut off from myself, I am out of touch with a most important source of experience. My growth comes to a near standstill, integration ceases, and my spiritual growth is blocked. Once puberty sets in, guilt and fear about body functions and sex are exacerbated. My body reacts whether I like it or not and despite what I learned about such things. All growth ceases until I get beyond this roadblock. How many lesbians and gays spend years treading water in life because they cannot come to grips with their homosexuality?

Furthermore, expected sex roles may not square with my individual uniqueness. The experiences of artists, handicapped people, and all of us, all sensitive people, offer poignant examples. Under social pressure, I try to conform, but I hardly do well. I may lose confidence in myself, develop self-hatred, and internalize rejection. My self-esteem plummets. Now out of touch with my real self and cut off from my most precious gifts, I am insensitive to the movements of my spirit; I am numb to the thrust toward honesty and love within me. I have learned not to trust or risk such urges. I do not trust myself. The energy I expend in suppressing aspects of my self depletes the energy I could use for personal growth and social contribution. If I am not at home in my body, I am fighting against myself. This fight is costly.

By contrast, sexual sharing can also have positive effects on personal and spiritual integration. Consider the possible value of genital stimulation. Bodily stimulation and sexual excitation have a healing effect since they relax us, calm the body, and release tension. Furthermore, the intense experience of orgasm temporarily ruptures the world of ideas in which we often live, and orgasm brings us back to awareness of our bodies. Lovemaking and orgasm open us to the raw data of experience apart from preprocessed concepts and, thus, allow for a new way of seeing and thinking about life. Experienced in honesty and love, orgasm opens us anew to reality and its spiritual dimensions.

The intensity of sexual experience also opens up the channels of the psyche. Feelings, memories, fears, dreams, fantasies, regrets, and hopes, all are released into conscious awareness. How often during intense sexual arousal have you had the experience of remembering things that were absent from your mind for years and even decades? This release of psychic material fosters integration, wholeness, and spiritual growth.

From another point of view, the state of intense arousal that accompanies sexual experience allows you to focus on one thing. Distractions are gone; your mind stops flitting about. If you focus on awareness itself—not by deliberate focusing, but by relaxing, letting go, and simply being more aware—you can experience your own spiritual nature. Such mindfulness appears to be the emphasis in tantric sex.

It should be noted that new openness to reality, release of the channels of the psyche, and focus of the mind are also the effects of regular meditation. Similar to meditation, sexual experience can be considered a spiritual practice.

Certainly, because of its intensity, genital sharing binds people to each other even apart from the moment of sex. It makes people long for each other and, thus, draws people into continuing relationship. Their mutual affection, clarified expectations, and practical responsibilities demand continual personal change and growth. When a couple faces life together in honesty and love, supported and bonded by sexual intimacy, the path of daily life becomes the path of spiritual perfection. Chapter 5 explains these spiritual effects of sexual sharing in more detail.

CONCLUSION

After reviewing some past attitudes regarding the relationship of sexuality and spirituality, this chapter presented a positive understanding that sees the two as intimate friends. In many different ways this chapter made the same point: sexuality and spirituality are complementary aspects of the human individual, and the basic issue overall is personal integration.

More specifically, human growth depends on integration of the aspects of the human being: body, psyche—with its "feminine" and "masculine" dimensions—and spirit. Acknowledgment of the distinctively human factor, spirit, introduces explicit concern for fidelity to a built-in movement toward the true and the good. The spiritual factor explains the importance of honesty and love in human sexual relationships. Conceived in this way, sexuality and spirituality are complementary aspects of the same phenomenon—human integration and personal growth.

This understanding is wholly humanistic. It addresses spirituality in terms appropriate to a pluralistic, secular, and global society. This understanding treats the essential factors that explain spirituality apart from the presuppositions of religious faith.

For those who want it, this understanding is also open to belief in God insofar as the ultimate goal of the dynamic human spirit, full Truth and Goodness, could be named "God." Likewise, this understanding is open to Christian beliefs insofar as they acknowledge actual attainment of this goal, deification or oneness with God, as a real possibility through the Holy Spirit and in Christ. Hinduism has its own approach to union with God, as do other religions. Thus, within these religious viewpoints, honest and loving human living—including sexuality—is the vehicle not only of personal integration but also of divine life. Sexuality and spirituality go hand in hand.

Chapter 4

Sexual Self-Acceptance
and Spiritual Growth

For spiritual growth, how important is it for you to be comfortable with your sexuality? In the case of homosexual people, religious groups actually argue that uncomfortableness would be preferable and that people's comfort with their homosexuality is precisely the problem. Of course, this conclusion depends on what those groups mean by spiritual health.

If from the beginning homosexuality is deemed sick, deviant, and sinful, and if "holiness" is defined as living according to those religious groups' teachings, then comfortable acceptance of homosexuality will never be seen as good. The conclusion depends on how these groups set up the question. Their arguments are completely circular: they define the question is such a way that a particular answer is inevitable.

Moreover, these groups rely on personal religious belief as their main source of knowledge—"God's will," the Bible, revelation, the pope, tradition. Therefore, the definitions they propose cannot be challenged. Their definitions are correct because they say so—or, more subtly, because *they* claim that "God" tells them so. How could anyone ever prove such a claim wrong—or right?

This chapter takes a different tack and, of course, arrives at a different conclusion. Here spiritual growth is defined in terms of observable positive changes in people. Even Jesus sorted out true prophets from the false on the basis of observable evidence: "by their fruits you

This chapter was originally published with documentation in *The Journal of Sex Education and Therapy* (American Association of Sex Educators, Counselors, & Therapists), 1989, volume 15, number 3, pages 200-210, under the title "Self-Esteem, Sexual Self-Acceptance, and Spirituality." Reprinted with permission.

will know them" (Matthew 7:16, 20). In such an evidence-based approach, the answer to the question of whether comfort with your sexuality is important to spiritual growth depends on knowledge about sexuality and psychology; it depends on the results of research into these matters.

People have mused about sex for millennia, but the scientific study of sexuality is amazingly recent. Only in 1854 was it clearly understood that the union of both egg and sperm is necessary for conception. In Germany and England, late-nineteenth-century and early-twentieth-century endeavors—by Richard von Krafft-Ebing, Sigmund Freud, Wilhelm Reich, Iwan Bloch, Magnus Hirschfeld, and Havelock Ellis— broached the study of sexuality. But not until 1948 and 1953 was the publication of significant, sexual survey research a reality: Alfred Kinsey's studies, *Sexual Behavior in the Human Male* and *Sexual Behavior in the Human Female* (surpassed in the United States only by Edward Laumann's 1994 *National Health and Social Life Survey*). And only more recently was actual observational research in human sexuality reported: William Masters and Virginia Johnson's 1966 *Human Sexual Response* and their 1970 *Human Sexual Inadequacy* founded the modern field of sex therapy.

Beyond the knowledge of sexual practices and physiological sexual functioning, issues of interpersonal relationships and intimacy are also central to human sexual experience. So, borrowing the theory and techniques of psychotherapy in general, attention to these has also become a standard part of sex therapy. However, further questions remain.

Current interest about the relationship between sexuality and spirituality is growing. Of course, by *spirituality* different people mean different things. When, for example, spirituality was thought to refer to heavenly fulfillment, it was the concern of nuns, priests, and monks. Understanding sex basically as a physical procreative act, the "theology of marriage" explained the meaning of sexuality in terms of "sacred" marriage, and the realm of licit sex was very narrow, indeed. Concern for love and romantic fulfillment in this world—indeed, concern for personal fulfillment of any kind in this world—was virtually unthought of. Questions about the relationship between sexuality and spirituality could hardly arise.

Now, however, we are beginning to understand spirituality differently. We realize that spirituality entails the integration of all aspects of the person, and its this-worldly goal is the actualization of a person's fullest potential. In light of this contemporary understanding, the role of sexuality in a person's spiritual growth becomes obvious and pressing.

This chapter attempts to bring empirical evidence to bear on this subtle and complex topic. The approach is roundabout. The argument is that acceptance of one's sexuality is critical for positive self-esteem, that self-esteem is a prerequisite for advanced human development, and that such development is synonymous with spiritual development: sexual self-acceptance leads to self-esteem, which advances human development, which includes spiritual development. Thus, sexual self-acceptance is important for spiritual development. The key is the connection between sexual self-acceptance and self-esteem. The conclusion will be nothing other than a restatement of the argument just sketched, for existing relevant evidence is scarce. Still, delineation of this argument will clarify some issues regarding the relationship between sexuality and spirituality.

SPIRITUAL DEVELOPMENT AND HUMAN DEVELOPMENT

In *Spiritual Development: An Interdisciplinary Study,* I argued that spiritual development is nothing other than human development viewed from a particular perspective. Four elements characterize this perspective.

- First, that one dimension of the human mind is spiritual needs to recognized. The human spirit constitutes "an intrinsic principle of authentic self-transcendence." In wonder, marvel, awe, and with openness, honesty, and goodwill, this inner principle allows us to constantly go beyond our former selves. Because of this spiritual nature of ours, our horizon is unlimited. We are geared to the universe. Then, granted that we human beings are in part spiritual, spiritual growth is simply a matter of allowing our spirit to take the lead more and more. Spiritual growth is a natural aspect of human growth and development.
- Second, a person must be open to this inner spiritual principle. Unfortunately, we humans are capable of shutting ourselves off

from our own inner workings. When we are shut off from ourselves, whether deliberately or unawares, we are also partially shut down. We do not grow. Growth requires openness.

- Third, spiritual growth has to do with the whole person, not one aspect or another. For example, psychologists speak of emotional development, intellectual development, and moral development. To add spiritual development to this list would be a mistake, for spiritual development includes all the others. Spiritual growth is about the integration of all aspects of the person.

- Fourth, spiritual development is something that occurs only in adults, in people mature enough to take their lives into their own hands and courageous enough to begin to deliberately form and re-form themselves. To be sure, children are spiritually sensitive and have spiritual experiences. Likewise, solid psychological development in childhood is necessary before a person can go on to pursue spiritual development in adulthood. Nonetheless, until at least late adolescence, people are not yet psychologically equipped to begin consciously forming themselves. Self-formation is the task of an adult, and it is synonymous with spiritual growth.

Thus, spiritual growth can be defined as the growth that results in a mature person who is open to the urges of his or her own spiritual nature. Said in more technical terms, spiritual development is "the ongoing integration that results in the self-responsible subject from openness to an intrinsic principle of authentic self-transcendence."

Emphasis on an intrinsic principle of authentic self-transcendence allows us to understand spiritual growth as a completely human affair. This understanding cuts two ways.

On the one hand, it challenges religion. Most discussion of spirituality in the West involves religious faith and God or some other supposed metaphysical being, which is external to, and different from, ourselves. In contrast, the understanding of spirituality that I am presenting relies on a built-in dimension of humanity—the wonder, question, or desire that urges people to seek ever-further meaning, to achieve ever-deeper insight, and to affirm ever-surer values, that is, the need to construct a life worth living and worth dying for. The ideal goal of the human spirit is to know and love all that there is to be known and loved; therefore, the human orientation is cosmic, and the adjective *spiritual* is appropriate.

On the other hand, this understanding also challenges secular thinking. If spirituality is a fundamental human need, in one way or another it is a concern of every human being. It is not something that requires or belongs to organized religion. Everyone, whether religious or not, must attend to spiritual matters. Secular people, secular movements, and secular societies may not ignore these matters and leave them to religious believers as if spirituality were an "extra" in life. Society needs to address the full range of human concerns, and among these is the spiritual.

Spirituality is fundamentally a human, not a theological, phenomenon. It depends on an intrinsic principle of authentic self-transcendence. My forthcoming book *Spirituality for a Secular Society* is about the universal human need to attend to spirituality and the hope for a unified world on the basis of a common, core spirituality.

I use the word *authentic* to describe self-transcendence. Use of this word serves as a reminder that not all change is useful; some can be destructive. To leave home and explore the world because you are tired of parental discipline is not necessarily a good thing. Then again, leaving home may be the best thing you could do. By leaving home, you certainly produce change in your life, you transcend your former state, but whether change is growth or regression is always an important question. We can misuse our spiritual capacity. We can err in shaping our lives. Talk of spiritual growth assumes that the change moves in a positive direction. The word *authentic* makes sure this assumption is not overlooked.

Emphasis on openness to this intrinsic spiritual principle implies that response to it is not automatic. Urging us to ever-further questioning, evaluating, refining, and self–re-formation, this principle represents a constant challenge buried within ourselves. To heed the challenge and to respond with growth requires the courage to examine ourselves, to explore the world, to take risks, and to change ourselves, our life, and our world.

From this point of view, the role of self-esteem in spiritual development becomes obvious. The person of low self-esteem, one who does not feel good about himself or herself, cannot be open to such a challenge and, thus, cannot achieve spiritual growth. More to the point, the person uncomfortable with his or her sexuality cannot achieve spiritual growth.

Emphasis on the self-critical, self-responsible subject leads to the same conclusion. The point is that spiritual growth is an adult phenomenon. Granted, it will not occur without a solid base in childhood and adolescence, and self-esteem is an important part of that base. Still, spiritual growth itself is essentially an adult affair—for which adulthood is defined, not by chronological age, but by personal maturity.

In their stage theories of human development, Lawrence Kohlberg, Jane Loevinger, James Fowler, and Robert Kegan, all include a stage, first possible in young adulthood, that is characterized in some way or other as "postconventional." It is a stage at which people begin to criticize themselves and their culture; they transcend their upbringing. They go beyond the conventional, the usual, the expected. They become universal people. They identify with humanity, as such, and not with some particular slice of humanity or other—such as nation, race, or ethnicity.

It is to this postconventionality that the self-critical and self-responsible character of spiritual development points. People at this stage of development are no longer bound by the mores—the meanings and values, the ideas and ideals, the understandings and commitments—of their social world. Rather, they are capable of taking a critical stance toward the social world and toward themselves, and on the basis of such criticism they structure their lives as they know to be best. On the basis of their own open, honest, and goodwilled explorations, they choose to make themselves what they will be. They become their best, and they do so on their own authority. They take full responsibility for themselves. They take their lives into their own hands.

Such an enterprise is risky. It opens onto absolute freedom. That is to say, within certain obvious limits, you can become whatever you want; you are your own boss. The sky is the limit. However, in the sky you're on your own: you have nothing on which to stand! As the existential philosophers liked to point out, the experience of such open-ended freedom is frightening and even paralyzing. Most people actually prefer to have someone else tell them what to be and how to act. Therefore, few people choose the threatening path of self-directed self-transcendence—the spiritual path. As Jesus said, "The gate is narrow and the road is hard that leads to life, and there are few who find it" (Matthew 7:14).

In fact, without a high level of self-esteem, a person is incapable of choosing this path, so people psychologically damaged in childhood are at a major disadvantage. When people with low self-esteem feel threatened to engage even in everyday social life, personal growth must be all the more difficult. They simply cannot break away from the pack and trek beyond the standard and create their own selves on the basis of their own authority. Thus, self-esteem is a prerequisite for postconventional development. Accordingly, it is a prerequisite also for spiritual development.

This understanding is quite different from older Western spirituality. Traditionally, to grow spiritually you were supposed to be humble, deferential, self-sacrificing. You were to submit yourself to God and let God sanctify you. Holiness required passivity.

In contrast, the newer understanding recognizes that, to a large extent, we are masters of our own lives. Indeed, even according to traditional theology, God cannot change us if we are unwilling to be changed: this is the illusive "sin against the Holy Spirit" that cannot be forgiven, about which Jesus spoke. This sin cannot be forgiven because we are unwilling to budge. We become our own worst problem. Again, according to traditional theology, whatever God does God does through us. We should not look to God to work miracles for us; God uses the natural processes of creation to get things done. Even according to traditional theology, the buck stops with us. Wisely playing the cards that we have been dealt, we make our own destinies.

SEXUAL SELF-ACCEPTANCE AND SELF-ESTEEM

Is there a connection between acceptance of yourself as a sexual being and the level of your self-esteem? By *sexuality* I do not mean gender, the stereotypical masculine and feminine roles that society requires of men and women. Gender roles are certainly an important consideration—because they have to do with role-playing and can be inauthentic—but they are not the point. My focus here is biology, sexuality as a physiological dimension of the human organism. Focus is on the body, as such, on the male or female gonads and genitals, on the physiological functioning of the sexual system.

Biological sexuality makes demands on a person. Especially in puberty, sex becomes an unavoidable reality that has its own schedules and requirements. Menstrual cycles occur, erections occur, orgasms occur, venereal feelings and sexual tensions occur, and heterosexual, homosexual, or bisexual desires occur. You have no choice but to experience them.

If you were lucky enough to have been told about sex, you might be ready for these physical changes when they occur and easily be able to make them a part of your self-understanding. On the other hand, you might be taken by surprise, be frightened, or even be appalled by these sexual experiences and left, to some degree, trying to escape from a part of yourself. Parts of yourself might become a repulsive intruder to you. Or, as is more likely, your experience would fall somewhere between the two extremes.

Does your capacity to accept, or your need to reject, the sexual dimension of your humanity bear on your level of self-esteem? The obvious intuition is that it emphatically does, and theorists support the intuition. George Herbert Mead points out the necessity of having basic physical needs met before one is even capable of socialization. Abraham Maslow's hierarchy of needs—physiological needs, safety needs, belongingness and love needs, esteem needs, and the need for self-actualization—makes the same point. The physical level is the basis on which all else rests; even being able to relate well to others in a social world depends on having your physical needs met.

William James likewise indicates that the physical "me," that is, the physical self, is the most fundamental. And Sigmund Freud lists oral, anal, and phallic stages as the bases of personality and, thus, suggests the importance of bodily experience for the developing self.

Such theory is not recondite and obscure; it is based on the observation of infant behavior. The obvious activities of the infant are physical: eating, sleeping, eliminating, learning to use the body. With all due respect to Freud, this is not to say that the physical drives are the ultimates in life. Recent research makes clear that, even while performing these physical activities, the infant is also learning to relate with others, and the infant depends on this social interaction for survival itself. Indeed, these more subtle aspects of infant development, the social aspects, unfold from the earliest moments of human life. They develop precisely by means of physical encounters. That is the point. As James Mark Baldwin notes about infants, any interpersonal regard and, thus, any sense of worthiness or unworthiness is conveyed bodily—through touching, holding, cuddling.

A professor of mine, Philip Powell, relates the case of a runaway boy who lamented that his parents did not love him. When asked how he knew, the boy blurted out tearfully, "Because they never touch me!"

At the earliest stages of development, no other means of communication exist except for the physical. For the infant and child the feel of the body is the feel of the self. So comfort with your body is the ultimate basis of all self-esteem, and throughout life bodily issues—such as your looks—remain most important to self-esteem. No wonder plastic surgery is such a growing industry!

It's obvious how sex comes in. Sexual experience is bodily experience. Discomfort with sexuality is discomfort with your body, and at a very basic level discomfort with your body works against self-esteem. Lack of self-esteem blocks advanced human development; therefore, it blocks spiritual development. Sexuality and spirituality are closely related, indeed.

Does any research evidence support those connections? Not very much—because nobody's been asking questions about the body, self-esteem, and spirituality. An Internet search indicates few references that bear on this question at all, and from them no firm conclusion can be drawn. Nonetheless, I will discuss two relevant areas of research that shed some light on the topic: sexuality among the physically disabled and acceptance of one's homosexuality.

SEXUALITY AND THE HANDICAPPED

According to professionals, comfort with sex is an important aspect of self-esteem in the handicapped. Honest and open discussion of sex is an essential aspect of therapy. In addition to sex, another physical activity, work, is also critical. Both enhance self-esteem in handicapped people, and the self-esteem plays back on these physical activities. Increased self-esteem leads to more effective work and more enjoyable sex, which lead in turn to increased self-esteem, and so on. Caught in this positive spiral, people also show a decrease in the negative features of their disability: less general dependency, fewer medical complaints, less feeling of castration, less social withdrawal, and less need for medical and social support.

One therapist reported this general observation: paraplegics who are sexually dysfunctional do worse at vocational training than they actually could and secure less gainful employment than they actually could. Another team of therapists observed something similar: their patients' "avoidance of realistic consideration of their sexuality" went hand in hand with their "avoidance of a realistic acceptance of their disability." It is as if sexuality stands for the whole physical person. To address the one is to address the other.

The main thrust of these reports is clear. Frank discussion of sexuality and the possibility of sexual experience are important for the psychological well-being—the self-esteem—of handicapped people. One case in particular stands out, that of a twenty-five-year-old woman suffering from severe cerebral palsy. She had a brief but satisfying sexual liaison that ended abruptly. As a result of this liaison, this woman became aware that she had sexual feelings, and she wanted to be able to give herself sexual pleasure. Her therapists agreed. So she spent nine weeks in therapy learning about sex, assessing her physical capabilities, exploring her sensual and sexual feelings, and developing sexual fantasies. Her therapists also adapted a vibrator and taught her how to use it. As a result, Deborah J. Dewolfe and Carolyn A. Livingston report,

> Her sense of self-worth and self-esteem were markedly enhanced. These changes in her behavior were noticed by her peers, her social worker, and the staff working with her. She was much more verbal about her angry feeling of her brief affair, much more positively assertive in asking for what she wanted, and just all around "much easier to get along with." She was much less hostile to her peers and more outgoing in taking part in activities around the residence.

Here is a poignant example of how enhanced comfort with one's sexuality can have a positive impact on self-esteem. Through supportive therapy this woman had experiences in matters of supreme importance for bodily self-acceptance: she received extensive information about her body and its functioning; with a mirror she was able to view her genitals for the first time and, with the aid of her therapists, to touch them; and she did acquire some control over her own orgasmic possibilities. These sexual achievements enhanced her self-esteem.

ACCEPTANCE OF ONE'S HOMOSEXUALITY
AND SELF-ESTEEM

The acceptance of one's homosexuality is another topic whose investigation might link sexual self-acceptance with self-esteem. Indeed, the very issue of coming out is a matter of sexual self-acceptance. Homosexual people must accept same-sex erotic feelings as part of their own selves before they can be comfortable with themselves. Seemingly, before such self-acceptance is achieved, homosexual people are at some variance with themselves, so their self-esteem is debilitated. Routinely, men and women just beginning to deal with their homosexuality say that they do not like themselves. Accordingly, self-acceptance must bring them an increased satisfaction with themselves, and an increased self-esteem.

Several reports on homosexuality and self-esteem suggest that, as a group, homosexual people do have a level of self-esteem equal to or higher than that of their heterosexual peers. But the matter is complex. A number of different sexual factors impact a person's self-concept: gender, social sex role, sexual orientation. People are different, and their situations are different. In *Homosexualities* Alan Bell and Martin Weinberg actually classify homosexual males into different types. Some types tend to have lower self-esteem than heterosexual males. The situation would be different again for women. Clearly, it is difficult to isolate self-esteem and all the sexual factors that impinge on it.

The studies I consulted all dealt with people who had already accepted themselves as homosexual. Having had to face familial, societal, legal, and religious opposition, these people would naturally have already developed high self-esteem. Or perhaps an already high level of self-esteem is what allowed them to accept their homosexual orientation in the first place. From the point of view of rigorous research, no firm conclusion can yet be drawn.

However, what studies have not yet officially confirmed seems obvious to gay and lesbian people. Surely, a survey of those who are now comfortably out would reveal an array of positive changes. At least according to persuasive anecdotal evidence—except, unfortunately, for those still racked with irrational religious guilt—since coming out, these gay and lesbian people are happier, less neurotic, more productive, and more grateful, overall, for being alive. Their self-esteem must also be higher, and they must have achieved a higher degree of personal integration. If these outcomes are taken as indicators of spiritual growth, as I argue in this book, these people are also more spiritual people for having become more accepting of their homosexuality.

CONCLUSION

The insistence of this chapter has been that sexual self-acceptance is critical to a person's self-esteem and, therefore, to a person's spiritual growth. In the depths of a person, sexuality and spirituality are intricately related. Intuition suggests that things must be so, but intuition is difficult to demonstrate. Perhaps it is not possible to isolate factors that are specifically sexual from others that surround them. Perhaps to some degree sexual self-acceptance and self-esteem are one and the same. Perhaps self-esteem is a prerequisite for sexual self-acceptance, not vice versa. We can draw no firm conclusions regarding these technicalities.

Nonetheless, the overall connections seem sound. In past decades, psychological research has shown how central bodiliness and sexuality relate to a person's self-concept and self-esteem. Without comfort with one's sexuality, a person cannot be a fully functioning person, for such a person would always be running from himself or herself. Contemporary awareness also adds the corollary: Only a fully functioning person can be spiritually developed.

Chapter 5

Sexual Pathways
to Spiritual Growth

What does sexuality have to do with spirituality? The previous chapters have discussed this question. This chapter goes into more detail.

The general idea is that both sexuality and spirituality are built-in aspects of our humanity. This fact is obvious in the case of sexuality. It pertains to our physical bodies insofar as we are males or females, equipped with internal and external sex organs of the male or female—and sometimes mixed—kind. Sexuality pertains to our mental life, our psyches, insofar as we take on masculine or feminine ways of thinking about ourselves and of behaving.

I have argued that spirituality is a built-in aspect of our being, as well. In addition to psyche, our minds also include a self-transcending dimension: spirit. It expresses itself in our experiences of wonder, marvel, awe. It leads us to question and to want to understand as we move more deeply into our experiences and ever further into reality. It makes us even question our answers because we want to be sure we are right; we know we are doomed if we construct our world on falsehoods. It leads us to ponder—and sometimes even agonize over—decisions or choices we need to make.

These abilities—awareness, understanding, judgment, and decision—are spiritual. They open us up to an unlimited world of meaning and value, and they force us to live within a world of ideas and ideals. They come into play in sex when, almost despite ourselves, our sexual involvements lead us to share our ideas and ideals and to

This chapter was originally published with documentation in Daniel A. Helminiak's *The Human Core of Spirituality: Mind As Psyche and Spirit,* Albany, NY: State University of New York Press, 1996, pages 254-266. Reprinted with permission.

weave dreams and make promises: Our physical sex and emotional liaisons involve us in setting up a life with one another.

Most people think of spirituality as something to do with God and religion, and this understanding is correct, as far as it goes. However, from my point of view, the order is reversed: We create religions and believe in God because of the spiritual dimension of our own being. It is our spiritual nature that opens us up to the big questions of life: Who are we? Why are we here? Where do we come from? Where are we going? What is worth living for? Belief in God and adherence to religion supply answers to these questions. So, yes, religion and God are related to spirituality for many or most people. But religion and God need not be involved, and they are not the starting point of spirituality. Our inherent spiritual nature comes first; matters of God and religion follow. Spirituality is a completely natural and essential aspect of our being. Religion and awareness of God grow out of this essential aspect.

Accordingly, the integration of sexuality and spirituality is nothing other than the integration of oneself. To the extent that a person brings together all the dimensions of his or her being—body, psyche, and spirit—this person also integrates sexuality and spirituality. The matter is as simple as that. This integration depends on harmonization within oneself, not on the attempt to meet requirements imposed from outside, whether from family, peers, religion, culture, or society.

What follows fills out this understanding of sexuality and spirituality more concretely. The following exposition revolves around six general themes. In the first four themes consideration opens onto broader and broader perspectives: It begins with the individual and moves to the couple and then to the human family, and finally it focuses on our human longing for the infinite. These first four themes are limited to a strictly human point of view. They unfold apart from any consideration of belief in God.

This initial presentation shows how a nontheist understanding of spirituality can deal with most of the issues that come up in standard "religious" accounts of spirituality. It is useful to underscore the contrast, and it is also important to consider what difference "religious" elaboration can make.

Accordingly, themes five and six move into religious considerations. They treat the specific contributions to an understanding of sexuality that belief in God—theist belief—can make and then the contributions that concern for union with God adds. I call concern for union with God "theotic" (from the Greek *theosis,* deification, becoming godlike).

The end result of this six-step approach is a most illuminating example of human and spiritual integration. This chapter treats sexuality as it relates to spirituality not only in a merely human perspective but also in a theological perspective. Of course, all that is said here applies equally well to hetero- and homosexuality. In these matters, trying to make a difference between homosexuality and heterosexuality is simply mistaken.

SEXUAL AROUSAL AND ORGASM: FOCUS ON THE INDIVIDUAL

Concern for the individual person focuses on sexual arousal and orgasm. As William Masters and Virginia Johnson have shown, physiologically sexual arousal depends on two processes, vasocongestion and myotonia: the swelling of organs because of the inflow and accumulation of blood, and the increase of tension in muscles. Orgasm results from the release and relaxation of this arousal and tension. Talk of orgasm here applies whether the orgasm is shared with another person or experienced alone.

The experience of sexual arousal and orgasm has a physical healing effect. It reduces stress and relaxes and calms the body. During sexual arousal, there occurs in the psyche the concomitant release of emotions, images, and memories. Dreams and fears, hopes and anxieties, memories of past experience, images of fantasy worlds—a whole flood of powerful psychic material may flow out of psyche's secret caverns. Especially during orgasm itself, this intense organic and psychic experience short-circuits rigid rational control. It brings you down to earth out of the heady idea world in which people often live. It invites the healthy acceptance of your bodiliness. After all, the experience of pleasure requires letting go.

Such letting go, such losing oneself, is a blessing amid stressful and hectic contemporary living. However, as Saint Augustine and Saint Thomas Aquinas saw it, such letting go was a threat. It entailed momentary loss of rationality and was thought to be dehumanizing.

This experience was to be tolerated only for the sake of a higher good, the possibility of procreation.

The sexual experience does, indeed, entail an altered state of consciousness. Its enticing intensity and narrowing of focus, effected by bodily chemical changes, can even result in pathological compulsive and addictive sex acts, because the lure of sex preoccupies the mind, and driven people become wholly oblivious to its social, moral, and physical consequences. Nonetheless, in more integrated and responsible people, that altered state of sexual arousal holds promise for a personal integration that Augustine and Aquinas were unable to appreciate.

In Eastern traditions the understanding and use of sexual arousal are very different. Orgasm is hardly a concern. Rather, attention is on prolonged and intense (but nonorgasmic or sometimes nonejaculatory multiorgasmic) sexual arousal, and it serves an explicitly spiritual purpose. Techniques of breathing and sexual stimulation intensify the altered state of consciousness concomitant with sexual arousal. Thus, a natural human activity, sex, frees and opens the mind to experiences similar to those induced through other spiritual practices (such as fasting, sleep deprivation, meditation) or induced chemically (by peyote, mushrooms, or other "sacred" psychedelics). Sexual arousal becomes a doorway to profound psychic and spiritual experience. Intense physiological arousal supports awareness of the transspatial and transtemporal dimension of one's nature. Sex becomes an occasion for spiritual experiences.

In people who are open, honest, and loving—in a word, authentic—sexual arousal and orgasm offer the possibility for personal renewal. The momentary breakdown of controlling patterns of thinking and the inflow of material from the psyche allow you to restructure your outlook and, in the process, yourself. There may be new data to be taken into account or old data once again to be remembered. You might relive past traumatic experiences or achieve insight into a longstanding problem. With a torrent of painful tears or the gasp of unexpected realization, the experience of sex can reproduce the personal transformation associated with psychotherapy.

As if taking a long and needed vacation, the sexually induced experience of openness and relaxation calls you to make recreation a more integral part of your lifestyle. In orgasm you experience that you are really not in total control. This may be a welcome and reassuring realization. Sex entices you to let go and then rewards your surrender. You face your finitude and may be able to find delight in "lowly" and earthy things: bodily rubbing and organic slicks, tears, groans, and pained ecstasy. That ecstasy may, indeed, include profound psychic and spiritual elements.

Such return to your roots, such experience of your whole humanity, holds the possibility of increased integration. Note well, this is all talk of possibility. For people can make of things much what they want. People can use sex for abuse and manipulation, for degrading others, or for obliterating their own awareness; or people can use sex to open up their hearts and to achieve more wholesome personal integration. When integration is the result, spiritual growth is also at stake, for integration entails increasingly spontaneous flow of the open-ended, self-transcending dynamism of human spirit.

LOVING ANOTHER PERSON:
FOCUS ON THE COUPLE

Focus on the couple that shares sex expands the possible spiritual implications of sexual experience. In a sexual encounter, you meet another person on a deep and secret level. Two people stand exposed to each other, all opened up. They have different dreams, memories, preferences, beliefs, and values, so they inevitably and interminably challenge each other—inevitably, because no two people can ever be identical, and interminably, because, if their relationship does not stagnate but continues to grow, the couple will uncover ever more deeply rooted differences to enrich or subvert their sharing. All the while thick bonds of sexual desire, physical and emotional, hold them entwined and force them to resolve their differences: They can't let go of each other! Thus, organic and psychic sexual processes serve spiritual ends. Sexual togetherness serves interpersonal sharing and growth.

Such sharing, continued authentically, with openness, honesty, and love, is as much a spiritual discipline as any fasting, prayer, retreat, spiritual counseling, or vigil. It partially dismantles the personality; it unearths the secrets of the heart. It presents a possibility for a more wholesome, more authentic, restructuring of oneself. This fact explains, in part, why religions tend to consider marriage something sacred. Although the religions speak in terms of God and grace, their teaching highlights the fully human spiritual integration that an honest and intensely committed relationship fosters.

Honestly loving another person confronts us with reality. It makes us clarify and purify our values, view things more objectively, surrender our prejudices, learn to repent, and be moved to forgive. Repentance and forgiveness must be a part of any deep relationship and especially when sexual sharing enters into the picture. Such profound physical and psychic self-exposure to another person leaves you very vulnerable and inevitably hurt—just as your dealing with the other in such a situation inevitably hurts the other. The complexities of the human person almost guarantee that, despite the best of intentions, misunderstandings will occur and people will be hurt. So sexual involvement bids you be more humble, compassionate, and concerned. Sexual sharing involves you in a process of human integration that naturally unfolds in accord with the demands of the human spirit. Authentically lived sexuality is itself part of one's spirituality.

THE POLLYANNA EFFECT:
FOCUS ON THE HUMAN FAMILY
AND THE COSMOS

Beyond the individual and the couple, sexual sharing involves the family and, indeed, the cosmos. Inherent in the experience of sexual love is movement beyond yourself.

A popular song of the 1950s, "Everybody Loves a Lover," suggests a name for this aspect of human love: The Pollyanna effect. The lyrics of the song celebrate the notion that, just as everybody loves a lover, so, in return, a person who is in love loves everybody. A lover is a Pollyanna.

Some say love is blind, but from another point of view, love opens our eyes to a world of beauty beyond ourselves. Loving another person opens you to identify with all people. A seeming paradox exists here, for my emphasis all along has been on personal integration, on the integration of the individual. The seeming paradox is that as you become more and more integrated, you identify more and more with other people. The more you become yourself, the more you know yourself to be one with others. Increasing individuation results in increasing sociality. Then, since holistic, authentic human love is an integrating experience, it leads you to identify with the whole human race—and the cosmos.

However, that effect is not naive, as the term *Pollyanna* might suggest. Nor is that effect, that seeming paradox, difficult to explain. If human integration entails integration of the spirit and if the spirit's very nature is to transcend itself, then human integration entails a movement beyond oneself and toward all that is true and good, all that is. The spiritual nature of the human both makes you be yourself and orients you to the universe of being. The human spirit, like sex, is essentially outgoing. Human love, including sexual sharing, expands beyond the loving couple. The conception, birth, and nurturing of children provide the obvious example.

Mothers and fathers find in themselves surprising ability to forget their own needs and wants and to attend to those of their children. The very process of parenting elicits deep love that results in ever further challenge and ongoing personal integration. This process continues through the years as infants grow into children and children into youths and youths into adults, often soon becoming young parents themselves. Mother and father, now grandparents, must continue to contend not only with their own individual differences but also with the realities of their children, each a unique person. So the challenge to personal growth inherent in the engendering couple relationship now expands as parents raise and release their children to be their authentic selves. This interpersonal experience—family, and likewise faithful friendship—is life's occasion for all of us to transform ourselves for the better in interaction with one another.

Parents have a unique occasion for personal, and thus spiritual, growth as they watch their children mature. In their children they may recall and relive their own childhoods. In this way, they may be healed of hurts they carried through life. Parents may recognize the difference between a child's understanding and the understanding they are developing as the responsible ones, so they may wisely opt to be even more responsible. They may catch themselves responding as their own fathers or mothers did, so they have a chance to decide for themselves how to act and what to be. Then they may know the exasperation of trying to change oneself, so they may develop compassion in the face of other people's shortcomings. They may recognize in their children a diversity inherent in people, so they may come to be more tolerant. Experiencing the succession of generations as their own lives unfold, they may become more comfortable with the limited course of human life and be grateful for whatever life they have had to live. Thus, in many different ways, parents have an opportunity to grow in wisdom, integration, and spiritual depth.

Fathers and mothers share a common experience in begetting and raising children, yet some aspects of the experience are gender specific. The experience of mothers is particularly rich in sexual dimensions.

The mother carries the child in her womb for some nine months while hormonal changes make her emotionally vulnerable and especially open to tenderness. In many ways sharing a common biological and emotional world, mother and child are bonded in a way that only a mother can fully comprehend. The pain and the subsequent hormone-induced "high" of the birth experience forge another bond between mother and child.

Breast-feeding continues the bonding in a most remarkable way. As in other sexual activities, a fully aware human adult performs a fully animal function, this time sustaining the life of an offspring with the products of her own body. In this procreative function women are challenged in a unique way to be comfortable with their bodies. The baby is fully one with the mother in the biological and mental symbiosis typical of early infancy. The infant's sucking stimulates in the mother the release of hormones that not only start the flow of milk but also bring the mother a pleasurable calming experience. In turn, the mother cuddles and caresses the baby, gratifying the infant with what satisfies. From this biological point of view, talk of love between mother and child takes on a new range of meaning. Natural organic functions elicit, foster, enhance, and reward love between mother and child. For the child this love is a foundation for adult experiences of falling in love and loving.

Here is undoubtedly some explanation of the incredible loyalty and self-sacrifice that a mother often shows in regard to her children. Here is another kind of long-term relationship enhanced by a physical component, a relationship that pulls a woman out of herself, bonds her with another, and launches her on a path of unimagined self-transcendence. Lived with honesty and love, the mother's experience with her child is an occasion for deep personal and spiritual development. This is another instance in which uncomfortableness with one's animal nature and fear of the full range of sexuality can limit a rich occasion for personal integration and spiritual growth. Indeed, uneasiness about the processes of pregnancy, birth, and nursing can pass on to yet another generation the uptightness about the body that too often colors contemporary "civilization"—because without any words ever being spoken, the infant picks up the feelings of the mother as she holds the infant. Body-to-body communication is more honest and goes more deep than conceptual communication expressed through words. If the mother is uptight about physical closeness and bodily feelings, the child will also become uptight and carry that uptightness in his or her gut through the rest of life.

In those same maternal experiences, the father also has a great opportunity for his own personal and spiritual development. Bonded in differing ways with the mother and child, he may enter into their intense experience as he supports, protects, admires, and nurtures the widening circle of love. The father's own physical contact with the child will carry the same kind of power as the mother's.

Other broad concerns also show how sexual sharing, inherently self-transcending, moves people far beyond themselves. Children, one fruit of our love, deserve a world worthy of them, so loving adults take concern for the world as well as for the children. Loving adults, with or without children, become interested in politics, in neighborhood, school, and world affairs. Loving eyes are open to human suffering and social injustices all around. Those who allow themselves to love in body and psyche as well as in spirit know vulnerability and pain in their own hearts, so they can feel the pain of others' oppression. They themselves suffer when others hurt. So a spirituality of sexuality opens onto a spirituality of social justice and onto a spirituality of environmental concerns. The earthiness of sex keeps our feet on the ground, lets us know that we are matter and slime. It attunes us to the music and rhythms of life that we share with other forms on this planet. As another popular song has it, I would have never been aware of the birds in the sky "Till There Was You."

In the ultimate case, loving each other, lovers sometimes experience themselves and the other and the whole universe as one. Some might pooh-pooh this experience as a caprice of Cupid and Venus or as a remnant of some childhood fairy tale. However, granted the mystery of unbounded spirit within us, this experience is a moment of mystical ecstasy, a fleeting glimpse of what we really are and, therefore, want more to be. That orgasmic self-experience of body, psyche, and spirit, in harmony and completely "turned on," may be an anticipation of the attainment of spirit's ultimate goal: to be one with all that is.

LONELINESS, THAT ENDLESS YEARNING: FOCUS ON THE INFINITE

Human sexual love expresses humanity's endless longing. The human heart aches for, and reaches out to touch, the infinite.

Self-transcending, self-constituting humanity is a rolling snowball. Its power grows more mighty as it moves along. The more open you are, the more open you become. The greater your capacity, the more poignant is your longing. In the integrated human being, even sexual desire is an expression of our spiritual dynamism.

Sometimes a person strikes us with astounding beauty, and we can but stand transfixed. Oh, how we want that Venus or that Adonis! But the beauty that pierces to the heart may be only a symbol of the goal of our own spiritual longing—the one, the true, and the good, in all perfection. She or he pierces precisely by touching the human spirit and its capacity for unbounded fulfillment. So in the end, that Venus or Adonis cannot be had. Scheming, grasping, or clutching—lusting—is counterproductive. Rather, you must reach out and hold on gently, if at all. You must restrain yourself and remain open, else you shut down the very longing that alone holds promise of fulfillment.

Of course, indulged lust will extinguish the desire and free you temporarily from the longing, but such a base response blunts the deeper source. Cheap sex reinforces imbalanced psychic patterns that restrict the free flow of the human spirit.

In contrast, sometimes in deeply committed relationships, in which the couple has actually walked through life together, a person can momentarily release that endless longing and share it in the arms of the beloved. Then lovemaking becomes a blatantly spiritual experience. The whole universe seems to fuse as lovers share their hearts, and *mystical* is an appropriate name for the experience.

Nonetheless, nothing finite ever finally satisfies, for the reach of the human spirit is unlimited. Through all the yearning, the more subtle joys, the simple enjoyments of life that do touch the heart, are more lasting and more fulfilling than the passing excitement of a sexual encounter. The quiet pleasures are a person's promising experience of his or her own spirit. The aching of the heart is really the longing of the soul. Sexual desire is partly an expression of a spiritual need. One must allow the longing and make friends with the yearning, for to do so is to make friends with oneself.

THE GOODNESS OF CREATION:
ENTER BELIEF IN GOD

Belief in God has further considerations about sexuality and spirituality to offer. For the theist believer, sex is a gift of God. That is, horniness, romance, and caring—human body, psyche, and spirit, with their implications for love—are inherent aspects of human life designed so by the Creator. Therefore, they must be good and wholesome. Their authentic experience inserts us ever further into, and opens us to, the ultimate Mystery of the unfolding universe, which is of God. God is the source and the sustenance—as well as the goal—of human sexual love.

Accordingly, for one who believes in God, the endless longing of human sexual desire points ultimately to God. The theist understands the one, the true, the good, and the beautiful to be an expression of the Divine. The whole of the universe is God's good creation, and the ultimate desire of the human heart is the Creator-God of the universe. So the theist can pray with Saint Augustine, "Lord, you have made us for yourself, and our hearts are restless until they rest in you." Sexual desire is somehow a longing for God.

Moreover, believers find hope in knowing that God made human love sexual—whereas angels, in contrast on the one hand, traditionally understood to be unembodied spirits, know no passion or physical arousal in their spiritual love; and other animals, on the other hand, have sex but do not make love and cannot savor the beauty and goodness of their sexual experiences. So believers continue to hope in the face of sexual frustration. They trust that somehow the good God, who in drawing the universe forward to its fulfillment, does heal the flaws, accidental or culpable, that foul our attempts to experience sexual integration and satisfaction. They believe that God at work in the universe does want us all to have fulfilling sexual experiences.

Those are the contributions that authentic theism makes to this matter of the integration of sexuality and spirituality. Those contributions are not numerous, but they are significant. That they are not numerous highlights a central argument of this book: Most of what is called spiritual can be treated apart from mention of God. That they are significant, nonetheless, highlights another valid consideration: A fully comprehensive account of the human situation naturally opens onto considerations about belief in God and union with God. In humans, sexuality—bodily and psychic—is geared toward the spiritual; and the spiritual opens onto the theological.

SEXUAL FULFILLMENT IN GOD: ENTER CONCERN FOR UNION WITH GOD

Finally, the theotic viewpoint also makes its contributions. The key to the theotic viewpoint is concern for deification, human participation in divinity, becoming one with God. Classical orthodox Christianity offers the only coherent account of deification that I know, so I will have to limit consideration to the Christian example. Extensive discussion of this subtle theological question is available in my books *The Human Core of Spirituality* and *Religion and the Human Sciences,* including a contrast with the Hindu understanding.

Christian concern for human deification relates to a number of specifically Christian themes. These have implications for an understanding of sexuality and spirituality.

Traditional Christianity affirms the Incarnation, the belief that the Eternal Son of God became human in Jesus Christ. This belief confirms the goodness of humanity: If humanity was good enough for God, it must, indeed, be good. Therefore, despite the overwhelming bulk of Christian practice, Christian doctrine must radically affirm that sex is good. Indeed, the Eternally-Begotten of God, Jesus Christ, as a real human being, certainly experienced sexual responses of one kind or another. In Jesus Christ, God became sexual.

On the other hand, according to Christian belief, as exemplified in Christ and promised to all in the Holy Spirit, every human being is destined for divine glory. Humanity is to share in divinity—and this humanity includes sexuality. Thus, from both points of view—divine and human: God becomes human, and humans become divine—Christian belief insists that human sexuality is worthy of God.

Accordingly, a person's personal unity of body, psyche, and spirit, and a loving couple's unity with each other are actually a growing participation in the very life and unity of God. Sexuality is geared not only to interpersonal human communion but also to human deification. Sexual encounters will have their ultimate fulfillment in human union with God. So human lovers, sometimes frustrated in their sexual experiences with each other, may look forward to an ultimate fulfillment of their aching for each other. Their deepest longings will be satisfied. Their unity is to be like that of God, about which John 17:21-23 has Jesus say, "May they all be one; even as you, Father, are in me and I in you, may they also be in us. . . . May they be one even as we are one: I in them and you in me, may they become perfectly one."

It is important to recall and insist that, according to Christian belief, heavenly fulfillment in God is not merely spiritual. It involves more than the human spirit, for it depends on "resurrection of the body." Belief in resurrection of the body means that the human being, as such, body, psyche, and spirit, is to be restored and fulfilled. Accordingly, resurrection of the body implies not only some transformation of the human body but also some perfection of the human psyche.

Thus, Christian belief affirms perfect human integration as the heavenly destiny of every human being. In heaven one's human spirit is to reach its ideal fulfillment through participation in divine knowledge and love. Because of the unity of the human person, the psyche and body must also be perfected. The human spirit could not reach its perfections apart from the perfection of the body and psyche, which support and sustain the human spirit. Human fulfillment depends on the harmonious integration of all three facets of the human being. So Christian faith expects full human integration—according to the model of Jesus: resurrected from the dead, united with God, and living as human in a glorified body.

Christian resurrection means perfection of all three: body, psyche, and spirit. Specific focus on sexuality highlights another implication of this belief. Full actuation of the human body and psyche along with perfect integration of the human spirit would be nothing other than eternal orgasm. Then heaven would be an ongoing sharing in divinity, which would entail ever fuller spiritual fulfillment, which, in turn, would entail never-ending arousal and actuation of the body and psyche—a continuous experience of peak "turn-on." Heaven could be conceived as making love with God and in God with everyone else and with the whole universe—all at the peak of never-ending arousal, eternally. Heaven is a never-ending orgasm.

Such graphic sexual imagery is actually very Christian. Ephesians 5:23-32, for example, compares the Christian's union with Christ to the marital union of husband and wife. In addition, a long-standing, though prudish, Christian tradition—almost despite itself—insisted on reading the Bible's Canticle of Canticles, a blatantly obvious love poem, as a spiritual meditation on the soul's love for God.

Admittedly, the conception of eternal orgasm is somewhat fanciful, but it has its validity. It is fanciful because it presumes that a resurrected body would still function as human bodies now do. However, Jesus himself said that in the resurrection there would be no marrying and taking in marriage and all would become like the angels (Matthew 22:23-32; Mark 12:18-27; Luke 20:27-38). However, Jesus' point was merely to insist on the resurrection, not really to explain its mode, for he was refuting a counterargument whose absurd core was an elaborate tale of multiple marriages. Besides, the question Jesus was answering asked to whom the woman would belong. But Jesus did not endorse a possessive form of marriage. Part of his point was that no one can really belong like property to anyone else. So, understood in its own context, Jesus' teaching in this case does not eliminate the possibility of orgasm in heaven.

This conception of eternal orgasm also has validity because it merely insists on the happy and wholesome actuation of the human body and psyche in heaven. The experience of sexual arousal and orgasm is as valid an example of such actuation as any other that could be presented. Indeed, among all the biological and psychic functions, because of its radically outgoing nature, sexuality seems unique in its ability to express the spiritual dynamism within the human—and hence, within the theotic viewpoint, to express union with the divine.

The conception of eternal orgasm in heaven is also very useful, for in Christian terms it highlights an aspect of humanity that Christianity has tended to minimize: sexuality. This conception puts sexuality at the heart of Christian belief. An elaborated understanding of resurrection of the body includes perfection of both the body and the psyche. So sexual fulfillment must be part of human deification in Christ and the Holy Spirit.

Exemplified in the case of Christianity, concern for union with God envisages earthly sexual experience as some anticipation of human fulfillment in heaven, and in heavenly fulfillment we see the continuation and perfection of our sexual experience on earth. Because of the unbounded reach of human spirit and in light of belief in union with God, the ongoing integration of sexuality and spirituality must be seen as a process of deification.

SUMMARY ABOUT SEXUALITY AND SPIRITUALITY

These six themes illustrate how bodily and psychic experiences are linked with spiritual development. In this holistic understanding, sexuality is an intrinsic part of a person's spirituality. The human spiritual capacity emerges from its psychic and organic underpinnings. The human spirit can soar in its open-ended embrace of the universe only if the body and the psyche support it. Functioning healthily, they do. By their very natures, the biological dimension of human sexuality is outgoing, and the psychic dimension is bonding. They anticipate and foster the open-ended outreach of the human spirit and the attainment of the unity of all things, which is the spirit's goal. When sexuality is the focus and human genuineness or authenticity rules the field, the human body, psyche, and spirit all move in one direction. Body and psyche instigate and support the ever self-transcending extraversion of the human spirit. Orgasm and romance sustain human caring. Interpersonal sexual sharing is spiritual communion. Human spiritual communion points to a fulfillment in what believers call "God."

Whereas a former Western era saw sexuality as opposed to spirituality, contemporary understanding insists that the two move hand in hand. Thus, a consideration of human sexuality provides the ideal example of human integration and shows that human integration is the sum and substance of spiritual integration. By its very nature, the human is spiritual, so in humans sexuality powers and expresses spirituality.

Chapter 6

Sexual Ethics Without Religion

In the popular mind, ethics is linked to religion. Religion teaches that God determines right and wrong and that doing what religion teaches is following God's will. This teaching is true in some way, but it is not straightforward.

We come to know right and wrong only gropingly. Especially when new issues arise—such as genetic engineering or cloning or chemical contraception or sexual orientation—we struggle to decide what the right response is. When we finally decide, if we have acted honestly and in goodwill, we say that our decision, such and such, is the will of God. For surely, what is good, as best we can determine, is what God would want.

But attributing ethical conclusions directly to God does not guarantee that they are correct. And imposing them on others in the name of God may be the ultimate abuse of power.

With the advent of gay liberation, and for absolutely valid reasons, many lesbians and gays rejected the religions that formed and bound them. In the process, some rejected not only the sexual ethics they were taught but also the very notion of valid sexual ethics. The problem of linking ethics with religion is that when the one goes, so does the other. When experience makes clear that religious requirements must be wrong, all requirements go out the window, and sexual expression becomes a free-for-all.

This chapter was originally published as "Sexual Ethics Without Religion" in *Open Hands,* Chris Glaser, ed., 1998, volume 13, number 4, pages 21-22. Reprinted in *DignityUSA Journal,* 1998, volume 30, number 4, pages 11-13, under the title "Loving Thy Neighbor and Thyself: Sexual Ethics for the New Millennium." Reprinted with permission.

THE TRUE NATURE OF ETHICS

The fact of the matter is that ethics is built right into human nature. Our very minds demand that we only affirm what is true—and you cannot dispute this point without confirming it by your very arguing. Similarly, our minds demand that we do only what is good—what is positive, upbuilding, enhancing, what opens onto growth.

In the depths of our hearts is a spiritual core. We are geared to embrace the universe, so we spontaneously marvel at beauty, and we long to love and be loved. The lasting fulfillment we desire, of course, always eludes us, but our very desire leads us ever more deeply into the experience of life.

Still, only goodness has a future; falsehood and evil inevitably self-destruct. Only what squares with the nature of things can hope to survive long-term. Our spirits sense this fact, so they flee the disorder that is evil, and they gravitate toward the harmony of the good. Experience of this inner movement is called conscience. We ourselves, the very structure of our being, are the source of ethics. Our inherent desire to live ever more deeply urges us to choose what brings richer life.

Thus, the ethics that cultures and religions propose is only the goodwilled application to specific issues of the spiritual longing for fulfillment that is built into the human heart. Doing what is right means genuinely serving our own best interests. It might have nothing to do with God and heaven, for what is right must be equally right for the agnostic as for the believer.

Then the general ethical question is simply this: What contributes to the good? What furthers ongoing growth? What makes for lasting satisfaction? This multifaceted question also governs sexual matters.

PHYSICAL, EMOTIONAL, AND SPIRITUAL DIMENSIONS OF HUMAN SEXUALITY

Sex in human beings is complicated. Earlier thinking—built on Stoic philosophy and funneled into the Western tradition through Saint Augustine—held that, animal-like, sex equated with procreation. However, human sex includes not just physical response and biological function; it also entails emotional entanglements. Moreover, it opens onto the spiritual in us so that *having sex seduces lovers into dreaming dreams and making promises.* The physical, the emotional, the spiritual—in humans these connect to one another. Sex in humans opens onto the meaning of life and a universe of shared experience. This is the way human sex is. So "what furthers ongoing growth" in sex must respect all these dimensions.

That broader understanding implies that sexual sharing can be completely ethical even outside the confines of heterosexual, child-bearing marriage—as long as, to some degree, as appropriate in each case, the sexual sharing unleashes its life-enhancing potential. Thus, allowing pleasure, fostering bonding, and triggering shared visions and virtues, lesbian and gay relationships, though biologically non-procreative, might express the essential and distinctive nature of human sexual experience as much as heterosexual relationships might. No inherent reason exists why gay and lesbian relationships cannot be fully ethical—which is to say, loving, constructive, life-giving, up-building, growth-producing, fruitful, productive.

Such broad understanding of sexual intimacy differs from other commonly heard opinions. Some myopically limit sex to the physical. They argue that pleasure is sovereign and it legitimates any sexual experience. Others, more subtle, but still narrow, move on the emotional plane. They insist on being "in love" or at least having feelings for someone before engaging in sex.

In fact, both those emphases are on target, and they are acceptable—but only if they are incorporated into the broader picture. Once incorporated, they get nuanced. Not any pleasure, not any emotional bonding and delight, but only those that truly serve ongoing growth are allowed. Only those respect the full nature of human sex, and only those are genuinely fulfilling: we are more than bodies and emotions; the human spirit also requires its due.

ETHICAL GUIDELINES

With this understanding, basic ethical rules fall easily into place—not come down from heaven; not imposed by parents, society, or religion; but built right into our own sexual natures and interpersonal relationships: no disease, no physical harm, no unwanted pregnancy, no coercion or manipulation, no abuse of the immature and naive, no emotional harm, no violation of commitments, no betrayal of personal values. These negatives are there because violation of them is destructive.

Positively, human sexual sharing requires honesty, trustworthiness, mutual enjoyment, mutual support—some degree of concern and commitment. These requirements may seem restrictive, and in some ways they lead to the same kind of behavior that religion at its best traditionally advocated. Yet these requirements are more freeing than the traditional.

If they require concern and commitment, they do not stipulate eternal vows. The nature of each relationship will specify how much concern and commitment is possible and necessary for the relationship actually to be loving not only in the present moment but also in its long-term effects. It is certainly possible that a passing sexual encounter could respect all these requirements and really be for the overall good of the people involved. It is also possible that a relationship might involve more than two people, whether in sexual intimacy itself or in some configuration of interweaving relationships, and really be for the common good. The "open relationship," the ménage à trois, and the mistress or gay lover alongside a heterosexual marriage are typical examples. All are possibly ethical, but all are also questionable. Real relationship tends to break down in these cases. Almost inevitably someone gets badly hurt. Then again, people inevitably get hurt in any relationship. Everything human is messy.

Whether those involvements are actually good is the telling question. Answering this question is not always easy, and imposing blanket answers is not helpful. Being willing to ask the ethical question and to follow the required answer in each case—this is what makes people and their behavior ethical. Again, if room is made for homosexuality and for a contemporary understanding of sexuality in general, the honest answers will usually not fall far from where traditional morality placed them.

THE PERSONAL AND INTERPERSONAL NATURE OF HUMAN SEXUALITY

A key complexity of human sex is that it is not just a physical encounter. Humans are persons. In addition to bodies, we have emotions and we have spirits. This is what it means to be a person. So human sex is an interpersonal enterprise. The interpersonal dimension of human sexuality is entwined with the ethical requirements. Indeed, *ethical, personal,* and *interpersonal* begin to sound like synonyms.

Ethical requirements are not simply a matter of altruism, of being concerned about others. This simplistic me-versus-you view of morality is totally misguided. Ethical requirements are a matter of wholesome self-serving that is inextricably entwined with the good of others. Doing good is to everybody's advantage.

Our whole constitution is outgoing. The horniness in our loins, the longing of our emotions, the dreams and promises of our spirits—all impel us unrelentingly outside ourselves. We fulfill ourselves through interaction with what is beyond us. When we fulfill ourselves in the good, we actually become that good even as we share it with others. What we are and what they are in honest and loving living—what we stand for—becomes one and the same. All talk of selfishness versus altruism is a bugaboo.

The sexual act symbolizes this distinctively human state of affairs: when sexual sharing proceeds well, what is good for me is good for you, and vice versa. The physical pleasure, the emotional bliss, and the spiritual self-transcendence—yours and mine—are mutually enhancing. It's a win-win situation.

THE SOCIAL IMPLICATIONS
OF HUMAN SEXUALITY

We are social animals. We live in and with one another. Human sex cannot be extricated from a social context. Even solo sex usually involves fantasies, memories, and longings about others.

It is therefore insane to protest, "My body is my own," "No one has a claim on my life," and "I have the right to do with myself whatever I please." Such claims for a new "ethics" are appearing of late in the gay community.

Weary of the restriction on free-for-all sex that the AIDS epidemic sanely imposed, some free spirits are mounting a campaign to restore the irresponsible days of yore when gay liberation was struggling to be born and had desperately thrown off all restraints. They claim that physical pleasure is the meaning of sex. They claim the right to high-risk behavior in the pursuit of pleasure. Fetishizing HIV, they use risk of infection to heighten the excitement of sex. They claim the right, with consenting partners, to do whatever they wish.

Under many circumstances, they certainly can do whatever they wish. After all, there's truth in the standard schoolyard protest of "It's a free country." However, that they actually have the right is mistaken. The matter is not worth discussing in these terms. The language of rights is part of the bugaboo of "me versus you."

This cut-off-my-nose-to-spite-my-face mentality misunderstands the nature of human beings and of society, for both coincide. This mentality mistakenly thinks laws and morality are restrictions imposed from without and fails to see that valid ethics arise from, and serve, our own selves. We are not always sure what the valid ethics are, but pretending no ethical requirements exist in life is not the solution.

No one belongs solely to himself or herself. Family, teachers, neighbors—all have an investment in us. The extreme example is the GI, who is "government issue," property of the state. He or she will be punished for self-destructive behavior because it costs the military money. Similarly, family, friends, and society at large pay the price for irresponsible sex that results in HIV infection and other harm. It is an illusion that the sex of consenting adults is solely their own business. The notions of adultery, infidelity, and sacred vows have long expressed other societal implications of sex.

Like it or not, human sexuality is a social reality. Its inherent ethical nature has social implications built right into it. People may kick against the goad and refuse to accept the human state, but such refusal is simple stupidity. One can only lose. Religions call that refusal sin and relate it to God.

THE PROMISE OF ETHICAL LIVING

Understanding what the religions were attempting to do and taking up the task in their place or as a part of them—for the task is really our own—will provide a new ethics that actually meets the needs of the third millennium. Then we might also hope to see a fourth millennium—and individual and social fulfillment, as well.

Chapter 7

The Right and Wrong of Sex,
Queer and Otherwise

The 1960s brought a sexual revolution. For straights "the pill" effectively separated sex from procreation, and, for the first time in human history, it was possible to comfortably have sex simply for the sake of personal sharing and enjoyment. Building on the civil rights and feminist movements of the era, gay liberation was soon on the scene, and homosexual people began claiming a right to same-sex relationships up front and unapologetically. There emerged an attitude that is widespread today: Any sex is okay as long as it's safe, as long as it's responsible. People seldom propose real arguments against this attitude—although, for reasons of "faith" (which basically comes down to personal opinion and preference, if not downright prejudice), religions continue to reject it.

But what does *responsible* mean? This is *the* ethical question. It asks what is right or wrong in sexual practices. This question interests many of us as our generation faces the challenge of constructing a sexual ethics for ourselves. This question is important, I believe, especially for lesbian and gay people. How can we avoid wondering about morality when religion and society continue to insist that we are wicked, perverted, sick, immoral, ungodly, and destined for hell?

THE CHALLENGE OF ETHICS
FOR THE GAY COMMUNITY

Sexual ethics or sexual morality, the right and wrong of sexual behavior, is not only important to the gay community. The matter is also

This chapter was originally published in *Pastoral Psychology*, 2004, volume 52, number 3, pages 259-267, under the title "The Ethics of Sex: A Call to the Gay Community." Reprinted with permission.

challenging. Gay liberation had its saving beginning in the bold rejection of standard morality. Not only did we need to throw off the mores of society. We also had to reject the teachings of religion. With these also went the restrictions of sexual ethics.

In fact, we had no choice. By the standards of the day, we were outlaws and sinners. To be ourselves and have our relationships, we had to disregard the morality of everyone around us. Unfortunately, as a movement, we threw out the baby with the bathwater. In our struggle for liberation, we threw off all concern for ethics, and being gay often meant doing whatever we wished.

But times have changed. Matured in the School of Hard Knocks, the ongoing AIDS pandemic, and feeling somewhat more secure in our battle for legal status, we have risked criticizing ourselves and begun to set necessary limits. Safer sex was an important part of this package. We may think of safer sex as simply a matter of sanity and survival, but that matter is precisely what ethics means. Ethics is really about what is ultimately to our own greatest individual and collective advantage.

REASONS TO CONSIDER SEXUAL ETHICS

The result of our rethinking will be a new sexual ethics, an ethics for everyone, gay, bi, or straight. Gay sex does not usually involve procreation, but procreation and child rearing were the backbone of traditional sexual ethics. Take the sexual focus off of conception and put it on intimacy and relationships—as "the pill" did for straights—and you get the situation with which we have been dealing from the beginning. Under contemporary circumstances—including reduced infant mortality, early sexual maturity and delayed marrying age, increased human life span, and overpopulation—the imperatives that bear on a sexual ethics have changed. We need to redo sexual ethics, and what wisdom the gay community has gained should be valuable to everybody.

Besides, we are basically good people. We sang that fact in the early Pride marches: "We are a gentle, loving pe-e-eople, singing, singing for our li-i-i-ives." We've never been out to be wicked. We just wanted to be honest and allowed to love. At our best, we have always been out to do the right thing, so we can trust our own best judgment where ethics is concerned. We need have no fear that attention to ethics will box us in.

However, we have avoided this matter. We are afraid of it. Despite ourselves, the guilt-inducing rhetoric of society and religion has seeped into our sensitive souls. In the quiet of our own consciences, we sometimes still experience "the guilties." We are not sure in ourselves about what is really right and wrong. Often after the passion of the moment, we wonder if we should have "done it."

All the way around, we stand to benefit from squarely facing sexual ethics. We would all rest more content if we explored the matter.

I propose three principles to guide this exploration. First, a principle of affirmation: Gay is good. Second, the principle of science-based ethics: Do what is humanly healthy and wholesome as best as we can determine. And third, the principle of development: Do your personal best.

On the basis of these principles, it is hard to say precisely what may or may not be ethical in a wide array of sexual situations: solo sex; sex within committed relationships; singles' sex with a friend, acquaintance, or stranger; "open" relationships; use of prostitutes and hustlers; group sex; sex via the telephone or Internet; activities at bars, bushes, bathhouses, and bookstores; B&D or S&M scenes; the use of pornography, drugs, and toys; and all the rest. The three principles do allow much more latitude than did traditional sexual ethics. Apart from second-millennium Christianity, tacitly most of the world's cultures already allowed such latitude—including Old Testament Israel and, arguably, New Testament Christianity, understood in their own historical contexts. Modern Western society has been unusually uptight about sex, especially in the twentieth century and especially in the United States: How is it possible that in the twenty-first century the federal government is spending millions of dollars to support abstinence-only sex education, which has been shown to be ineffective? Still, if these principles are applied honestly, the results would often fall close to where traditional guidelines, if open to homosexuality and our new understanding of sex, also point. Why? Because morality at its best has always been concerned not only to curtail harmful behaviors but also to help people thrive.

GAY IS GOOD

I take it for granted that nothing is inherently immoral in being gay or in having gay sex. Every consideration points to this ethical conclusion. It should be taken for granted at this point in history. No argument, religious or philosophical, coherently concludes otherwise.

- Homosexuality is *not* a sickness. More and more surely, the research evidence of the social sciences shows that homosexuality is a natural variation, widespread throughout the animal kingdom, a part of virtually every known human culture, and, thus, a natural part of the world—which, according to religious faith, God created.
- Homosexual people are *not* irreligious. In fact, many describe their coming out as a moment of grace and subsequently find themselves psychologically healthier, more productive, and closer to others and to God.
- The Bible does *not* condemn homosexuality as such but is, rather, neutral on the matter. My book *What the Bible Really Says About Homosexuality* confirms this point.
- Throughout its history, Christianity has *not* always opposed homosexuality. On the contrary, in the high Middle Ages, a gay subculture thrived, and a standard body of gay literature was studied in the church-run universities. John Boswell's *Christianity, Homosexuality, and Social Tolerance* and Mark Jordan's *The Invention of Sodomy in Christian Theology* confirm this point.
- In church practice, procreation is *not* essential to sex. Marriage and sex between sterile or aged couples has always been allowed.
- The argument of "complementarity" of the sexes—that somehow man and woman were made for each other exclusively—is *not* coherent. Inevitably, it is an appeal to biological plumbing and, as such, reverts back to the duplicitous argument about procreation.

It is important that we affirm our legitimacy as lesbian and gay people. This stable affirmation secures the ground on which we can explore sexual ethics. Self-assurance—healthy self-esteem, as discussed in Chapter 4—leaves us free to try to know how we can best live our gay lives.

SCIENCE-BASED ETHICS

My principle of science-based ethics says to do what is humanly healthy and wholesome as best as we can determine. Be responsible. Do the right thing. The challenge is to determine what *right* or *responsible* means.

To specify what is right, some people appeal to religious teaching or divine revelation as received, for example, through the Vedas, the Bible, the pope, the Koran, or the Book of Mormon. Others rely on family upbringing or cultural traditions or social expectations—mores. The problem with these approaches is that they lead to the ludicrous notion that right and wrong are whatever people want to make them.

Mores differ, and religious teachings differ. If they are what determine right and wrong, then right and wrong differ for different people. Then nothing about what is wholesome or destructive is inherent. Morals become just a matter of opinion and people are free to do whatever they want as long as they think it is right. However, honesty and good sense tell us otherwise. If nothing else, the experience of September 11, 2001, should have taught us this lesson: Believing that God is on your side does not make you right. The universe does not bend to our fancies. Imagining positive outcomes will not alter a dead-end course of events. Actions have consequences.

Because of the very nature of things, some things are helpful, and others are harmful; some things are sustaining or upbuilding, and others are destructive; some things alleviate pain and suffering, and others cause them. This difference is what we mean by saying that some things are good and others are evil, and this set of circumstances is the ground of a science-based ethics. The idea is simple, straightforward, and down-to-earth. The idea is that right and wrong are built into the functioning of the universe and human intelligence is able to discern them. Right and wrong are part of the nature of things. The challenge is to determine what exactly is the nature of things.

In this regard, in addition to philosophy, personal experience, and common sense, the social sciences can come to the rescue. Today we know more, by far, about sexuality than ever before in human history. On many sexual questions the hard evidence of extensive research reveals what is helpful or harmful. This very evidence is a basis for determining right and wrong. In this sense, *science-based ethics* is just another, more accurately descriptive, contemporary name for *natural-law ethics*. The idea is simply to determine right and wrong on the basis of the evidence.

Granted, the Catholic Church has co-opted the notion of natural law and uses it to oppose sexual liberation. In the popular mind, natural law is the name for the Vatican's teaching. However, the Vatican misrepresents natural law. The concept was around before the Vatican existed. Natural-law theory had its earliest beginnings in Sophocles's play *Antigone* about a woman who appealed to an authority more ancient than kings and defied King Creon's decree that her brother not be buried by burying him. Aristotle understood that authority to be the law common to all peoples (*jus naturale:* natural law) in contrast to the laws of particular nations (*jus gentium*). Stoic philosophy elaborated this notion by appeal to the order or *Logos* that is built into the universe and that human intelligence could discern: to follow this order would be to live reasonably, ethically. Thomas Aquinas provided the most comprehensive summary of this theory, and, thus, it became a hallmark of Catholic ethics. But natural-law theory is hardly the property of the Catholic Church. Virtually all classical moral philosophers have held some theory of natural law.

The Vatican mistake has been to ignore recent developments in the understanding of human sexuality and, with the ancient Aristotelians, Stoics, and Neoplatonists and with the medievalists, to insist that procreation is the essential purpose, the ultimate meaning, of human sexuality. The mistake is to reduce sex to a mere biological function and turn human sexuality into a barnyard-animal affair. To be sure, the Vatican has recently nuanced its position, now acknowledging also an interpersonal, "unitive" dimension of sex. Yet, the Vatican consistently downplays the interpersonal dimension of sex—as is blatant in its statements against gay marriage—and the Vatican's insistence on openness to procreation in every sexual act remains a central facet of its official teaching that it proclaims as "natural law."

Rejecting a science-based approach to ethics simply because the Vatican misrepresents natural law would be a major mistake on our part. Long-standing natural-law theory is our strongest ally, and we need to claim and clarify it. Only it—the appeal to reasoned conclusions based on scientific evidence—can dispel the clouds that religions, cultures, personal tastes, and arbitrary opinions stir up around sexual ethics.

In fact, scientific research has contributed to our understanding of sexual ethics. The overwhelming bulk of scientific evidence has shown that gay is good, that nothing is inherently harmful or abnormal about homosexuality. Medical research has discovered the cause of AIDS—not homosexuality, but a virus—and has required the use of condoms. Psychological studies show that the *distinctive* function of human sex is intimacy and relationship, not procreation. On all these fronts, scientific research supports homosexuality as a fully healthy and fully acceptable natural variation.

Likewise, research also shows, for example, that masturbation is in no way harmful. Rather, people who engage in solo sex tend to be more comfortable with themselves and others and tend to be socially more outgoing than people who do not masturbate. Other research—as well as common sense—shows that rape, the sexual abuse of children, and sexual manipulation or coercion are profoundly destructive. Research-grounded conclusions of this kind objectively determine what behaviors are good or bad, helpful or hurtful, right or wrong, as best as we can determine.

Of course, questions about the adequacy of scientific studies will always arise. Professionals debate such matters constantly. Nonetheless, in many cases, an open, honest, and goodwilled survey of the available evidence results in conclusions that are virtually indisputable. Only people who are pushing another agenda would seriously suggest that we do not yet know enough about sex to arrive at responsible conclusions in many important areas and that we have to rely on "revelation" or some such other, fanciful source. Besides, the very fact of debate about the adequacy of scientific studies strengthens the reliability of the conclusions that are eventually accepted. Science is a self-correcting enterprise.

Thus, the science-based approach to ethics—natural law—simply states that what is destructive, as best as we can determine, is wrong, and what is helpful is right. Application of this principle depends on the openness, honesty, and goodwill of everyone involved.

ONE'S PERSONAL BEST

Finally, the principle of development calls for every person to strive to do his or her best. The point is not that certain acts are inherently evil and we ought to try to avoid them—as the old morality taught—but that sex has consequences in our lives, and, for the sake of our overall experience of life, we should be concerned about the quality of our sexual activities. Of course, we are not all capable of the same achievement; we cannot all maintain the same high quality, not even in matters of morality. We tolerate in children what we prohibit in adults; we overlook in the disadvantaged what we denounce in the gifted. As Jesus in Luke 12:48 phrased the matter, "From those to whom much has been given, much will be required."

If sexual activity on some occasion or other is only to the good, as best we can determine, how could it be wrong? It could not. But is it really to the good? Is it my personal best? Does my sexual activity help me and my partner(s) achieve our full potentials? Or does our sexual activity distract us from facing the real issues in our lives? Overall, is my life and are the lives of others better because of my behavior? Or are our lives worse? These are the telling questions.

Not everyone is capable of the same depth of personal integration and interpersonal relationship. Unfortunately, some of us have been damaged since childhood. In many cases the damage is severe, and little hope exists for advanced development. It would be unrealistic, unfair, and counterproductive to require that everyone be involved in a highly developed relationship before they were allowed to share sex. Who is to say of adults what a sufficiently high level of development would be, in any case? Besides, sharing sex can actually foster personal growth.

Sometimes a passing encounter is the only relationship of which a person is capable. Such an encounter is already a kind of relationship, and it provides precious human contact. Sometimes a passing encounter is to the benefit of all concerned. A one-night stand could be a good thing. Sometimes a passing encounter is the beginning of something much better. It can happen that a full-blown, long-term relationship results from casual sex. However, let's not delude ourselves about the frequency of positive outcomes in such cases.

In general and according to the research, human sex is ultimately geared toward interpersonal relationships. Not the mere biological functions of physical pleasure and possible procreation, not even the psychological experience of fantasy, romance, and emotional delight, but a spiritual matter, interpersonal bonding, is the prime objective of human sexuality—connecting with other people, sharing dreams and promises, building a life with others, finding meaning amid uncertainty and ambiguity.

Apart from all involvement with religion or reference to God, I call this facet of sexuality *spiritual* because it results from the distinctively human capacity for wonder, marvel, awe, and from the subsequent pursuit of meaning in life and commitment to the values inherent in that meaning. These aspects of human experience transcend space and time and point to an open-ended and coinciding personal and interpersonal fulfillment. The capacity for such fulfillment is the human spirit. It is spirit that makes the human animal a person. Hence, while indeed involving physical contact and emotional attachment, the essence of interpersonal bonding is spiritual. This emphasis on the spiritual—on the interpersonal, not the biological or emotional—is precisely what legitimates homosexuality and other nonprocreative sexuality as fully valid expressions of human sexuality. Of course, the interpersonal objective of human sexuality includes the biological and psychological dimensions of sex, too.

Accordingly, sex is better the more it involves genuine intimacy and sharing across life's activities; and it is worse insofar as it is a passing event, isolated from the rest of one's life. Sex is better the more it integrates the three emphases of physical, psychological, and spiritual; it is worse insofar as it dissociates them and keeps them apart—because, as social science indicates, such dissociation sets up walls within a person and blocks personal fulfillment and, perforce, diminishes societal contribution. Such matters lie on a continuum, a range from least to most desirable. The principle of development requires that, in the face of this range, we strive for our personal best.

ETHICAL GUIDELINES

Because people and circumstances differ, laying out specific rules for sexual behavior is difficult. Negative guidelines are the easiest to propose. The following is a list that runs from the physical through the psychological to the spiritual requirements:

- No disease.
- No physical harm.
- No unwanted pregnancy.
- No deception, manipulation, or coercion.
- No abuse of the immature or naive.
- No use of others for simply selfish enjoyment.
- No emotional harm.
- No violation of commitments.
- No betrayal of personal values.

Simple compassion and basic goodwill—recognizing the consequences of our actions—automatically excludes the negative options. Compassion and goodwill would likewise require judging as wrong other behaviors in the contemporary sexual world:

- being cruel in turning down a proposition;
- tricking with a stranger to spite your lover;
- looking for a new lover while you are still in a relationship;
- violating the sexual contract or agreement that you made with your partner, husband, or wife;
- misleading a prospective sex partner about your availability or interest in developing a relationship;
- being mean to somebody just because you don't think she or he is sexy enough for you;
- dismissing the attentions of "older" people and interpreting their compliments as the seductions of "dirty old" men or women; or
- leading people on by misrepresenting yourself on the Internet.

These contemporary "sexual sins" have nothing to do with procreation, the "waste" of semen, or violation of a bodily orifice—as in the old morality—yet, as interpersonal offenses, they are hurtful and, therefore, wrong.

The negatives arise because violation of them is humanly destructive on some level. These are not restrictions imposed arbitrarily by some foreign or outside authority; they emerge from the very nature of the sex in which we engage. Sex is a shifting, sensitive, and powerful thing. It opens us up and makes us vulnerable, so it not only fosters profound personal growth; it also easily hurts. Those restrictions express only what is for the best interests of all concerned. To intelligently serve our own best interests, individually and collectively—and these two are opposite sides of the same coin—is the fundamental meaning of all ethics or morality.

Overall, this much can be said outright. In every case only what is helpful to all involved should be done, and what is harmful to anyone involved should be avoided.

Interpersonal relationship is the key to responsible sex. The enhancement of persons is the ultimate meaning of *human* sexuality. Respect for this lofty nature of sex results in healthy and positive sharing; disregard of this nature is inevitably somehow humanly destructive, whether physically, psychologically, or spiritually. Ethically responsible sex means precisely sexual sharing that is helpful, positive, enhancing, and upbuilding for all concerned and on all levels.

Of course, it would be difficult to make blanket statements about exactly what might be helpful to different people at different points on their developmental journeys and on different days of the week. For example, a relaxing physical release does qualify as a positive good. So does just having fun. If you can find someone who wants to have fun with you, and you both understand that only fun is at stake, and no other negative considerations exist, why not enjoy each other and be grateful for the experience? However, such casual sex would shake the emotional lives and burden the consciences of some people I know, both men and women. For them such sex overall would not really be fun. Besides, the constant pursuit of only casual sex—tricking—could become a habit that keeps a person in only shallow associations and relationships. As a result, perhaps out of fear of deeper involvement, a person could settle for nonthreatening, noninvolved sex and, thus, limit personal growth. In this case, "just playing the field" or "being a player" becomes a liability and a moral concern.

According to Abraham Maslow, self-actualized people will often opt only for affection or friendship and pass on a chance to have sex—simply because the idea of sex "just doesn't feel right," and they want to feel good about themselves. Sensitive to their own souls and to the needs of other people, self-actualizers recognize a potentially hurtful situation and avoid it. On the other hand, they will often share sex in cases that more conventional people would condemn. Not hung up on abstract rules, self-actualizers are concerned for the genuine well-being of others and themselves and tend to see these two as intertwined. I would like to believe that the hard process of coming out in honesty and goodwill puts many lesbians and gays in the category of self-actualized.

THE ETHICAL ATTITUDE

To what extent any sexual activity might be ethical needs to be something we think about. To what extent a sexual activity is beneficial to all concerned is something to ponder regularly. No easy, ready-made answers exist. Pretending that they do is not helpful. Matters of individual preference and personal growth are complex.

In any actual instance, only the people involved will be there to make the decision. Unless we are, ourselves, ethical people, committed to the good in every situation, ethical behavior will not follow, and we will not learn over time what is truly moral, what actually works for the good.

More important than claiming to know outright whether this or that practice is moral—more important are attention to our behavior's ethical import and our concern to act in a responsible way. The essence of being an ethical person is not necessarily having all the answers but pursuing the questions in openness and honesty and following through in goodwill.

Perhaps the most important thing for the gay community—and all others—is to begin discussing these questions. As authentic human beings, more than "practicing homosexuals," we need to be practicing ethicists.

Chapter 8

The Spiritual Crisis
in Religion and Society

The Crusades, the Inquisition, witch burnings—a shameful side to Western religious history exists. At the beginning of a new millennium, circumstances should be better, but they are not. The times are confused. A new world is in the making. And religion still fosters violence.

The destruction of the World Trade Center on September 11, 2001, is the obvious example. Others are the mass suicides at Waco, Texas (despite whatever role a bungled government maneuver played in the case), suicide bombings by Hamas and Islamic Jihad in the Near East, the Israeli occupation of Palestinian territories, the "Troubles" in Northern Ireland, the subway gassing by the apocalyptic cult Aum Shinrikyo in Japan, the assassination of Prime Minister Yitzhak Rabin in Israel, terrorist bombings in Madrid and London. And more are occurring, are closer to home, and are ongoing.

There are bombings and murders of personnel at abortion clinics. There are bashings and murders of gays and lesbians. There is incendiary rhetoric from white supremacists and anti-Semitic paramilitary groups. There is the subtle but systematic suppression of women. There is the physical abuse of children in the name of discipline. There is the virtual enslavement of women in polygamous marriages. And religion supports them all.

This chapter was originally published with documentation in *Pastoral Psychology*, 1997, volume 45, pages 365-374, under the title "Killing for God's Sake: The Spiritual Crisis in Religion and Society." Reprinted with permission.

THE SAD RECORD OF RELIGION AND VIOLENCE

Vanity Fair chronicled the 1995 murders of ten gay men in Texas. The article comments: "These youngsters relish the obvious terror they create in their victims and are emboldened by the firm conviction that the Bible and their Lord Jesus are on their side."

In an article in 1995, the *National Catholic Reporter* wrote about white supremacist David Lane and Aryan Nations leader Mark Thomas. Associated with a group called Christian Identity, Lane sees himself in a messianic role: "I'm that man." But unlike Jesus, he brandishes a sword: "We are backed into a corner. . . . We are denied white nations, schools, organizations. . . . All destructive institutions must be destroyed." Thomas likewise speaks in religious terms: "We believe that today we are living in the kingdom of Satan and that war does involve the taking of human life. . . . The Spirit of God can only inhabit an Aryan body. The eternal enemy of our race is found among the Jews."

Similarly, Biblical Fundamentalists support their antifeminist position with quotes from the Bible, such as the words in Ephesians 5:22-23: "Wives be subject to your husbands as you are to the Lord. For the husband is the head of the wife just as Christ is the head of the church." Religious support for the pro-life movement also is well-known.

To be sure, most mainline religions deplore these violent trends. Still, religion often subtly condones or approves them. When the first of the physicians, David Gunn, was shot at an abortion clinic in Pensacola, Florida, the gunman's minister, interviewed on national television, could not bring himself to condemn the act. Though the Vatican did condemn violence against lesbians and gays, its 1986 letter added an aside about the violence: "Neither the church nor society should be surprised."

Certainly, it would be hard to prove that religion causes violence. However, similar to television and movies, some religion obviously fosters violence in those so inclined and provides them with easy, self-righteous excuses. This is so because much religion becomes an ideology, a closed and rigid set of ideas that support a particular worldview.

The danger of such abuse is particularly great for the religions of the book—Judaism, Christianity, and Islam. Appealing to divine revelation, they claim to have a hold on absolute truth. In the face of God's truth, it does not make good sense to be concerned about making good sense. As the great, early Christian theologian Tertullian boasted, "I believe because it is absurd." The eighteenth-century Christian philosopher-theologian Søren Kierkegaard echoed this same sentiment in his *Either-Or.* So for those who want it, Western religion offers ample reason to reject reason in deference to blind faith.

THE POLITICAL SIDE OF RELIGION

But another consideration plays into the mix. Religion has always been intertwined with political movements and cultural trends, and such involvement is to be expected. No society can hold together without some commonly accepted mores. One important task of religion is to supply them. Thus, religion inevitably gets contaminated with the political concerns of the day—bloody crusades, inhumane inquisitions, atrocious religious wars, grisly exterminations of indigenous cultures, barbaric policies of "ethnic cleansing," murderous pro-life demonstrations. Sleeping with strange bedfellows, religion unwittingly fosters in practice the very violence it may officially abhor. This state of affairs provides a clue for a solution to the problem. Wrapped up in religion is a whole swath of things. The need is to sort them out.

Religion is not only concerned about God and the afterlife. Religion also says how this present life should be lived. Though religions name God and appeal to heaven, they are really teaching beliefs and ethics for living in this world. Said otherwise, credos and commitments, or meanings and values, or visions and virtues, or ideas and ideals—or in the words of Erich Fromm, orientation and devotion—are at the heart of every religion. Every religion has some set of them, and supposedly God has revealed and required them. God's revelation of the Ten Commandments to Moses on Mount Sinai is a clear case in point.

Are these guidelines directly from God? Or, more humbly, are they instead the expressions of the goodwilled beliefs and ethics of the day in this or that particular culture? For example, one of the Ten Commandments reads, "Thou shalt not covet thy neighbor's wife." Interesting that nothing is said about coveting a neighbor's husband! The reason is that these commandments reflect the political state of early Mosaic society wherein the woman was a piece of property, similar to cattle, slaves, and children, and adultery was an injustice against the owner, the man. The commandments were not addressed to the women, but to the men, who held the power in that society.

Of course, some would argue that, based on a "revelation from God," society should be structured exactly in that Mosaic manner. Still, if patriarchy represents God's ultimate blueprint for life, God begins to appear quite shortsighted. Even Jesus' first-century treatment of women broadened the Mosaic view. Jesus expanded and qualified what was supposedly God's final word. Contemporary biblical scholarship understands the texts in their original cultural setting. On this basis, it is clear that Jesus forbade divorce because he was concerned for the fate of women in a patriarchal society. Still concerned for women, in many cases today Jesus would undoubtedly endorse divorce. Likewise, in its commentaries and ongoing rabbinical discussions, Judaism itself often retains a broad and tolerant teaching on these matters.

Something similar can be said about the biblical view of the cosmos. Though some true believers continue to insist on creationism or, more recently, intelligent design as an alternative to evolutionary theory, not even the staunchest Biblical Fundamentalists maintain that the earth is flat. Yet, as even a close reading of Genesis 1 makes clear, the Bible pictures the earth as a disk of land set on pillars in the primordial waters, with the sun, moon, and stars hung on a hammered-metal-like dome covering the earth.

The credos and commitments of religion are often the social products of the day. They do not in themselves merit a divine and eternal seal of approval. What is of God in them is the openness, marvel, honesty, and goodwill that lie behind the teachings. However, these perennially valid and godlike virtues are clothed in the cultural opinions. Much of religion is really human, not divine. The need is to sort out the difference.

RELIGION, SPIRITUALITY, AND THE CURRENT DILEMMA

Common to every religion and to every society are sets of visions and virtues. This is so because to have beliefs and morals is an inherent requirement of the human mind. Paraphrasing Erich Fromm again: other animals live by instinct and are driven by genetic requirements; humans, on the other hand, need some map of life by which to live and some commitment to values worth living for. Unlike other animals, humans ponder the meaning of life and deliberate the implications of their behaviors. Inherent in the human situation is concern for the big questions of life: Where did we come from? Why are we here? Where are we going? How should we live?

These questions are spiritual concerns. For this reason they are also religious, for traditionally religions foster and nurture such concerns. However, once they are recognized as spiritual and as common to all human beings, whether religious or not, the distinction between spirituality and religion emerges in full force.

Until the modern era, religions were not just the carriers of spirituality; for all practical purposes religion and spirituality actually overlapped. In the divorce between church and state, religion naturally got custody of spirituality. Thus, along with religion, concern for the credos and commitments that govern wholesome living was shunted to the sidelines of everyday life. Now secular society is free to go its own way. Meanwhile, on the sidelines, the religions quarrel with one another, each claiming a privileged God's-eye view of things.

In effect, modern secular society is left a ship without a moral rudder. For the first time in history we find a society that, more and more, has no shared experiences, no shared understandings, no shared beliefs, and no shared commitments. Routinely my college classes, for example, are unable to agree on a single moral principle that ought to govern sexual behavior. We have no shared vision of what life and society should be. No society can hold together long under these circumstances. The problem is a crisis, and it is spiritual.

The solution is not once again to religionize secular society as the religious Right would suggest. The solution is not to reestablish religious dominion over popular culture. This reversal could never be achieved. Besides, the religions cannot agree among themselves about what ought to be believed and lived. In the desperation of the times, the religionists become more strident and more totalitarian. Hence, they foster and condone the very violence they claim to oppose. The solution is not in religion, but in spirituality.

Spirituality is an inherently human matter. It is a facet of every human being, every human institution, and every human society. The roots of spirituality are in the human heart; it is only the branches that reach up into the heavens.

The solution to the current impasse is to tease apart religion and spirituality and then to elaborate a spirituality based on the universal inner makeup of the human being. Such a spirituality would surely respect the concerns of religion at its best while also, because it is simply human, addressing secular society at large. The outlines of such a spirituality can be sketched.

HUMANITY AS INHERENTLY SPIRITUAL

A dimension of the human mind exists that can rightly be called *spirit*. Philosophers and theologians through the ages spoke of it under different names. Plato called it *nous*. Saint Augustine spoke of it as *memoria*. Martin Heidegger referred to it as *Lichtung* (an opening or clearing in the mind). Franz Brentano, a pre-Freudian psychologist, referred to it as *innere Wahrnehmung* (inner perception). Bernard Lonergan, the late, Canadian, Jesuit philosopher-theologian, spoke of it in terms of intentional consciousness. The following discussion of the human spirit follows Lonergan's analysis.

This dimension of mind makes humans self-aware. This self-awareness is the basis of marvel, wonder, and awe. From it arises questioning, conceiving, theorizing, judging, pondering, deciding, and planning. Intentional consciousness is operative in the simplest question that a child might ask, the elaborate programs of a modern legislative body, the eternal pledge of a lover's vow, and the silent wonder of a mystic's contemplating the stars. An everyday aspect of ordinary human experience, this dimension of mind nonetheless reaches out to embrace the universe. It would know everything about everything; it would love all that there is to be loved; it would become one with the immensity and beauty of the cosmos.

This very dimension of the human mind is the source of the meanings and values—or credos and commitments, or visions and virtues, or ideas and ideals, or orientation and devotion—that all humans devise and that we find enshrined in religion. But these things also concern philosophers, the lovers of wisdom, and psychologists, sociologists, anthropologists, politicians, and social planners, all whose interest is human living and its wholesome organization. This dimension of mind lies on the border—it is the link—between the things of earth (the humanities) and the things of God (religion and theology).

This dimension of the human mind makes humans in part spiritual beings.

Once the nature of human spirit is delineated, another dimension of the human mind stands out in contrast. This other dimension concerns more palpable things: emotions, images, memories, and personality structures. These are also mental, but their texture is different. They are earthier, more primitive, and more obscure. They do not share the self-transcending quality of lucid human spirit. Lonergan calls the aspect of mind that includes these things the *psyche.*

Psyche and spirit cohere in one human mind. Though they function hand in hand, they are not the same thing. You may not have an insight or intuition, a spiritual act, without the help of an image, a psychic reality. Still, simply to have an image is not the same as to question and understand. You may not in spirit make a decision without a press of emotion in psyche; still, simply to experience anxiety or excitement is not the same as to deliberate and decide. Psyche and spirit really are two different aspects of the human mind.

Nonetheless, psyche and spirit are not LEGO blocks that piece together to form a mind. Psyche and spirit can no more be dismantled than the mind and the body can be separated. Psyche and spirit ever collaborate in the ongoing functioning of the human mind. The spirit cannot soar in open-ended unfolding when defense mechanisms in the psyche healthily require stability. Still, sometimes dysfunctional emotional responses in the psyche can dissolve as the urgings of the open-ended spirit push for broader expression. Together psyche and spirit maintain a shifting equilibrium that both preserves mental health and allows for ongoing growth. The result is ever advancing human integration—the harmonization of inner human functioning and the continued actualization of inherent human potential. This process is nothing other than spiritual growth, for at its heart is the ever further incorporation of the self-transcending human spirit into the structures of the personality.

BUILT-IN REQUIREMENTS
OF SPIRITUAL FULFILLMENT

In line with the analyses of Bernard Lonergan, more can be said about the human spirit. Most important, the human spirit has its own norms of proper functioning. An open-ended dynamism that would embrace the universe, the spirit contains a built-in homing device. It is geared toward reality, toward what is. So its longing is for the true and the good. Only these open onto continued and unlimited fulfillment. Falsehood provides no basis for a lasting future, and it is the nature of evil eventually to self-destruct. Geared toward an infinite universe and wanting to have it all, the human spirit would avoid such dead ends.

The human spirit is inherently inclined toward the true and the good. Indeed, the unfolding of the human spirit itself defines what is meant by the true and the good, for whatever shuts down the open-ended unfolding of the human spirit cannot be good.

In a word, Lonergan names the criterion of the true and the good *authenticity,* and he provides a technical definition for it. His analysis shows that the human spirit has a four-level or four-facet structure: awareness, understanding, judgment, and decision. Rooted in the spirit, the requirements of authenticity parallel this structure. Four "transcendental precepts" result: Be attentive, be intelligent, be reasonable, and be responsible. They are precepts because they are requirements of the human spirit. One violates them at the cost of one's own self, at the cost of one's "soul." They are transcendental because they apply across the board to any and every human activity.

In an age when absolutes are unwelcome, the transcendental precepts stand as absolute requirements. Yet also sympathetic to the tenor of the age, they prejudge no inquiry, they predetermine no outcome. They never say what exactly must be done; they only prescribe how anything and everything ought to be done: attentively, intelligently, reasonably, and responsibly. Thus, they insist on an absolute without being absolutist. Only "the devil" would protest that insistence on them biases human functioning.

Though similar, this term *authenticity* does not completely square with the more popular sense of the word, which comes from existential philosophy. The popular usage is broader and vaguer. For better or worse it could mean something as banal as "doing your own thing." It could allow for full-blown relativism wherein "You have your truth and I have mine" and "Good is whatever anyone sincerely believes to be good." According to this popular usage, a person could qualify as authentic for behaving as the obnoxious pest that he or she claims to be.

In contrast, Lonergan's notion of authenticity has dogged honesty and universal goodwill built right into it. It leaves no room for selfishness, egotism, or solipsism. Rather, it envisages the point at which being true to oneself and being loving toward others overlap and coincide—much as in Aristotle's account of true friendship or in Augustine's famous phrase, "Love, and do what you like," or in Abraham Maslow's description of the self-actualizing person. Lonergan's authenticity reaches out toward what is objectively true and good. Thus, apart from religion, God, or theological speculation, this understanding of the human being can solidly ground spirituality.

SCIENCE THAT IS OPEN TO GOD

A spirituality built on authenticity is also fully open to theist religion. According to traditional Western theism, God is the Fullness of Truth and Goodness. If so, human authenticity leads Godward, and this-worldly expressions of authenticity can rightly be called godlike. Thus, making authenticity their standard, believers and nonbelievers alike could join hands in peace and walk together toward spiritual fulfillment.

However, there is no need to bring God into the picture at this point. Emphasis on authenticity allows us to bracket religion's otherworldly concern about God even while respecting religion's this-worldly concerns for truth and goodness. Focus on authenticity roots concern for spiritual things in the human mind. Therefore, this focus can ground concern for spirituality in a wholly secular society.

Spirituality lies on the border between theology and psychology, so a clearly conceived, humanistic spirituality cuts between the two and beyond. On the one hand, a humanly grounded spirituality challenges the religions to release their monolithic claim to the spiritual and to begin dialoguing among themselves and with secular institutions about the spiritual concerns that all people have in common.

On the other hand, such spirituality challenges psychology and the other social sciences to begin addressing questions of normative meaning and value, the true and the good, and thus to help formulate universally valid guidelines for wholesome living. At the same time, such spirituality also makes clear that even secular society needs to address spiritual concerns and that society can look to open-minded religion and an expanded psychology for direction. Focusing spirituality as the link between theology and psychology can be a major breakthrough in addressing the problems of our age.

A SPIRITUAL RESPONSE
TO RELIGIOUSLY MOTIVATED VIOLENCE

Such spirituality offers a solution to the problem of violence in religion. Grounded in the human spirit with its inherent requirement for authenticity, spirituality actually advocates the same guidelines as most religions at their best. However, precisely because it is grounded in our common human nature, spirituality also has an empirical basis from which to criticize religion.

When church and state were separated, religion lost the leading role in society's drama, but religion was granted hefty severance compensation—immunity from criticism. Except for egregious excesses, democracy finds it unacceptable to fault religious practices or beliefs: Who has the right to tell other people what to believe and how to worship? Yet precisely such immunity from criticism allows religion to preach bizarre and dangerous teachings and in the process to cozy up to violence. Appeal to a human-spirit–based spirituality could check extremist religious leanings. Faulting religion for misguided spirituality would disqualify it as the voice of God.

Of course, actually correcting the problem could never be that easy. People have criticized religion for centuries, and no lasting improvement has resulted. It is the nature of religion, secure in its claim to divine revelation, to stand firm against "mere" reasonable argument. When naked blind faith backs a religious crusade, rationality simply carries no weight.

Nonetheless, today new hope exists. A middle ground is emerging, and on it a new coalition can stand. Not all religion is irrational, and not all secularity is without conscience. Sane and reasonable religion can ally with responsible secular forces and with spiritually attuned social science, and all can rally around authenticity. Together they can isolate the dangerous facets of religion—whatever is close-minded, unthinking, unreasonable, and irresponsible. Just doing this much, naming and containing the problem, is already a major contribution.

A swelling majority of goodwilled people united around respectful and wholesome living will relegate the foolishness of the radical religious fringe to the oblivion of obvious irrelevance. Offering a concerned but confused generation a sane and saintly vision will drain off the support for narrow and unthinking religion. A spirituality of authenticity provides this vision. It can become the consistent public message of an array of different religions. It can address the spiritual needs of a pluralistic and secular society. It can remedy the religious violence of our desperate age.

Chapter 9

Jesus: A Model for Coming Out

They went to Capernaum; and when the Sabbath came, he entered the synagogue and taught. They were astounded at this teaching, for he taught them as one having authority, and not as the scribes. Just then there was in their synagogue a man with an unclean spirit, and he cried out, "What have you to do with us, Jesus of Nazareth? Have you come to destroy us? I know who you are, the Holy One of God." But Jesus rebuked him, saying, "Be silent, and come out of him!" And the unclean spirit, convulsing him and crying with a loud voice, came out of him. They were all amazed, and they kept on asking one another, "What is this? A new teaching—with authority! He commands even the unclean spirits, and they obey him." At once his fame began to spread throughout the surrounding region of Galilee.

Mark 1:21-28

Mark begins his Gospel with that composite vignette from the life of Jesus. A provocative question runs though that passage: who is this "Jesus"? In fact, as a real human being, Jesus had no way of knowing his deepest identity or ultimate mission. Like all of us, he had to struggle to be himself. Thus, Jesus offers an example to anyone who is "coming out" in whatever way. But to recognize this example in Jesus, we need first to get behind the stories written about Jesus and achieve some insight into the experience of Jesus himself. Then we can realize how much the challenge he faced in life was like our own. Then we can understand how Jesus also had to deal with coming out. Then we can see how Mark's telling us something about Jesus also tells us something about ourselves.

MARK'S PICTURE OF JESUS

Mark's Gospel is thought to be the earliest of the Gospels. It was probably written in the early 60s CE, just one generation after the time of Jesus, so this Gospel, though a theology in itself, does not exhibit highly speculative theological reflection on Jesus—as, for example, John's Gospel does. Besides, the Gospel's text shows that Mark did not know his Greek very well, so he was not able to write with elegant style—as, for example, Luke did. As a result, Mark is the most down-to-earth and straightforward of the Gospels, and in Mark we find our most concrete picture of Jesus during his time on earth.

A comparison of the Gospels makes clear that Matthew and Luke were following Mark in certain places as they wrote their own Gospels. It is also clear that they tended to tone down Mark's human details about Jesus. While Mark 3:5 relates that Jesus was angry at the Pharisees, Matthew 12:9-14 and Luke 6:6-11 omit the note about anger. Relating the cure of the woman who suffered from hemorrhages for twelve years, Mark 5:24-34 recalls the aggressive exchange between the disciples and Jesus, who foolishly asked who had touched him in the crowd. Luke 8:42-48 tones down this exchange, and Matthew 9:18-22 never reports it. Neither Matthew nor Luke even mentions the cure of the blind man at Bethsaida. Mark 8:22-26 reports that Jesus had to make two attempts to accomplish this cure. Thus, overall Mark presents a much more human Jesus than the others do, a Jesus who gets angry, who is irritable and impatient with his disciples, and who has to work at performing miracles.

The Jesus that Mark presents is simply one who came with authority, the Messiah, who, surprisingly, had to suffer. Mark shows that, in both his teaching and his actions, Jesus had power. Such is the interpretation or theology of Jesus that Mark presents.

JESUS AS GOD INCARNATE
IN LATER CHRISTIANITY

Christians today say much more about Jesus. We have gone far beyond Mark's simple picture. We not only say that the suffering Messiah, Jesus, had authority, but also go as far as to say that he was God come among us. Ours is not the rather unsophisticated picture of

Mark. However, to arrive at our current theological picture, much of history had to go by.

As Christianity developed, Christians thought about Jesus, and only gradually did they come to make sense of the early disciples' experience of Jesus. Little by little, step by step, Christianity proposed a coherent understanding of who Jesus was and what he was about. The understanding kept shifting and adjusting until it reached final clarification. The progression of understanding can be traced out.

After the resurrection experience, the disciples had a much better understanding than they had had earlier. Evidence to this effect is found in Acts of the Apostles, which reports very early preaching about Jesus. Peter's Pentecost sermon proclaims that *in the resurrection* "God *has made him* both Lord and Messiah, this Jesus whom you crucified" (Acts 2:36). The same thinking surfaces in Romans 1:3-4, in which Paul appears to be quoting a very early doctrinal formula. Paul says that he is writing about Jesus Christ, "who was descended from David according to the flesh and *was declared Son of God* in power according to the spirit of holiness *by resurrection from the dead.*" The implication is that during Jesus' lifetime the disciples did not actually recognize him as Lord and Messiah. Some would take this fact to mean that he became Lord and Messiah only through the resurrection and was not always so. A more careful statement would be that Jesus was not yet Lord *for the disciples* and what he was in himself was still being determined.

In contrast, Mark's Gospel writes the recognition about Jesus' Lordship back into Jesus' life and locates that recognition at the time when John the Baptist baptized Jesus. Mark 1:10-11 reports that "just as he [Jesus] was coming up out of the water, he saw the heavens torn apart and the Spirit descending like a dove on him. And a voice came from heaven, 'You are my Son, the Beloved; with you I am well pleased.'" Some of the early manuscripts that we have recovered containing Luke's Gospel make this same point even more forcefully. For Luke 3:22 they read, "A voice came from heaven, 'You are my Son, *today* I have begotten you.'" According to this account of the matter, Jesus was already Messiah during his lifetime. Mark finesses the difference by suggesting that a secrecy surrounded the matter. Though Jesus was the Messiah, the fact was kept quiet until after his resurrection.

Then, John's Gospel, written some time around the late first century, pushes the understanding of Jesus' real identity even further back and presents Jesus as already with God from the beginning. John 1:1 and 14 read, "In the beginning was the Word, and the Word was with God, and the Word was God. . . . And the Word became flesh and lived among us." According to John, Jesus "preexisted" his earthly life.

Still, it was not until 325, at the Council of Nicaea, that an absolutely clear statement finally emerged that Jesus is, literally, the eternal God. He is "God from God, light from light, true God from true God, begotten not made, consubstantial [or one in being or of one substance] with the Father." These words come from the Nicene Creed, which the churches still profess and which, one could argue, defines Christian orthodoxy.

It took a long time for Christians to understand who Jesus was. Of course, the earliest of the disciples reverenced him from the beginning, and in practice they even revered him as they would God. After all, God had made him Lord (Acts 2:36) and "gave him the name [Lord] that is above every other name, so that . . . every knee should bend, in heaven and on earth and under the earth, and every tongue should confess that Jesus Christ is Lord" (Philippians 2:9-11). Such reverence toward Jesus is actually astounding given that the early disciples were Jews, committed to the oneness and absolute sovereignty of God. Yet the understanding of the early Christians' minds lagged behind the commitments of their hearts, as is often the case with us humans when we face profound and important matters. In a major step toward consistency, the Council of Nicaea finally proclaimed Jesus, who was always reverenced as God, actually to be God.

JESUS' SELF-UNDERSTANDING

How about Jesus himself? What did he know about himself? Who did he think he was?

Scholars who have studied the Gospels in-depth conclude that Jesus did not think of himself as God. His most preferred term for himself may have been "Son of Man." More certainly, however, he thought of himself as a prophet.

Surely, Jesus resisted being called the Messiah (or the Christ: *Messiah* in Hebrew and *Christ* in Greek simply mean "Anointed"). At his trial, when asked if he was the Messiah, according to Mark 14:61-62 Jesus does reply "I am," but then he goes on to talk about the Son of Man, not the Messiah. However, in this same situation, Matthew 26:63-64 has Jesus distance himself from the matter by saying, "It is you who say so," and Luke 22:67-69 has Jesus evade the question altogether and go on to talk about the Son of Man. It would appear that Mark added those words, "I am," to fit the lesson of his Gospel about Jesus actually being the suffering Messiah.

In the famous scene at Caesarea Philippi in Mark 8, when Jesus asks the disciples who they think he is, Peter answers, "You are the Messiah." As the passage stands, Jesus tells them not to tell anyone and then goes on to explain that the Messiah must suffer—to which Peter objects. Scholars trying to get behind this passage suggest that, to make his point that Jesus was the suffering Messiah, Mark reinterpreted this event.

The instruction *not to tell anyone* that Jesus is the Messiah is actually a theme that runs through the whole of Mark's Gospel. Scholars call this theme "the messianic secret." Mark used it to explain why, if Jesus was the Messiah, nobody during his lifetime recognized him as such. Mark introduced this theme in the very first chapter of his Gospel when he has Jesus order the unclean spirit to be quiet and stop calling him the "Holy One of God."

Moreover, in that scene at Caesarea Philippi, Jesus' predictions about his coming suffering, death, and resurrection are so detailed that one wonders how the disciples could have ever missed the point, yet, you will recall, the apostles were baffled when the time for Jesus' capture, trial, and crucifixion actually arrived. Then, we must conclude that these details were written into the story after the fact—or else the apostles were all dimwits. Besides, that the Messiah would suffer was a radically new idea. None of the Hebrew Scriptures portrayed the Messiah as a tragic figure. Suffering was simply not a part of the notion of *Messiah*. Trying to make sense of their experience of Jesus, the early Christians constructed the notion of a suffering Messiah by combining the idea of Messiah with that of the Suffering Servant in Isaiah 52-53. No wonder the Jews resisted the idea that Jesus was the Messiah. To make the idea fit Jesus, Christianity had to reshape it.

Thus, there is good reason to believe that Mark construed the story of Caesarea Philippi—and the trial scene—to teach the Christian understanding that Jesus was the Messiah. In the process, Mark also obscured Jesus' own attitude toward being called Messiah. If Mark's edits are taken out of the Caesarea Philippi passage as it stands, the passage reads quite differently. Actually, Jesus rebuked Peter for calling him the Messiah, not for objecting to his suffering. Apparently, Jesus did not think of himself as the Messiah, nor did he want others to think of him in those terms.

Apparently, too, a theology is weaved into even Mark's down-to-earth Gospel. After all, the Gospel writers, all of them, were portraying the meaning of Christian faith, not giving a blow-by-blow account of events as we would have wanted to have it. As was the style of the day and to make their point, they took considerable liberties with the historical facts. Their intent was to give a religion lesson, not a history lesson. The Gospel writers report what they had come to understand about Jesus, not what was evident on the spot or even, necessarily, what Jesus thought or said about himself. This fact is made clear in a simple comparison of, for example, Mark's Gospel with John's. In Mark, Jesus speaks in short, pithy statements and clever parables; in John, Jesus proclaims long, circular, and poetic discourses that can go on for chapters. Are we to suppose that Jesus has multiple personalities and preached in radically different ways on different occasions? The more sensible conclusion is that the evangelists wrote up their stories of Jesus in ways that best served their own different purposes. The Gospel writers were concerned to inspire faith, not to answer our historical queries.

This discussion is showing how, by getting behind the writing of the Gospels themselves, contemporary scripture scholars also open a new window on our understanding of Jesus. Thus, it appears that during his human lifetime Jesus had no clear and simple idea of who he was or what his role was to be. Why should we expect that he did? He was human, after all, was he not? What human being do you know who has life all figured out—and is not either bluffing or naive? Was Jesus, as Hebrews 4:15 says, similar to us in all things but sin, or was he not? If he was human like us, why do we suppose that he knew from the beginning what his life was all about? Moreover, if he, as a human being, did not think of himself as God, does this fact necessarily mean that he could not have been God? Aren't we all more and less than we think we are and than we could ever know? Though accurate human knowledge relates to what actually is, the full facts of any matter far surpass what humans can know.

Evidently, even Jesus has to struggle to understand himself and his life. This assertion is precisely the intent of that passage in Hebrews 4 and 5. Though places in the scriptures, especially in the Gospel of John, make it seem as if Jesus had everything worked out in his mind, the early Christians wrote those things in after the fact so that we would not miss the point. They wanted to be sure that we would not miss what they had *come to understand* about Jesus. However, during his life as it actually unfolded, Jesus did not have it so simple. He, too, like all of us, had to grapple with the meaning of his life.

JESUS' CLAIM TO UNPRECEDENTED AUTHORITY

Then, how very peculiar! Mark writes that Jesus spoke with *authority*. The word could also be translated as "with *power.*" It is a very important term in the biblical tradition because, of course, the only power that the Jews recognized was God's power. If Jesus was teaching with power and authority, it means he had the power and authority of God.

That Jesus had authority comes out in many other places. Mark summarizes the matter for us in his first chapter: "He [Jesus] taught as one having authority," and he presented "a new teaching—with authority." In that same chapter, Mark also notes Jesus' mighty works: Jesus cast out an evil spirit, cured Peter's mother-in-law and many others, preached powerfully, and cleansed a leper. If you read through all the Gospels, over and over again you will find that same theme: in word and deed, Jesus was the man with authority, the one who acted with power.

Remember, for example, how Jesus taught using the word *amen*. He would proclaim, "Amen, amen, I say to you." That is weird. The word *amen* was not used in that way. It was used as we use it today. *Amen* is a response that somebody makes to what somebody else says. In Pentecostal churches, for example, the people in the pews encourage the preacher and affirm the teaching. They shout out, "Amen, sister!" "Amen, brother!" "Amen." Or when we assent to a prayer, we respond with "amen." Our "amen" confirms what someone else has prayed. But along comes Jesus affirming himself: "Amen, amen, *I* say to you." He is saying, in other words, "On my own authority, I tell you this."

What did he say? The Sermon on the Mount, in Matthew 5-7, notes some striking examples. Jesus, the new Moses, proclaims God's commandments on the mountain top: Moses said this to you, but I say that. On his own authority, Jesus challenges the Mosaic tradition, which means that he challenges Judaism itself!

Understand what Judaism means. It is a religion with a highly refined sense of God. God is not like us. God is beyond us. When God's word does come to us, it is holy and sacred. For this reason, the Jewish tradition is firm in keeping the Law of Moses. In Jewish belief, this law came from God.

Now along comes Jesus saying, "On my own authority, I say to you such and such." Whereas the prophets said, "This is the word *of the Lord*," Jesus comes along saying, "Amen, amen, *I* say to you."

How very peculiar! Jesus did not say he was God, but he acted with an authority that could have suggested as much in his first-century Jewish circumstances. His words and deeds could easily lead someone to ask, "Who does this man think he is, anyway?"

JESUS' "CRISIS OF IDENTITY"

Jesus never outright claimed to be God. Well, think about it. How could he have? What could he have said? He knew full well that he was not the One he called "the Father in heaven." The words, "I am God," would have meant that he was claiming to be the Father.

Then, how could he have phrased the matter? Could he have said, "I am the Son of God"? He could have, but his listeners would have misunderstood and simply agreed, saying, "We know that you are, Jesus. You are greatly blessed. You are God's son." You see, in Jesus' day it was not a particularly monumental thing to call someone *son of God*. It did not mean that someone actually was God. Anyone who appeared blessed would have been considered a son of God.

In contrast to Son of God and just the opposite of what we would expect, the title *Son of Man* could have a much more sublime meaning—especially if read in light of Daniel 7:13-14: "I saw one like a son of man coming with the clouds of heaven. And he came to the Ancient One and was presented before him. To him was given dominion and glory and kingship. . . . His dominion is an everlasting dominion that shall not pass away, and his kingship is one that shall never be destroyed." Yet even this title *Son of Man* was obscure. It is not clear what or who this "son of man" is in Daniel. Besides, in addition to the lofty meaning in Daniel, the term *son of man* was commonly used to mean simply "a human being." Son of Man was, indeed, one title with which Jesus may have referred to himself. Still, this fact does not necessarily suggest that he considered himself to be God or even one who would come with the clouds and sit at the side of God, the Ancient One. If Jesus did refer to himself as Son of Man, his usage would have been more provocative than clarifying.

In Jesus' day no words could define what Jesus was. As with each of us in our individual situations, he had never happened before. He was unique to history. How could there have been words to name him before he had appeared? Even after his life on earth, it was not until 325 that the Christian church finally found the precise words to express the matter, a Greek phrase with a checkered history, *homoousios to patri,* "consubstantial with the Father."

Could Jesus have proclaimed that Greek formula about himself? Surely, he did not know those words. Even if he did and even if he had spoken them, no one would have understood what he was trying to say. Had he insisted, nonetheless, people would have thought him demented, a raving lunatic babbling incomprehensible nonsense.

What a fix Jesus was in! No way for him to name his unique experience existed. No way for anyone to really understand him was possible. Indeed, without concepts and words, he could not really understand himself. Even though Christianity did go on to proclaim that he was God, consubstantial with the Father, it should come as no surprise that Jesus just never claimed to be God. First, he had to *be* himself before anyone, including himself, could later go on to *say* who he was.

JESUS' EXPERIENCE OF BEING HIMSELF

Then, what do you think it was like being Jesus? What do you think was going on inside him? What do you think he was thinking about when he spent those days and nights in prayer? What do you think he shared with his friends in intimate, quiet moments?

Mark gives us a clue when he tells us that Jesus taught and acted with authority. To follow up on the clue, we need to ask where his sense of authority was coming from.

The answer is no great mystery. His sense of authority must have been coming from within himself. It must have been rooted deeply in his heart. From where else could it have come?

The evidence is clear: He was not acting with authority because he had everything figured out. He was not sure who he was; he did not have everything figured out. Evidently, too, then, he did not have any special "revelations" showing him who he was and what his every daily decision was to be. If he did, was he really human, really one of us, really "like us in all things but sin," as Hebrews 4:15 declares? What is *revelation,* anyway? Do we actually believe that God "speaks to us" through clear words and distinct images? Surely, if God is speaking to us at all, God speaks through hunches, intuitions, insights, the everyday ordinary workings of our own minds—although someone who did not believe in God would never think of associating God with hunches, intuition, and insights. Then, in practice, what difference would bringing in God or not make in the experience of hunches, intuitions, or insights?

The fact is that Jesus did not know precisely where his life was leading and what the exact outcome would be—although, as circumstances unfolded, it would not have taken a rocket scientist to figure it out, and toward the end he must have realized that his sense of authority was on a collision course with the authorities. Still, he was making his way day by day, responding as events arose. No script laid out all the details of his life. How could there be a script? He hadn't lived it yet. Or are we fatalists? Do we really believe that Jesus' life and our own are preordained? If so, why do we bother to think at all or to read books such as this one? If everything is preordained, we are robots moving through a make-believe, mechanical world. Is that the kind of life we want to attribute to Jesus? As it is, Jesus must have found his sense of authority within his own self.

Another way to make the same point would be to say that he lived by faith. He trusted in the inklings that were coming up from inside himself. He used whatever knowledge he had and whatever new insight arose, and he pieced a plan together. Day by day, with an open mind and with a generous dose of goodwill, he pursued his course, seeking ever to make the best of things. He lived with good sense and trust. In the big questions of life, he had little certainty to go on. He took his best shot, hoped for the best, and trusted. No naive fool, he was ever ready to readjust his steps when new evidence arose. He was a person of profound goodwill. He was deeply committed to life in all its challenge and mystery. He lived by faith.

Oh, to be sure, he was who he was. Although he could not put the marvel of his own self into words, it was in him; he was himself. Just by being in touch with himself, if he was really the Only-Begotten-of-God, he must have been in touch with that reality, his own self, at some level. He could not have expressed his reality in the words that I just used, but he must have felt it; he must have sensed it; he must have experienced it in some way. If he was in touch with himself—and he must have been, that alert, sensitive, vibrant human being—at some level and to some degree, he must have been in touch with who and what he was. Maybe he had no clear ideas or thoughts on the matter. Surely, he had no words to express the matter, but in his heart, in his dreams, in his quietmost moments, he must have had hunches, inklings, intuitions.

My point is this: All Jesus had to go on was what was inside himself. He let himself sense it. He communed with it. He was true to it. He trusted it. He let it lead him. This is surely the reason he went around saying and doing the things he did. This is why other people, looking at him, came to the conclusions that they did. They put into words what they saw him living. They named his experience. Don't we all need others to look on from outside and tell us who we are? In the meantime, his living was just the expression of his deepest inner experience. He was a man true to himself.

Here is a picture of Jesus, our brother, a fellow human being, in all his humanness. Here is a picture that religion, with its easy after-the-fact answers, does not give us: what he was really like, this human being walking around ancient Palestine. He lived in faith, lived in trust, lived in radical honesty. He was a very good person. Others did not understand him. He did not really understand himself. Not only did others not understand him, but they also pursued, persecuted, condemned, and eventually murdered him—because of the things he was doing and saying as a result of just being his honest and loving self. He was not even able to fully explain himself to them. He could not even rationalize himself to himself. He was just being who he was in all honesty and goodwill. He would not betray his own self, not on your life—or his own! Moreover, ever true to himself, he could not help but, by the same token, be ever faithful also to God—since he, according to Christian orthodoxy, was God, the Eternally-Begotten. Being who he was, he ran no risk of sin whatsoever in living his life on the principle of fidelity to himself. Fidelity to himself meant fidelity to God.

JESUS AS EVERYMAN—AND EVERYWOMAN

I said that Mark's Gospel tells us something about Jesus and also something about ourselves. Do you see any connection between Jesus and us when we get down to what he was really like? In my mind, the connection is obvious.

In fact, everybody who lives is unique. No one else is you. No one can live your life. No one can, in the final analysis, tell you what you need to do. Just as Jesus had to live out his own life, even though no one understood him and even though he did not fully understand himself, so each of us has to live out our life, not really understanding what it means or where it is going or why. As a real human being and also a God come among us, as portrayed in orthodox Christian belief, Jesus becomes relevant to every human being who ever lived.

Using the language of our own day, we could say that Jesus had the problem of "coming out." He sensed deep and unique moments within himself, but he was not able to easily share them with others. Attempting to share them was dangerous.

To that extent, Jesus was very similar to people in the lesbian, gay, bisexual, and transgender community of our day. They live with an issue that is very similar to Jesus' own issue—something that nobody can see on the outside but that they sense on the inside. In our oh-so-repressive Western Christian society, until very recently, when gay liberation came along, most people did not know how to name what was going on inside them, just as Jesus could not possibly have named what was going on in himself. Gay people only knew—and many are still in this situation—that something about themselves was different. They knew that, if they were going to be honest and be themselves, they just could not speak and act as everybody else was doing. They quickly came to learn that, if they dared being themselves, they would face fierce opposition and, in some cases, a horrible death. The parallels with Jesus' life are striking.

It takes courage to come out. It takes faith and trust to come out. It takes radical honesty to come out. It takes goodwill to make the best of what you learn about yourself. Whoever you are—gay, straight, the Son of God, the artist, the athlete, the klutz, or whatever—you have to become a really good and very strong person to be your God-given self. You have to be a person of deep faith and trust to accept your being as it really is, and you have to be deeply committed to the good to make the best of that reality, to use well whatever gifts, talents, and propensities you find in your unique makeup.

The challenge to "find yourself," to "be who you are," is a recent development in human history. In former ages, people had no doubts about who they were and how they fit in. The eldest son would inherit the land or business; the second eldest would go into the ministry; the third eldest would join the military or in some other way go off on his own. The girls in the family were destined for marriage, and their fathers or husbands ever determined the female fate. Life in a convent was the only somewhat liberating option for women who did not want to be bound to a man. A person's identity was linked to the family name and locale. The meaning of life was well-known: One was to fulfill one's earthly duties as laid out by social expectation, and, so doing, one looked forward to eternal reward in heaven. After all, this whole social system was the plan of God.

Today we live with incredible personal freedom, and also with much painful uncertainty. Free "to be ourselves," we also have to determine what we will be. In a globalizing world in which close community is scarce and traditions are ever more shallow, the challenge simply to be oneself often weighs heavy, indeed. It is no accident that the suicide rate among adolescents grows alarmingly higher.

The challenge that each of us faces in coming out as ourselves gives us all an intimate connection with Jesus. After all, according to Christian belief, Jesus must be the paradigmatic instance of the challenge of coming out: His case was absolutely unique in all of human history. He provides a prime example of someone's being himself in the face of unprecedented uncertainty and uncontainable opposition.

This connection with Jesus needs to be emphasized particularly in the case of lesbian women. Working with women, I have become very aware of the fact that Jesus was male. Oh, the fact is obvious, of course, and for this reason we just take it for granted, but I have recently had to take note of the obvious fact that Jesus was male.

Jesus' maleness is a great thing for men, straight and gay. In one way or another, they find it easy to identify with him. But what about women—and especially women who were sexually abused or women who are lesbian? Jesus's maleness makes it very difficult for them to identify with their "savior." His maleness puts women in a definitely subordinate position, and it may leave some women out in the cold altogether.

Let's face it. We do not like to talk about the sexual dimensions of religion. Supposedly, sex does not enter into religion, for religion is about much more "lofty" things. (What does this sentiment imply about our attitude toward sex?)

However, if we are honest with ourselves, we all know that physical attraction and affectional ties have much to do with religion. In fact, because religion engages the depths of a person, sexuality is surely more involved in religion than in, say, business or education or government. Mystics describe their experiences in sexual terms, and gentle sexual arousal is often a passing component in deep prayer or meditation. College students in my human sexuality course object when I make this point. They presume such a chasm between religion and sex that they cannot imagine sexual arousal associated with prayer. Yet it often is. Therefore, to the extent that we are uncomfortable with our sexuality, we will be unable to pursue deep meditation and prayer: Fear of sexuality is a block to sanctity. More than business, education, or government, religion is similar to art. People in artistic circles are known to raise sexual issues. If the same does not occur in religious circles, it is only because religion is less honest about the matter.

Like it or not, Jesus' maleness is a dynamic in the Christian religion. This dynamic may be a problem for some women, and there is no way around the problem. The sexual dimension is real. Jesus was male. This fact cannot be changed. From a psychological point of view, no easy solution exists. From this point of view and in all honesty, it must be admitted that Christianity's central emphases do not make for a universally relevant religion. Christianity is tainted at its core with sexism.

However, from a strictly theological point of view, Jesus' gender is not important—though one would never know this fact in light of many churches' reactions to the ordination of women. The important theological point about Jesus is not that he was a man, but that he was one of us, a human being. Until the question of women's ordination came up, throughout Christian history document after document in both Greek and Latin—which easily focus the difference—have always emphasized Jesus' humanity, not his maleness.

Therefore, every human being can identify with something in Jesus—honesty, soul-searching, self-affirmation, deep faith, courage, goodwill. In this sense, the male but human Jesus can also be a model for women, women compelled to seek equal status in society or ordination in the churches.

Deep in their hearts women sense a movement that may well be in conflict with current policy, yet they identify with Jesus precisely in being true to that inner sense, true to their own selves, true to an inarticulate urging that might challenge the status quo and result in realities new to history. Religion might suggest that they be "obedient to God" by denying their "selfish interests" and, on the supposed example of Jesus, sacrifice their personal well-being for a greater cause: Women are always told (by men) to sacrifice themselves for others (men). However, such religion distorts the example of Jesus to which it appeals.

If we understand Jesus to be one of us rather than fancy him to be a celestial visitor in human disguise, women are similar to Jesus precisely to the extent that they express the calling that they sense in their souls. If, according to Christian belief, they do not have, as Jesus did, a very identity with God urging them from within, they do have the urging of Jesus' own divine Holy Spirit, poured out in their human hearts and prompting them from within. To this extent and on the point that really matters, as much as any man, they are similar to Jesus.

Theologically, Jesus' self-affirmation in faith is the most important facet of his human life and death. Precisely the self-affirmation of this wondrous human being, even in the face of death, is Jesus' saving contribution. Away with other notions—for example, that God intended Jesus' gruesome murder and delighted in it or that in justice God demanded Jesus' blood or that Jesus was born precisely to die in sacrifice for others or that Jesus' painful death was the price paid to God for sin! These notions, widespread though they be, are without scriptural basis and are bad theology. They make God out to be an ogre. They are also bad psychology: They encourage unhealthy attitudes. Whereas Colossians 2:14 says that God *cancelled the debt* of sin, these notions, derived predominantly from a theory of Anselm of Canterbury and popularized by Luther and Calvin, suggest that God demanded payment of the debt and that Jesus paid it off for us.

No, not Jesus' death itself but, rather, Jesus' *virtue unto death* is what reconciled humanity with God. Death itself is hardly prized in God's eyes. Jesus' death was redeeming only insofar as it was the ultimate expression of his human virtue. Precisely his virtue restores human commitment to, and trust in, God. Jesus' human fidelity—first to himself and thereby to God, from whom he came—is what reconciles humankind with God. I elaborated this understanding of redemption in *The Same Jesus: A Contemporary Christology.*

It was only natural that our redemption in Christ unfolded in that way. For a human being, things could not be otherwise. In the case of Jesus as in our own, God is known in the only way that humans can know God, namely, in the life-giving flow of the universe that shows itself in cosmic wonders and, above all, in the human spirit. Said otherwise, we know God in the struggle of our own hearts, in the secret precincts of faith and conscience. All who, at whatever cost, engage this human struggle and enter into this same flow of the universe are one with Jesus in fidelity to the God who made the universe and us and who calls us to surrender to the supreme Mystery at work in and among us.

THE LESSON OF MARK AND JESUS

Thought about Jesus leads us to consider our own lives. Thinking about Jesus, we are led to think also about ourselves. Jesus and us, we go together. We live in unknowing, as he did. Our lives follow a mysterious path, as his did. For him and for us, good living takes courage, faith, honesty, and love. For all of us, life holds misunderstanding and uncertainty. For some, life may even bring outright persecution. For all, life inevitably brings death in one form or another, and similar to Jesus, most of us will know that death is coming, and we will have to come to grips with it.

If we really identify with Jesus, the unfolding of life also brings increased light. If we live with honesty and goodwill, the challenges of life give way to victories. Death brings resurrection.

Anyone who has faced a crisis in life knows that pain is the cost of the growth. Anyone who has gone through any coming out knows how much better things are after that step—the teenager (or middle-aged person) who names his or her homosexuality before self, family, and friends; the beleaguered wife and mother who finally says, "No more," and files for divorce; the spiritually repressed congregant who joins another church or another religion or, for salvation's sake, gives up on religion altogether; the graduate student who drops out of medical or law school and breaks the family tradition to pursue a career in art, business, education, or whatever; the American who finds that life in the States is simply insane and pulls up roots to become an expatriate in some far-off land; the university professor who gives up tenure to become an Albert Schweitzer. Life is always better after a daunting coming out. Materially and financially one may be worse off, but overall life is always better.

The image of Jesus that Mark's gospel portrays is that of the suffering Messiah, and Jesus suffered precisely because he dared to be true to himself: In his own soul he found his authority. Mark portrayed Jesus in this way to encourage the early Christians in Rome who were just then beginning to face persecution. Though suffering is an inevitable part of life, especially when we are determined to make our unique contribution, the achievement is worth the cost. Even death gives way to new life. Such is the courageous lesson that Mark sees in Jesus and commends to us.

Mark wrote specifically for the disciples of Jesus, but what Mark and Jesus have to teach is wisdom for anyone, believer and nonbeliever alike. The lesson of Jesus is a lesson about human living. The lesson is that fulfillment in life must come from our being ourselves. Whether "being ourselves" is understood in the religious sense of being what God made us to be or in the secular sense of merely being ourselves, if the project is honest and genuine, the practical result must be the same. As Jesus' experience shows, we know God and God's will only in probing our own hearts; we will be true to God by being true to our deepest and best selves.

The lesson is also that our being ourselves is our best possible contribution to others. Jesus "saved us" precisely by his fidelity to himself (and thereby to God) even in the face of death on the cross. In the flow of the universe, in which we are truly ourselves and in which the creative work of God is advanced, the affirmation of self and the salvation of others coincide. In authentic humanity and accurate theology, self and others are opposite sides of the same coin. The religious advice that we sacrifice our genuine selves for the sake of others is misguided and dangerous and, simplistically formulated, is diabolical. Lacking in faith, suspicious of creation, mistrusting the flow of the universe expressed in our guts, this advice deserves the response that Jesus gave Peter at Caesarea Philippi: "Get behind me, Satan!" (Mark 8:33). As Jesus resisted social pressure toward corrupt conformity, so must all of us who would be whole. We do our best for others by being our own very best.

If acceptance of religion could ever bring salvation, this religious lesson from Mark and Jesus surely presents one instance. It tells us to be ourselves. To follow it is to follow ourselves. In our common humanity, commitment to Jesus is commitment to ourselves. Being truly Christian, being a true disciple of Jesus, is a matter of being a genuine human being—and being genuinely human always requires some kind of coming out.

Chapter 10

The Trinitarian Vocation
of the Gay Community

All religious beliefs have this-worldly implications, and the doctrine of the Trinity is no exception. Consideration of the doctrine of the Trinity can shed light even on the gay experience, so this chapter uses this doctrine to highlight positive facets of the gay community.

The relevance of this chapter is not limited to Christians, and this exploration of trinitarian theology, which is so seldom discussed in any detail, will certainly fascinate Christians and others, as well. True to the down-to-earth emphasis throughout this book, this chapter aims to foster awareness of spirituality relevant to everyone, believer and nonbeliever alike.

John McNeill has repeatedly raised the question about homosexuality, "For what purpose? Why does God create homosexual people?" McNeill and others have begun to develop a Christian spirituality for gay people. This essay makes another contribution to the project by unfolding the positive possibilities in the homosexual experience. Developing a trinitarian answer to McNeill's question, this essay portrays positive living within the gay and lesbian community as an earthly parallel to the inner-trinitarian life of God. This essay presents the gay community as an earthly expression of the interpersonal life of God.

Evidently, this chapter makes a bold statement. It shows that, far from being godless and destined for damnation, lesbian and gay people may be engaged in a most sublime project, for central aspects of "the gay lifestyle" fit the pattern of Christianity's highest spiritual ideal: the unity of Three in One, the Blessed Trinity.

This chapter was originally published with documentation in *Pastoral Psychology*, 1987, volume 36, number 2, pages 100-111. Reprinted with permission.

CHRISTIAN BELIEF ABOUT THE TRINITY

Christian rhetoric always insists on one truth about the Trinity: It is a profound mystery. Most take "mystery" in a negative sense: something that cannot be understood—and they leave it at that. However, there is a more positive understanding of religious mystery: something so rich in meaning that its meaning can never be exhausted. Taken in this positive sense, the Trinity offers an overflow of meaning. This Christian doctrine provokes ever new insight—even as this chapter, in light of the recent emergence of the gay community, finds new meaning in the doctrine of the Trinity.

Within that wealth of meaning, this is certain: The Trinity is about the perfect unity of three Individuals in relationship, "three Persons in one God." This certainty will provide our point of comparison between the Trinity and the gay community.

Said in the simplest and most practical terms, the Trinity is a perfect community of love. According to traditional trinitarian theology, in God three distinct Persons—or Subjects or Individuals or Identities—share so perfectly that together They have only one life, one mind, one will, one being. They have everything in common except their individual identities. These three different "Someones" have only one, common being. They love so perfectly and share so fully that among themselves They have only one and the same life. Surely, this is an ideal about which all lovers dream.

Moreover, precisely their sharing this one life in different ways establishes the individual identities of the Divine Three. What makes them individuals is not *what* they are—for all Three are divine; all Three are God; all Three share the same one being, one knowledge, one love, one life, one mind, one will. They always are and always act together in complete unity. What makes them individual is not what they are. Rather, what makes them individuals is *how* they are what they are: Their relations to one another distinguish them from one another. The Son *proceeds from* or *is born of* the Father, so by sheer dint of logic, the Son cannot be the Father. Likewise, the Holy Spirit *proceeds from* the Father and the Son (Eastern Christianity says "from the Father through the Son"), so again, by sheer dint of logic, the Holy Spirit cannot be the Father or the Son. Because of the very relationships that these "proceedings" set up, the Three in God differ from one another in who each one is. The Son is the one who is born of the Father; the Holy Spirit is the one who proceeds from the Father and the Son. The Three are distinct identities.

Nonetheless, in their proceeding from one another, they share with one another all that they are, so by the very relationships that distinguish them from one another, they also share one and the same divine being with one another. The Father gives himself fully and perfectly to the Son, and the Father and the Son give themselves fully and perfectly to the Holy Spirit. What the Father is, this also the Son is, and what the Father and the Son are, this also the Holy Spirit is. What they are is exactly the same: Divinity. Therefore, only one God exists, only one Divinity—but Three exist who are this only one God, Three who in different and interrelated ways possess this only one Divinity. Since they each possess Divinity fully, They are identical in all aspects— except in the relationships with one another that make them Three different identities who possess one and the same Divinity.

To be sure, such an explanation is difficult to understand, for it is subtle. But it is not illogical. Nowhere does the explanation run into self-contradiction. The Three are only one God because all Three share the one and the same Divinity; and the Three differ because they share Divinity in different ways: as God without source, as God born of the Father, and as God proceeding from the Father and the Son. According to one consideration They are one; according to another consideration They are Three. No contradiction exists in this situation. Similarly, people sometimes say that they love and hate somebody at the same time. From one perspective, they love the person; from another perspective, they hate the person. No contradiction exists in this complicated set of affairs.

The doctrine of the Trinity is complicated because it expresses a lofty ideal. The Trinity presents the idea of three individuals who share so perfectly that they are one. Thus, the Trinity presents the image of perfect love. The doctrine of the Trinity suggests that love could be so perfect that the lovers become completely one without losing their individuality.

Granted this brief sketch of Christian trinitarian belief, four issues become the focus of this chapter: individuality, equality, relationships, and gender neutrality. In the Trinity there is (1) inviolable individuality (2) among equals who are (3) dependent on interpersonal relations but (4) unconstrained by gender. This chapter first notes how these same four issues may be found in the gay community, then spells out the parallels with the Trinity, and finally indicates some practical implications of this comparison.

HUMAN RELATIONSHIPS WITHIN THE GAY COMMUNITY

Friendships Beyond Gender Limitation

First, consider the irrelevance of gender stereotypes in the gay community. For example, well-known and prized within the gay community are female-male friendships that are free of all genital interest. Such friendships exist not only between male-female couples who are themselves both homosexual but also between couples, one of whom is homosexual and the other heterosexual.

In contrast, in society at large, men as well as women lament the difficulty of maintaining real friendships with each other. Erotic interest almost inevitably complicates or destroys their friendships. This outcome apparently results because these men and women are sexual beings with heterosexual interests. In a heterosexual culture—one that acknowledges the validity of only heterosexuality—men and women tend to be cast vis-à-vis each other as sex partners. Deep female-male friendships do not feature large in such a culture.

In contrast, gender is not a major issue within the gay community. So the frequent occurrence of precisely such friendships within the gay community represents a new hope for society at large. More can be said about the range of relationships possible in the gay community.

Equality in Relationships

Part and parcel of true female-male friendships is the acknowledgment of both friends as somehow equal. In contrast, typically our society still treats women as second-class citizens. Further elaboration need not be made. The point here is simply that in the gay community an alternative is emerging. In the frequency of its female-male friendships, the gay community grants the dignity, individuality, and worth of both men and women—alone and in relationship with one another. This dynamism points to the equality of all persons.

This statement of equality within the gay community holds true across the board—not only when comparing men with women but also when comparing men with other men or women with other women. At the present time, the stigma attached to homosexuality is still so strong that it acts as a leveling agent. Compared with one's homosexuality, one's social status, wealth, education, and renown often pale in significance. Unfortunately race (though to a lesser degree than in the straight community), physical beauty, and youth remain important criteria for evaluating people in the gay community, as in the straight community. Yet, beyond these, the gay subculture tends to see through most other externals sacred to the broader culture and to accept people on the basis of their personal worth. All persons are equal.

This equality of persons also reigns in lesbian and gay sexual relationships. The partners in each case—a man with another man, a woman with another woman—are equals from the start. In contrast, heterosexual relationships have historically been built on the subordination of the woman to the man: At the wedding ceremony, the woman's father "gives her away." She then gives up her father's name and takes her husband's name. In the extreme case, which can still be found in many cultures, the wife is the property and servant of the husband; she is there to bear his heirs and to tend to his needs. Such an imbalanced relationship could hardly work when the two entering the relationship are on the same social footing. So in the gay community a model of an interpersonal, sexual relationship in which both partners are equal and the relationship develops through true, mutual concern is emerging. Granted, this model of equality is happily also becoming the ideal in the heterosexual world, and granted, not all homosexual partners actually maintain a balanced relationship. Nonetheless, by the very nature of homosexual relationships, the ideal of equality is natural.

Personal Growth Through Interrelationship

By definition homosexuality implies intense, feeling-filled, same-sex relationships. Far beyond what the broader culture allows, the gay community permits affection and its expression between two men or two women. Especially two men's free expression of affection—even when nonsexual—strikes at the heart of the patriarchal culture. However, the issue here is not the negative gay challenge to a patriarchal system; it is rather the positive gay contribution to the dissolution of sex-role stereotypes.

Our culture raises little boys and little girls to fit the expected models. Girls are to be soft and delicate. They may freely express their own feelings and are to be sensitive to others' feelings. Their role is to serve and to accommodate others. To the boys they are to be attractive, even seductive. The girls are to be passive; their role is more to be supportive than initiating. They gain their influence through their men; they are the supposed proverbial "good woman behind every good man."

On the other hand, boys are to be rugged and aggressive. Boys learn to control their feelings. They are rational, not emotional; and this expectation sometimes means that boys are unfeeling and insensitive. They are the leaders, the go-getters. They cannot afford too much sympathy, and they may not cry. For girls, the boys are the prize, the assurance of security and protection, the coveted husband-guardian. For the boys, the girls are a comfort, a support, a plaything, a toy, an ever-willing respite from the battle of life.

Much can be said for or against such stereotypes. Many will object that the previous paragraphs are a caricature or that the times are changing or have already changed. Others, hopelessly ignorant of history and anthropology on all fronts, will insist that men and women have always been as just described and by divine decree are to remain this way. Whatever the case, the fact remains that society forms girls and boys to complement each other. The strengths of the one tend to be the weaknesses of the other. Then, working together, a man and a woman may easily achieve success, according to the culture's definition of success.

The complimentarity of sex roles benefits society at large. But what of the individuals? Are they to be sacrificed to society's goals? Unfortunately, the answer is yes; that such "sacrifice" occurs is necessary and even right. It is part of the human process of socialization. Wariness is needed only when socialization becomes dehumanization. But this danger is always real, and the stakes are always high.

Precisely because it touches these cultural issues at the core of our society, the gay liberation movement elicits strong emotional reactions. This liberation movement is saying that the gender stereotypes are demanding too much, debilitating men and women in general, and completely squelching the affectional life of lesbian and gay people in particular—not to mention bisexual, transgender, and intersex people.

As the gay community experiences them, personal relationships demand that people stretch beyond the standard sex-role stereotypes and move toward what has been called androgynous wholeness. At its best, the gay movement calls people to a fuller and richer human life. Through relationships people become their unique selves. Gay awareness insists on the right to interrelationships, the wholeness of each person, the value of every one, and the equality of all as people. The expected result of this interrelationship is the emergence of a more humane world.

Obviously, the main issue here is interpersonal relationships and personal growth. The issue is the same one that emerges from other contemporary movements, especially the feminist movement and its younger brother, the "men's group" movement. Lying behind them all is the twentieth-century breakthrough in psychological awareness. By contrast, the main issue is not genital activity, homosexual or heterosexual. Unfortunately, this point needs to be made explicit since many think only of sex when homosexuality is in question. The main issue is people and their relationships, not sex.

Preservation of Personal Uniqueness

The goal of the gay movement is not the homogenization of all individuals into androgynous blandness. From one point of view, relationships within the gay community transcend gender, but from another point of view they do not. After all, at the very core of the gay contribution is the insistence that men may love men and women may love women affectionately and sexually. It is important that it is really a man or really a woman that one is loving. In the contemporary gay community a man does not particularly want to relate to an effeminate man on the pretext that the relationship is then somehow heterosexual, and the parallel holds in the case of lesbians.

Likewise, all may have a basic equality in the gay community, but personal identity is not lost. On the contrary, gay liberation highlights and values the personal uniqueness of each individual. The gay community is noted—perhaps even notorious—for its support of colorful, creative, lively, self-expressive individuality. The very word *gay* bears this connotation. One implication of androgyny is precisely the validity of developing all sides of one's personality and becoming one's full and unique self.

Four points summarize the possible contribution of the gay community toward a richer understanding of people as male or female. First, the basis of human relationships is beyond gender. All relate to all, men and women alike, in the full breadth of human capacity. Second, all are basically equal; in friendship no subordinates exist. Men and women relate in profound friendship with one another, women relate with other women, and men relate with other men. The reign of patriarchy is ended. Third, all nonetheless retain their individuality. Men are men, women are women, and each is an individual, unique, gifted, and valuable as such. Fourth and finally, personal relationships are understood as growth producing. People become who they are through relationship with another. For this reason the gay community values relationships in all their possible configurations.

THE GAY COMMUNITY AS TRINITARIAN

We can now develop a comparison between inner-trinitarian life and the ideal of relationships developing within the gay community. I make no claim to actually know what God is or what God's inner and interpersonal life is like. As in all religious speculation, the comparisons made here are only suggestive. Yet the basic mutual relevance of these two topics will be clear.

First is the issue of gender. We call the First Person in God "Father" because that was Jesus' usage. *Father* is a male designation. Historical-critical studies make us well aware that Jesus was a product of the patriarchal culture in which he lived. Although according to Christian belief Jesus was the "Eternal Son of God," Jesus, was also truly human. Necessarily, then, he was limited in his human understanding and expression even about God. So, in the style of his day, Jesus referred to God as "Father."

However, later Christian thinking made it clear that the essential relationship between the "Father" and the "Son" is not one of male camaraderie, but one of generation. The "Son" is *born of* the "Father"; the "Father" *begets* the "Son." Once clarified, this essential issue can be expressed in terms other than those in which it originally arose. In fact, in a different cultural situation this issue needs to be expressed differently if the original meaning is to be retained.

Making its point, the Eleventh Council of Toledo, in 675, spoke of the Son's being born "of the womb of the Father." This image is undeniably feminine. Therefore, it must be possible to correctly express the Christian truth about the Trinity by speaking of the Father also as Mother. *Mother* preserves the essential relationship, generation. The term *Eternal Parent* would be equally correct, as would also be the term *Mother-Father.* This last term has the distinct advantage of being strange, so its very usage reminds us that God is not similar to us or similar to anything else that we know. God is neither male nor female, and God is neither mother nor father. God is both and more than both. On the other hand, the term *Creator* is not an adequate substitute for *Father.* God, Three in One, is the Creator of the Universe, so all Three Persons in God, in their respective ways, are Creator. Styling the Eternal Parent alone as Creator collapses the Trinity into one Person, the Mother-Father, and suggests that the other Two, since they are not the Creator, are not God.

Nonsexist alternative terms for the "Son" are also possible: Only-Begotten, Begotten of God, Eternal Offspring, Eternal Child of God. Finally, the term *Holy Spirit,* free of gender connotations, may stand. In sum, we have a genderless Trinity: the Eternal Parent, the Only-Begotten of God, and the Holy Spirit.

Well-meaning but uniformed attempts to insert femininity into the Trinity by making the Holy Spirit female are not helpful. They exacerbate the problem: They attach real gender to the Persons in God. Designating two of those Persons as male and only one as female, these suggestions continue to support male dominance. But God has no gender. Attempting to complement the Father in God by calling the Holy Spirit "Mother Spirit" is an even worse move. It completely muddles trinitarian theology. This usage suggests that the Holy Spirit, similar to a mother, is a source of generation in God, but the Spirit is the last of the Three Persons in God. Calling the Holy Spirit "Mother" suggests that the Only-Begotten of God is born of the "Father" and the "Mother" (the Holy Spirit), whereas the Holy Spirit proceeds from those other Two.

Though we may have difficulty developing a nonsexist trinitarian terminology, in the perfect community of love that the Trinity is, gender is simply not an issue. The relationships of distinct Subjects open to one another in complete self-giving are all that matters.

Here is a parallel with the personalist emphasis within the gay community at its best: Not gender, but true concern for other people, is the accepted criterion of human relationship.

Second, the Three in God are who they are by relationship to one another. The processions of the Only-Begotten from the Eternal Parent and of the Holy Spirit from the Eternal Parent and the Only-Begotten set the distinctions among the Three. These relationships of origin and only these determine the individuality of the distinct, divine Persons.

Such a state of affairs again parallels the personalist thrust within the gay community. There people are encouraged to be who they are and to become who they are through their relationships with others. The individuality of each is not thought to be predetermined or fixed prior to interaction with others. Rather, each discovers personal possibilities and becomes himself or herself in relationship with others. Limits are broadly drawn. One is what one is willing to risk in relating to another. In some way, then, this human situation is similar to the divine situation. Interrelationship is at the heart of one's being who one is: The Eternal Parent, the Only-Begotten, and the Holy Spirit are who they are because of their relationships to one another.

Third, the Three in the Trinity are equal; all are God. The perfect and complete self-giving of the Mother-Father results in the Begotten of God, perfectly equal to the Father-Mother in all things except for a distinct identity: "bornness" of the Eternal Parent. Likewise, the perfect and complete self-giving of the Eternal Parent and of the Eternally Begotten to each other results in the Holy Spirit, also perfectly and equally God as the other Two are. Expressing ideal love, the Trinity is a community of equals sharing one life, one being, in harmony and perfect unity.

That equality in God parallels the ideal equality among people open to one another in honest and loving relationship. As humans relate with one another in truth and love and learn to share more and more in common, what they are, what they stand for—but not who they are—overlaps. *They* become *one*. This theme was the topic of my doctoral dissertation *One in Christ*.

The gay community provides an environment that can foster such interpersonal relationships. Transcending the limits determined by sex-role stereotypes, women and men relate to one another in the gay community as friends, as equals. Likewise, stretching their personalities to androgynous wholeness, men with men and women with women relate in affection and love. They relate, not as half-persons—man or woman, supposedly formed to complement their opposite—but as themselves, each one fully and richly developed. They relate, not, then, out of personal inadequacy or societal expectation, but out of the fullness of their personhood. The opposites expand, overlap each other, and find equality. All share the same—now not male or female, but simply, authentically human—qualities. Again, this human situation of equality somehow mirrors that in the Trinity.

Finally, Eternal Parent, Only-Begotten, and Holy Spirit retain their distinct identities despite their absolute unity as God. Those whose very identities are determined by their generative relations to one another, identical though they be in all else, must be distinct subjects. They are not lost in nondifferentiation because they are all equally one God. Similarly, people in the gay community remain who they are, man or woman, this one and not that one, despite that all are equal and all are equally open to relating to all others. The ideals of the gay movement do not entail dissolving the differences between the sexes or between individual people. On the contrary, being gay forces people to find themselves and to be themselves. At the present time, at least, being gay—or transsexual or intersexed—entails a quest for self that straight people need never consider. Precisely by means of unifying relationships, unique to the people involved, the gay community supports this quest and preserves personal individuality. Again, the Trinity provides the model.

THE VOCATION OF GAY CHRISTIANS

On those four points and with varying degrees of strictness, divine life within the Trinity shows a parallel with an ideal fostered within the gay community. Viewed with an optimistic eye and accepted with goodwill, that ideal points to the vision of perfected Christian life announced in John 17:21-23: "May they all be one. Father, may they be one in us, as you are in me and I am in you. . . . With me in them and you in me, may they be so completely one that the world will realize that it was you who sent me."

At the heart of the lesbian and gay experience, lived honestly and deeply, is a movement toward mystical union. As detailed in Chapter 5, this mysticism is not just some airy-fairy spiritual matter but includes psychological and physical dimensions, as well. This discussion is about real human beings—body, psyche, and spirit—relating to one another and in various ways becoming one with one another and with God.

The essence of Christian belief is that authentic human growth on earth is ultimately the result of God's own love, the Holy Spirit, poured out among us, so that in Christ humans become like God; they are deified. Loving one another as coequal and codetermined, yet inviolably distinct people beyond gender limitations, humans grow into trinitarian life. Precisely because of these four distinctive aspects of the lesbian and gay community, life within this community is a growing participation in God's own life, the completion of Christ's work among us, and the result of the Holy Spirit's mission to us. Thus, the gay community has the possibility and, thus, the vocation of offering our world a model of ideal Christian life in practice.

Some may be surprised by these conclusions about the spiritual potential of the gay liberation movement. Such surprise would be likely especially among those who "know" the gay community only through the pejorative stereotypes and who are unfamiliar with the deeply spiritual segments of that community or whose depth of theological insight is limited by a biblical or doctrinal fundamentalism.

Regardless, members of the gay community who live deliberately in Christ-like ways—whether they are Christian or not—must be destined for that fulfillment symbolized as a sharing in the inner-trinitarian life, to which all are called in Christ. These people must grow in that life precisely by living their human lives on this earth. Since they are lesbian and gay, they must grow in that life precisely as gay and lesbian. No other possibility exists.

Therefore, since they are, indeed, growing in trinitarian life, it is completely appropriate that aspects of their particular situation be highlighted and held up to the rest of the Christian community as indications of how God's life among humankind may grow. This conclusion is especially true when certain values in their life, in contrast to the culture at large, may significantly foster that divine life—as in the present case. Although some may damn the gay community as diabolical and godless, this chapter suggests that the gay community is uniquely suited to embody the highest spiritual values. The very structure of this community points to Christianity's most sublime conception—union with, and as in, the Divine Trinity.

The possible surprise at these conclusions is merely that which always results from concrete application of the Christian message, especially from application to a particularly misunderstood and generally hated segment of the human race. The scandal is merely the scandal of God's love for us as revealed in Christ. It is the scandal of the Good Samaritan or the woman at the well or the call of the hated tax collector Matthew or the favor shown to cheating Zacchaeus or the Sabbath cure of the paralytic. It is the scandal of the five "shady" women in Matthew's genealogy of the Messiah and the scandal of the human life and bloody death of God's Only-Begotten. As the Bible teaches over and over, when God decides to become intimately involved with humankind, the result is seldom what humans would expect.

Of course, this potential for growth in God's life is no exclusive property of the gay community. What is true here of the gay community must also be said of all Christians and all people of goodwill. All are called to love all others, male or female, gay or straight, as equals, respectful of individuality, growing in both human and divine life by means of interrelationship. "There are no more distinctions between Jew and Greek, slave and free, male and female" (Galatians 3:28). This is ancient Christian teaching, so these themes are not unique to the gay community. The real issue is not sex acts or sexual orientation, but humanity and its potential for genuine love.

Nonetheless, the four themes of this chapter highlight the core of the possibility for positive social transformation that arises in a unique way within the gay community. As with everyone else, if they are to love at all, lesbians and gay men must love where they are able—and that is in gay and lesbian relationships. Unlike others, in order to love effectively, lesbians and gay men simply must expand their psychosexual self-images and develop relationships beyond those conceived in current sex-role stereotypes. Otherwise, their relationships will be hopelessly superficial and will never survive. Virtually no institutional support exists for those relationships; lesbian and gay people have no alternative: they simply must love deeply and truly. Therefore, for those who know it, the gay community is an obvious example of these Christian themes in actualization.

What is described here as part of the gay liberation movement is really part of a broader cultural movement. Today's concern for re-structuring sex-roles and deepening personal relationships goes well beyond the gay community. The question is a human one, not a gay or straight one. However, gay and lesbian people have a greater stake in this general movement than do others. If the movement fails, others stand to lose a possibly higher quality of human relationship and personal fulfillment. Gay and lesbian people stand to lose the possibility of love relationships altogether—as well as their jobs, their homes, their family ties, and even their lives: Homophobic prejudice runs deep. So it is no wonder that novel expressions of human love and re-lationship, now available to all, flourish especially in the gay community.

Not exclusively, then, but with a certain priority, gay and lesbian people are able—and so are called—to contribute to a central aspect of Christ's work, to reproduce on earth the inner-trinitarian life of God in heaven. Theirs is to further love among all people—coequal, growing by interpersonal relationship, respectful of ideal individual-ity, and beyond the stereotypical limitations of gender. The culmina-tion, of course, is nothing other than universal participation of all in divine fullness, the answer to Christ's prayer, "Father, may they all be one—as you are in me and I am in you. May they be one in us." Al-though expressed here in Christian terms, this ideal recurs in its own way in all the religions of the world. Indeed, it represents the pure spiritual longings of the human heart. Thus, this vision of unity per-tains to everyone, whether religious or not. In this matter in the twenty-first century, as our world struggles to form a global commu-nity, gay liberation plays a prophetic role: It anticipates and points to-ward a unifying human love that Christianity sees as worthy of God.

Chapter 11

Homosexuality in Catholic
Teaching and Practice

Not everybody is Catholic, but let's admit it: When the pope speaks, everybody listens. People may not agree, but they take notice. The influence of the Vatican is awesome—and for gay and lesbian people, frightening. So consideration of Catholic teaching is of interest to everybody. Besides, Catholicism has a well-developed sexual ethics. So, again, whether a person agrees or disagrees, consideration of Catholic teaching opens up important questions. Moreover, in light of the sex-abuse scandals in the Catholic Church, people are wondering how its teaching about sex and it sexual policies might have played into this scandal.

Overall, the official Catholic position on sex is not what most people think it is. Similar to so much else in the Catholic Church, appearances reign supreme. However, things are seldom what they seem, and what goes on in the back rooms actually determines public outcomes. So, of interest to everyone in one way or another, this chapter provides another look at sexual ethics—and how they are changing, even in the Catholic Church.

Where does Catholicism stand on homosexuality? Actually, all over the map. Catholic teaching on homosexuality is complex and nuanced, and it allows for differences between teaching and practice. Conscience is supreme in Catholicism: When individuals act for solid reasons and in good conscience, Catholic teaching defends their right to quiet dissent. In fact, many Catholics ignore the church's sexual teaching, finding that it makes no sense to them. Although they are

This chapter was originally published in *culturefront: A Magazine of the Humanities,* 1998, volume 7, number 3, pages 65-68, and republished in *DignityUSA Journal,* 1999, volume 31, number 2, pages 20-24. Reprinted with permission.

doing wrong according to this teaching, also according to Catholic teaching they are not guilty of sin if they have acted in good faith.

These subtleties of Roman Catholicism may surprise people on the street and many Catholics in the pew, but they are accurate. Catholicism's public image, monolithic and rigid, is an illusion. The Catholic Church has plenty of room for homosexual people. It's just that this room is kept a secret, and the spaces are cramped and uncomfortable. Now even these matters are coming out of the closet. As a result, despite hierarchical protest, Catholic sexual ethics are changing.

THE HETEROSEXUAL ISSUE: BIRTH CONTROL

Birth control offers an easier example than homosexuality, yet it raises the same ethical concerns as gay sex. Everyone knows that Catholic teaching forbids the use of artificial contraception, and everyone knows why: Sex must be left open to procreation. Still, some 90 percent of practicing Catholic couples use artificial contraception. According to Catholic teaching, if they act in good conscience, they do not sin, so they need not confess this matter, and they may continue to receive Holy Communion. And they do.

The pope continues to preach around the globe that their contraceptive practices are wrong, but almost nobody, either inside or outside the church, faults them for using birth control. In private, some bishops just shrug their shoulders over the matter.

THE NATURE OF SEX

The linchpin of Catholic sexual ethics has always been the insistence that the procreative capacity is essential to sex and may not be deliberately excluded. This insistence entered the church through ancient Stoic philosophy. It is not in the Hebrew or Christian scriptures. Rather than looking first to the Bible, as Protestantism is likely to do, Catholicism grounds its sexual ethics in "natural law." That is to say, Catholicism believes that right and wrong are built into the universe and can be discerned. One follows God's will by respecting the laws of nature. One uses the things that God created as their essential makeup suggests they were meant to be used.

When it comes to sex, the central questions are: What is the nature of sex? How was it meant to be used? The Stoic philosophers, Saint Augustine, Saint Thomas Aquinas, and a whole string of Catholic teachers have held that sex is for having children, period. Supposedly, such is the nature of sex.

Luther, Calvin, and Protestantism in general have long rejected that narrow understanding. Contemporary psychology also recognizes that sex is not just a biological function. Sexual attraction, arousal, and orgasm unlock depths of emotion, memory, and fantasy. Moreover, sex often seduces lovers into sharing dreams and making promises. Human sex, unlike sex in barnyard animals, opens onto spiritual concerns—the meaning and purpose of life. More than just conceiving children, sexual sharing binds people in a loving and loyal union that contributes to the wholesome functioning of society.

Since Pius XI's teaching in *Casti Conubii* in 1930 and especially with the Second Vatican Council in the mid-1960s, Catholicism has been broadening its understanding of sex to include an interpersonal dimension. Official Catholicism now freely allows that the interpersonal dimension is of equal importance with the procreative dimension, and some theologians—even conservative ones such as James P. Hanigan in his 1988 book *Homosexuality: The Test Case for Christian Sexual Ethics*—argue that the balance of emphasis has already shifted in the official documents, if read closely. As Catholic teaching more and more emphasizes the interpersonal dimension, it deemphasizes the procreative dimension as the sine qua non of human sex. As one senior Jesuit scholar, Richard A. McCormick of the University of Notre Dame, has speculated, the overall integrity of the sexual relationship, and not the biological integrity of individual sex acts, might be what really matters. Indeed, the Catholic Church has long blessed nonprocreative sex within the marriages of sterile and elderly couples.

These changing views are transforming the Catholic understanding of sex. In good conscience married Catholic couples are using contraceptives and lesbian and gay Catholics are entering into sexual relationships. Apart from matters of sexual plumbing, the cases are exact parallels. On the psychological and spiritual levels—the distinctively human levels—gay and straight sexual intimacy seem to mean the same thing.

"COMPLEMENTARITY" AND SEXUAL ANATOMY

However, sexual plumbing remains a focus of this discussion. In opposing homosexual relationships, the *Catechism of the Catholic Church,* for example, adds an argument that has long been prominent in Protestant circles: complementarity—the notion that man and woman are somehow especially made for each other. The difficulty is to specify exactly how this is so.

Strict complementarity of the sexes hardly applies on the spiritual and psychological levels. In this regard, any two people might complement each other. The argument holds only biologically. It is that matter of sexual plumbing: Only penile-vaginal intercourse is allowed. Catholicism teaches this very thing. In marital lovemaking, any foreplay is allowed, but the male seed has to be "deposited" in the "appropriate receptacle." (I don't remember any concern being given to the female orgasm until very recently.) Thus, when analyzed, the complementarity argument is really just another way of insisting on the procreative dimension of sex, and for reasons already mentioned, this insistence is not convincing. In fact, few people today would agree that penile-vaginal intercourse is the only acceptable expression of sex.

This recurrent conclusion causes major problems for Catholic sexual ethics. In fact, the official teaching offers a coherent and comprehensive position. Emphasis on the single matter of procreation determines the ethics of the whole array of sexual expressions—masturbation, premarital and extramarital sex, homosexual acts, birth control, and chaste marital sex.

Such coherent positions are hard to come by, and a simple and single-minded sexual ethic seems appealing, especially in the confusion of today's world. For this reason, official Catholicism vigorously tries to maintain its position. Unfortunately, for most people the position no longer makes sense, and it is not holding. One result is that lesbian and gay relationships are flourishing in Catholic circles, and some aspects of the official Catholic position fully allow them to do so.

THE NUANCES OF CATHOLIC TEACHING

On the inside, Catholicism is actually a very humane and tolerant religion. Among all the Christian denominations, Catholics "in the pew" are the most supportive of homosexual relationships. The Catholic emphasis on sacramentality—the use of water, oil, bread, real wine, music, candles, incense, bells, statues, medals, rosary beads, relics—hallows earthy things, and this "gut" teaching takes better than the heady kind. So, despite the subtly reasoned official prohibitions, as repeated studies have shown, Catholics allow and enjoy sex more than other Christians. Understandably, Catholics are also more accepting of homosexual love.

The official position is tolerant, as well. It does not regard homosexuality as a choice and does not see such an orientation as likely to change. Though it is called an "objective disorder," simply being homosexual is not, in any way, considered sinful. (Of course, one is not supposed to act on one's homosexuality.) Moreover, Catholicism condemns prejudice and injustice against lesbian and gay folk. The church is expected to welcome these brothers and sisters, have them participate fully in parish life, and offer them a "special measure of support" because of their "difficult situation." To be sure, homosexual Catholics find some of this teaching condescending or ignored in practice, but the teaching is more supportive than that which some other churches offer.

Catholicism even allows for gay and lesbian sex. The Catholic position includes what is called "pastoral application of official teaching." The notion is that, in practice, the general principles of official teachings need to be prudently applied to fit individual cases. People are different. No two cases are exactly alike. What is ideally required is not always attainable, so allowances need to be made in pastoral situations, in one-on-one counseling, or in the privacy of the confessional. People can be required to do only what they are able.

The Vatican mentality follows the Roman notion of law. Laws are thought to express ideals that people should strive to achieve. Laws do not, as in the English and American traditions, express minimum requirements that must be met. Catholic ethics propose ideals, and these apply variably in individual cases.

Thus, Father Jan Visser, a principal author of the 1975 Vatican document on sexual ethics, could write in the January 30, 1976, edition of *L'Europa,* "When one is dealing with people who are so deeply homosexual that they will be in serious personal or social trouble unless they obtain a steady partnership within their homosexual lives, one can recommend them to seek such a partnership, and one accepts this relationship as the best they can do in their present situation." This is authentic Catholic teaching. In practice, for the good of individuals and society, in certain circumstances Catholicism may even recommend lesbian and gay relationships.

The same conclusion can be drawn in another way. For Catholicism, doing wrong is not the same thing as committing a sin. Wrongs are in the objective order. They are violations of natural law. They represent destructive forces unleashed on our world. However, sin is a subjective thing. It depends on human understanding and free choice. It resides in the human heart. In Catholic teaching, it is fully possible that someone can do something wrong without being subjectively culpable.

Just as a parent would not punish a mere child for, say, playfully strewing pots and pans over the kitchen floor, so God would not condemn a person for something the person did not know or believe to be wrong. One may well be doing wrong, but unless one has neglected to inform oneself properly, one does not sin. One may be innocently ignorant, naive, stupid, or even dangerous, but one is not a sinner. Sin implies deliberately turning from the good, and thus from God. Contrariwise, then, you may do something that is not objectively wrong, but if you believe it is wrong and do it anyway, then your heart is corrupt: You are a sinner.

This understanding of sin is significantly different from that which is common in some Protestant, and especially Biblical Fundamentalist, circles. There, knowingly or not, deliberately or not, to perform forbidden acts is to sin and merit hell.

THE SUPREMACY OF CONSCIENCE

Many lesbian and gay Catholics do not understand what is wrong with their loving one another in sexual intimacy, so they do what, to them, seems right. Catholic teachings say they are doing wrong, but it does not accuse them of sinning. Thus, apart from public scandal, they may participate fully in the religious life of the church. At stake in this Catholic understanding of wrongdoing and sin is a profound respect for personal conscience. This respect is one of the best kept secrets in the Catholic Church—deliberately so, it seems.

In 1997, the National Conference of Catholic Bishops published *Always Our Children,* a pastoral message encouraging parents to love their lesbian and gay children. Several lines on personal conscience were deleted from the final draft. The bishops feared that those lines might mislead people. Maintaining the clarity of Catholic teaching was the highest priority. Nonetheless, some Catholics, including bishops, still found the document objectionable and protested it. So the document had to be revised in consultation with—that is, under the scrutiny of—the Vatican.

The Catholic Church walks a tightrope in balancing official teaching against individual conscience and private behavior. The balance is maintained by giving the official teaching top billing and putting conscience in the fine print. Commitment to public order is paramount. For official Catholicism, obedience is the supreme virtue.

Thus, when DignityUSA—a national network of support groups for lesbian, gay, bisexual, and transgendered Catholics and their friends—publicly protested Catholic teaching on homosexuality in 1987, bishop after bishop expelled local Dignity chapters from church property. Dignity's offense was, of course, not so much its endorsement of gay sex, but the public protest, the breaking of ranks, the challenging of authority.

Yet as Dignity saw the matter, the Church's repeated condemnations were doing severe psychological and spiritual harm to many individuals: teenagers committing suicide, adults repressing their affection and creative potential, people living in unrelenting self-loathing, guilt-driven compulsives acting out surreptitiously in irresponsible and unsafe sex acts. Counterproductive and downright destructive, the official teaching had to be challenged. Dignity saw itself as prophetic. The situation is symptomatic of tensions within contemporary Catholicism.

CATHOLICISM'S CONFLICTED OPENNESS TO GAYS AND LESBIANS

In many cities across the United States, many churches are well-known for being gay friendly. The spring 2005 issue of *Bondings*—a quarterly newsletter of New Ways Ministry, whose founders, Sister Jeannine Gramick and Father Robert Nugent, were censured and silenced by the Vatican for their educational ministry on homosexuality—provides "a partial list" including some 159 churches in 90 cities. In the churches on that list with which I am personally familiar, openly lesbian and gay people (including priests) exercise ministries, and same-sex couples—oftentimes with children—worship comfortably with the rest of the congregation. Ostensibly, these are standard Catholic churches, but similar to much of the American Catholic Church with respect to artificial contraception, they quietly ignore the prohibition on gay sex. The duplicity in the Catholic system looms large.

These gay-friendly churches clearly push the limits of Catholic teaching; yet even the bishops, who turn a blind eye, must be grateful that someone is realistically addressing the issues. Indeed, many bishops have established diocesan ministries to sexual minorities, some of which are excellent, others repressive or nominal. Among some of these ministries it is commonplace that, although the clergy publicly stand by the official Catholic line, congregation members freely engage in homosexual relationships, and everybody knows it. In Rochester, New York, and Richmond, Virginia, bishops sponsored public events to welcome lesbians and gays to the church—though, of course, still requiring celibacy from them. These events evoked inquiries from the Vatican and protests from conservative Catholic groups.

Run by an all-male, (supposedly) celibate priesthood and hierarchy, Catholicism still refuses to come to grips with the reality of sex. The official response is to sweep the topic under the rug and preserve *la buona figura,* that is, save face. This standard posture has obviously aggravated the Catholic sex-abuse scandals and shows itself in the Vatican's misguided effort to screen out—that is, force underground—gay seminarians.

CATHOLIC GAY MINISTRIES

The gay-friendly churches and official diocesan ministries often attract members away from the local Dignity chapters. Evidently, most Catholics just want to be part of the church and are not interested in the political activism needed to change the system. Compared to their Protestant counterparts, most Catholic laity are passive in their churchly lives.

At the opposite pole from Dignity is a conservative activist organization called Courage, a national network of support groups dedicated to promoting celibacy among homosexual Catholics. Of course, unlike Dignity, Courage enjoys the endorsement of the hierarchy. It is built on the assumption that homosexuality is an emotional debility. Based on Alcoholics Anonymous, Courage uses a twelve-step program to help people stop having sex. This ministry may serve a useful purpose for people who want to be celibate or who really are sexually addicted. Yet it can hardly be helpful that Courage, contrary to Catholicism's official respect for scientific findings, ignores the bulk of scientific evidence and equates homosexuality with psychopathology. In any case, the local Courage groups are small. People are not flocking to this hyper-Catholic association.

THE INEVITABLE CHANGE

Similar to other Christian churches, Catholicism is struggling to develop a new sexual ethic, and inevitably it will accommodate homosexual relationships. Although official Catholicism continues to insist that its sexual ethic is as clear and unchanging as ever, in thinking and practice a shift is occurring. The shape of the new synthesis remains to be seen. In contrast to the old emphasis on procreation, it will probably be built on the interpersonal meaning of sex.

Chapter 12

Gay Marriage:
A Response to the Vatican

In summer 2003, the Vatican issued a set of *Considerations Regarding Proposals to Give Legal Recognition to Unions Between Homosexual Persons.* In November of the same year the American Catholic Bishops followed suit and issued their own declaration, *Between Man and Woman: Questions and Answers About Marriage and Same-Sex Unions.* Unequivocally these Catholic statements reject unions for gays and lesbians and even call on Catholic legislators and all citizens to oppose any such proposals. The Vatican's arguments are the same as those used by most people who oppose gay marriage, so a discussion of these arguments is important for anyone concerned about gay marriage. Besides, for Catholics and non-Catholics alike, the voice of the Vatican carries awesome influence, so we must all have concern about the Vatican statements on current moral and political issues.

The Catholic position on gay marriage is so wrongheaded that it merits severe rejection. I believe that many Catholic theologians would agree, but they are not in a position to say so publicly. (In the Church, as elsewhere, politics, not open and honest debate, often determines policy, and the Vatican is a master of power politics.) As a Catholic theologian who is not dependent on church authorities for my monthly paycheck, I am free to make such a rejection, and I do so here.

This material was originally published as "Grace Builds on Nature: A Gay Catholic Theological Response to the Vatican's Statement on Gay Marriage" in *White Crane: A Journal of Gay Spirit, Wisdom & Culture,* issue 61, Summer (2004), pp. 14-18.

THE IDENTIFICATION OF SEXUALITY
WITH PROCREATION

The Vatican's core argument against gay marriage or unions can be stated in an equation: marriage = sex = procreation. The Vatican allows sex only in marriage and ultimately for the sake of procreation, so same-sex marriage cannot qualify. Supposedly, the linkage between these three elements is inviolable, and, supposedly, this linkage expresses the nature of sexual relationship itself. The appeal is to a version of "natural law" built on ancient and medieval speculation. Many others who oppose gay marriage unwittingly buy into this same argument.

Contemporary insight into the nature of human sexuality shows that the Vatican equation is wrong. The Vatican emphasizes the basest dimension of sex: the biological production of offspring; and it devalues the distinctively human dimension of sex: the bonding of hearts and minds in interpersonal relationship. In contrast to all animal species, only humans routinely have sex during infertile periods, only humans routinely have sex face to face, and only human females routinely experience orgasm. These biological facts in themselves point to nonbiological facets of human sexuality as the distinctively human ones. In humans sex is first and foremost about personal bonding and only secondarily, incidentally, about the procreation of offspring.

The official Catholic position on this point needs to be challenged outright. It is disturbing to realize that this skewed understanding governs all Catholic teaching about marriage and intimate human relationships. However, this rejection of the official Catholic conclusion is not a rejection of the Catholic presupposition. Natural law remains the basis of this whole discussion. However, as I argue in Chapters 7 and 11 and throughout this book, on the pivotal question, What is the nature of human sexuality? the Vatican is wrong.

Since the Second Vatican Council in the mid-1960s, official Catholicism has weighted the procreative and the interpersonal ("unitive") dimensions of sex equally, but this theoretical equality does not redress the imbalance in the Catholic position in practice. Insistence on procreation defines the Catholic teaching and controls its every practical application, whether to same-sex relationships or any other sexual question. The Vatican champions an understanding of sex as a barnyard-animal affair, and, as is blatant in the document on gay marriage, the Vatican downplays the interpersonal meaning of human sexuality. This position flies in the face of all that personal experience and the human sciences reveal about sexual intimacy.

The position of the Vatican is lucid and consistent, but it is also glaringly mistaken. Yet only it allows the Vatican and the bishops to reject lesbian and gay relationships out of hand. And only it supports the Vatican's call to secular society to reject gay unions. The Catholic hierarchy is pushing its sectarian agenda and, in the name of a misconceived "nature," expecting the rest of society to go along.

INCONCLUSIVE RELIGIOUS ARGUMENTS AGAINST SAME-SEX RELATIONSHIPS

Not only is the Vatican's basic teaching about sex off base, but everything the Vatican proclaims about homosexual relationships—except that they are not procreative—is wrong.

The standard theological arguments are all mistaken.

- The Bible does not condemn same-sex relationships. In light of widely available and stunningly convergent biblical scholarship, an honest person today must, in the very least, admit that serious questions surround the texts that supposedly condemn homosexuality. My book, *What the Bible* Really *Says About Homosexuality,* summarized this scholarship in popular form.
- As Catholic scholars John Boswell (*Christianity, Social Tolerance, and Homosexuality)* and Mark Jordan (*The Invention of Sodomy in Christian Theology)* have shown, Christian tradition has simply not always condemned same-sex relationships.
- In practice, Catholicism does not insist on the procreative dimension of married sex, for the Church continues to bless the marriages of known sterile couples and allows sex between couples who are beyond childbearing age.
- The argument about the supposed complementarity of man and woman is incoherent. It could not regard psychological complementarity, for psychologically any two people might valuably complement each other. The complementarity in question must regard biological plumbing, so insistence on complementarity is

but a covert insistence on the procreative dimension of sex, which, as just noted, is not a church requirement in practice.

- Repeated biological, anthropological, sociological, medical, and psychological research shows conclusively that homosexuality is not in any way an illness—or an "intrinsic disorder," as the Vatican phrases the matter—but is, rather, a natural variation. Indeed, same-sex pairing is rampant throughout the animal kingdom. As such, homosexuality must be part of the creative plan of God, an aspect of the diversity built into the universe.
- Gay and lesbian people are not godless or sinful in their relationships. On the contrary, they report their coming out as a moment of grace. Honest self-acceptance allows their lives to blossom in gratitude, love, generosity, and societal contribution.

MISREPRESENTATION OF SOCIAL-SCIENCE FINDINGS ABOUT SAME-SEX FAMILIES

The Vatican's biological and anthropological arguments are equally mistaken.

- It must constitute deliberate distortion of the documented evidence to suggest that gay and lesbian relationships enjoy no unitive or conjugal—that is, positive interpersonal—dimension. As do straight couples, gay couples find in each other affection, support, encouragement, companionship, spiritual enrichment, and meaning, purpose, and stability in the maelstrom of life. Gay and lesbian relationships clearly "express and promote the mutual assistance" of the couples. The fact that these relationships are not "open to the transmission of [biological] life" is another matter, and it is the ubiquitous red herring in this discussion.
- Similarly, it must constitute deliberate distortion of the documented evidence to suggest that living in lesbian or gay families developmentally harms—and, thus, supposedly, victimizes—children. Research studies have followed such children through their teenage years. The studies show that these children fare at least as well as children in more standard family constellations. The Vatican's accusation of harm and violence is outrageous—and especially in light of the fact that so many children in our value-skewed world would be happy to have any place at all to

call home and in light of the further fact that the Catholic hierarchy has lost all credibility when preaching about concern for children.

MISGUIDED CONCERN ABOUT THE SOCIAL ORDER

The Vatican's arguments about the social order are also distorted and mistaken.

- It is glaringly untrue that stable lesbian and gay relationships contribute nothing to the good of society. How could mutually supportive and life-enhancing relationships not benefit the social order overall?
- Likewise, how could the institutionalization of lesbian and gay relationships devalue the institution of marriage? Husbands and wives are hardly likely to divorce en masse so that they can find homosexual lovers. The possibility of same-sex unions is not going to seduce young people away from heterosexual marriage: As the Vatican officially admits, homosexuality is not a choice. Support for stable relationships all around will hardly undermine existing stable relationships. That lesbians and gays respect and desire marriage would seem only to bolster that institution.
- Supposedly, to institutionalize gay marriage would be to institutionalize an evil. This argument begs the question. It remains to be shown that homosexual relationships are evil. None of the Vatican's arguments convincingly makes that case, as already noted.
- Unless lesbian and gay relationships are sinful, institutionalizing them could not give bad example to the young or obscure moral values, as the Vatican claims. Consistent in its faulty logic, the Vatican again begs the question.
- That the civil recognition of gay marriage would imply a major change in the organization of society—this fact is beyond dispute. But whether that change would be good or bad is another question. Abolition of slavery, universal suffrage, racial integration, and women's rights also demanded the restructuring of society. Would the Vatican, on principle, turn back the clock on all social change?

A POSITION BUILT ON SAND AND BLIND FAITH

The upshot of the analysis thus far is clear: The Vatican has only one key reason for opposing gay marriage: It entails a nonprocreative use of sex. Gay marriage challenges the quaint Vatican understanding of human sexuality. If marriage = sex = procreation, gays cannot marry, obviously. However, whether sex does need to be procreative is debatable, to say the least. Other Christian churches, for example, have long abandoned opposition to the use of contraceptives, and some Christian churches bless gay relationships. The other Vatican arguments are all factually or logically mistaken, as well.

The Vatican's campaign against gay marriage stands on sand. Nothing supports the Vatican position except unquestioning acceptance of the Vatican's own teaching.

A VALID CONSIDERATION: CONCERN FOR THE CHILDREN

Nonetheless, buried in those Catholic documents is one concern truly worthy of note: the place of the children. Historically, marriage has been an institution dedicated to the rearing of children. So marriage, family, child rearing, and procreative sex naturally fitted together. From our current perspective in which sex can be nonprocreative, it becomes clear that marriage and heterosexuality were intertwined because the children—not necessarily the married couple—were the societal concern. Until recently in Western history, marriages were arranged. They served to draw lines of ownership, power, and inheritance rights. The lines ran through the children born to those marriages. Child rearing was the real but overshadowed meaning of marriage.

But a new ideal has emerged. Today people marry for love, not necessarily to sire offspring and to pass on property. In addition, the availability of effective contraception has further separated childbearing from the institution of marriage. Under the best of circumstances, marriages for love continue to serve those older economic and political functions. However, many marriages do not, and in many cases people no longer expect marriage to do so.

Today people contract for psychological intimacy when they marry, but as a society, we generally do not yet know how to sustain intimacy, so about half of all marriages fail. The reason is not some perversity afoot in contemporary society. The reason is a change in the meaning of marriage from what it used to be. The twelfth-century troubadours, the Romantic poets and novelists, the liberation of women, and the invention of the pill changed the meaning of marriage in Western civilization.

Today people marry for emotional intimacy, and when intimacy is not forthcoming, they dissolve the marriage. Even Vatican annulments acknowledge the legitimacy of this novelty. The recognition of gay marriage is but the logical unfolding of a historical process long underway.

Many heterosexual couples marry today with no intention whatsoever of having or raising children. In our society, child rearing and marriage have effectively been separated. In this new situation, the case of two childless heterosexuals is an exact parallel to that of two childless gay men or lesbians who enter a long-term, committed relationship. That the heterosexual arrangement should be called marriage but not the homosexual one is a claim that cries to heaven for reasonable explanation. Apart from appeal to the—here irrelevant— notion of child-rearing marriage, no explanation has been proposed. Consistency would require either that heterosexual relationships be granted the status of marriage only when children become part of the household or that any couple bonded for intimacy and mutual support be granted the status *married*.

Focus on the children recasts the discussion of gay marriage. The line should not be drawn between gay and straight relationships but between child-rearing households and childless households, whether straight or gay. This latter arrangement would better preserve the telling feature in the traditional Western marriage, the feature that, it seems, rightly concerns the Vatican: the rearing of children.

CIVIL UNION VERSUS SACRED MARRIAGE

A sane sorting out of the issues requires recognition of the difference between religious and civil marriages. Justice demands that civil society grant equal rights and responsibilities to everyone. So civil authorities need to craft laws that treat all coupled relationships equally and that, in addition, privilege those relationships that involve the rearing of children. Perhaps the former should be called unions and only the latter, marriage, but some intelligent resolution of the issue needs to be devised.

However, the secular resolution need not be the same as the religious. Although God-fearing religion must certainly support just and equitable laws within secular society, the religions are free to define their sacred rites however they wish. So the ever-reactionary Catholic Church (historian Adolf Harnack wrote that the particular charism of the Catholic Church was to be a drag on social change) can continue to ignore the facts and logic in this matter and define marriage uniquely as a heterosexual matter. Such is the right of religion in a free society. However, in the process, the Catholic Church will move even further from other Christian churches that already bless same-sex relationships, and the sexual ethics of the Catholic Church will become increasingly irrelevant to the world at large.

Above all, in the contrast between the secular and religious determination about marriage, this point must be emphasized: Catholic opposition to the legalization of gay marriage, in whatever form, is pure sectarianism; it is the attempted imposition of gratuitous religious beliefs on a pluralistic society. Apart from concern for the children, the Vatican's emphasis on procreative sex is wholly an in-house affair and has no valid relevance to the secular debate about gay marriage. Secular society has long moved beyond sex-for-procreation-only.

MARRIAGE AS A SACRAMENT

Catholic belief in the sacramentality of marriage also plays into Vatican opposition to gay marriage. Supposedly, only heterosexual relationships provide the appropriate "matter" for a valid sacrament. A number of considerations bear on this topic.

- The sacramentality of marriage is a strictly theological topic, but secular talk about the "sanctity of marriage," in fact, appeals to such theology. So the topic deserves attention.
- Not all Christian churches recognize marriage as a sacrament in any strict sense, so one must wonder what talk of the "sanctity of marriage" or the "sacrament of marriage" really means.

- Only in the Middle Ages did Christian thinkers list seven sacraments—Baptism, Confirmation, Eucharist, Reconciliation (Confession of Sins), Marriage, Holy Orders, and Anointing of the Sick (Extreme Unction)—in contrast to a host of "sacramentals"—minor sacred objects such as medals, statues, holy pictures, prayer books, candles, incense, and holy water. Only in the sixteenth-century Counter-Reformation did Catholicism solemnly enshrine the list of seven. This history suggests that room exists to rethink the meaning of "sacrament."

- Since Augustine, sacraments have been defined as outward signs that give grace. If grace is seen as God's power and love working among us—and especially to communicate God's own life to us—any nonsinful human situation could be an occasion of grace. For this reason, the distinction between sacrament and sacramental is difficult to specify, and in the last analysis the determination of the seven sacraments is a matter of somewhat arbitrary ecclesiastical decision: In contrast to others, some life events are deemed pivotal, and these are named sacraments—for example, marriage.

- If lesbians and gays, as well as objective outside observers, can recognize same-sex relationships as blessings from God—for all the positive reasons noted previously but denied out of hand by the Vatican—these relationships also qualify as means of grace. Then, for the same reason as in a heterosexual relationship—mutual sanctification to the partners—a homosexual marriage could also qualify as a sacrament.

- This line of reasoning calls for rethinking the whole of sacramental theology. But in the Catholic Church such rethinking has been underway for decades; it views Christ and then the Church as the primordial, core sacraments and sees the current seven sacraments and the many possible sacramentals as derivative instances of sacramentality.

- In the end, the religions must themselves work out their particular understanding of the sacramentality of marriage, including gay marriage. Secular forces that oppose same-sex marriage by naive appeal to the sanctity of marriage must acknowledge that, as intimated here, gay marriage can be on a par with straight marriage insofar as sanctity, grace, and sacramentality are concerned. Every wholesome relationship must be an expression of the Holy Spirit's action in this world.

THE REORGANIZATION OF SOCIETY

The Vatican is right to suggest that the legalization of gay marriage will result in "changes to the entire organization of society." However, that these changes will be "contrary to the common good" is a highly debatable proposition. In fact, the Vatican offered no convincing argument for its doomful claim. To the contrary, justice, fairness, mutual respect, and community building would seem to require the legalization of civil gay marriage, and such a change could only be ultimately to the good.

Gay marriage will restructure the social order, no doubt, but such restructuring is inevitable. We are at a turning point in history. Pluralism and globalization are forcing us to rethink our social institutions. No longer can limited perspectives and rivaling religions sustain isolated enclaves of humanity. History is requiring that we build a truly global community, and only a particular kind of vision will sustain such community—a vision that all people could affirm in honesty and good conscience. Forging such a vision will require every society and every religion to rethink its own cherished worldview and to purify its beliefs and customs of anything unworthy of humanity overall. Not even the Catholic Church is exempt from the requirements of unfolding history—or, said theologically, from obedience to the ways of God. The ongoing emergence of democratic government, religious tolerance, racial equality, women's rights, universal education and medical care—in sum, the God-given dignity and rights of every human being—have already been leading humanity along a path toward global community. Discussion about gay marriage is just another way station on this same, inevitable path.

THE GENIUS OF ROMAN CATHOLICISM
AND THE SALVATION OF THE NATIONS

The argument I am advancing is actually Roman Catholic through and through. A defining Catholic principle dating back to the earliest Christian centuries holds that "Grace builds on nature." My emphasis may seem naturalist and secularist, but I am only highlighting the earthly dimension in the composite Catholic vision. The genius of Catholicism is profound enough to sustain such emphasis. Indeed, an earthly emphasis is needed to balance centuries of Christian overemphasis on the otherworldly. A down-to-earth emphasis is precisely what our world needs today.

At this critical time in history, openness, honesty, and goodwill are needed, not reactionary dogmatism or hysterical conservatism. True concern for the common good is needed, not religious insistence on sectarian beliefs—such as the supposedly essential procreative nature of human sexuality. The Vatican preoccupation with procreation opens onto one positive contribution: concern for the children. As for the rest, the Vatican's limply argued opposition to gay marriage is embarrassing—at least it is to me, a Roman Catholic. It is unworthy of an institution that claims to speak of justice, for Jesus, and in the name of God. Perforce—and what is more crucial at this point in history—the Vatican's argument is unworthy of humanity.

Chapter 13

Why Biblical Literalism Is Not Christian

Without doubt, religion is the strongest opponent of lesbian, gay, bisexual, and transgender people. Scratch the surface of almost any argument, and underneath you find religion. Senator Rick Santorum's comments in May 2003 about the U.S. Supreme Court's rejection of all sodomy laws were downright insulting—and shamefully uninformed. He claimed to be voicing Catholic teaching. In fact, his knowledge of Catholicism was also shamefully uninformed, but his private religious beliefs were the basis of his legal opinion, nonetheless. Religion rules even in the U.S. Senate.

Surely, the most cited antigay argument is that the Bible condemns homosexuality. Of course, the Bible does not, but religious belief continues to provide cover for personal prejudice; widespread ignorance about the Bible and about homosexuality makes that cover almost impenetrable.

This religious bias needs to be addressed directly. Under the name of *Christianity*, preaching corrodes the sensitive souls of gay and lesbian people and inspires hostility against them. Their spiritual health requires rejection of the supposedly Christian claims. Chapter 14 projects a positive picture of authentic Christianity, which includes lesbians and gays and all people of goodwill. However, this chapter first takes a negative tack. It clears the field by challenging outright the Christian status of Biblical Literalism or Biblical Fundamentalism. Nonetheless, even here, the overall goal is positive: to clarify what true Christianity is and to protect "the glorious freedom of the children of God" (Romans 8:21).

This chapter was originally published in *Ecumenical Trends*, 1997, volume 26, number 8, pages 1-10, 113-122, under the title "Christian (read: Fundamentalist): A Case for Mistaken Identity." Reprinted with permission.

THE IDENTITY THEFT OF CHRISTIANITY

What is *Christian?* It has never been easy to answer this question, and recent developments further muddle the discussion.

The word *Christian* has taken on a new meaning. Propagated on the religious airwaves and on the street corners of the Bible Belt, USA, this new meaning now passes unquestioned in the media at large. Christian means Fundamentalist—just as surely as Catholic, Lutheran, and Methodist refer to other denominations.

Of course, terms such as *Fundamentalist Christian* or *Christian Right* can suggest some nuance. However, deliberately clouding the matter again, Fundamentalism has stealthily tried to soften its image by associating itself with the more moderate umbrella term *evangelical*—although much evangelicalism, but not all, is just Fundamentalism by another name. By organizing the "Catholic Alliance," the Christian Coalition has even tried to incorporate conservative Catholics—despite the fact that they are followers of the "Antichrist" (that is, the pope), according to widespread Fundamentalist opinion.

Through it all, this fact remains: Fundamentalists have seized the generic term *Christian* and turned it into the name of their denomination. And no one has raised an objection! In fact, for whatever reason, it took me ten years to first find a publisher for this chapter. I refuse to cede the name *Christian* to the Fundamentalists. As I argue in this chapter, the Fundamentalists have broken from the Christian tradition and constitute a separate religion. I will not even call it *Christian Fundamentalism* because it is not Christian at all. I propose to call this new religion *Biblical Fundamentalism* (or in context, simply *Fundamentalism,* or sometimes *Bible Religion* and the *Biblicists*), and I use these names in this chapter and throughout my writings. The ecumenical movement's welcome goal was to bring the Christian churches together, but this movement has had one negative effect: It made talk of heresy impolite, so no one would raise the issue. Here I raise the issue.

To profess to be Christian today is to identify as a Fundamentalist. Many who were baptized, bred, and will be buried as faithful members of traditional Christian churches no longer qualify as Christian. The vast majority of believers in a 2,000-year-old religion can no longer acknowledge their religious commitments. If they say without qualification, "I am a Christian," they appear to adhere to a reactionary, twentieth-century, minority movement. This significant religious and social phenomenon should not go unnoticed.

Nor should it go unchallenged.

Confusion about the very name *Christian* does call for clarification. What does *Christian* mean, anyway? Attention to Biblical Fundamentalism provides a remarkably useful approach to this question.

On the one hand, despite the scandal-provoked decline of biblical televangelism in the late 1980s, Fundamentalism quickly recovered, regrouped, and still stands firm. Its domination in the South is mind-boggling. Its control over the Southern Baptist Convention is now secure. The Christian Right stunningly captured the 1996 Republican platform committee, and with the installation of George W. Bush in the White House in 2000, this religious movement came to enjoy unprecedented political clout. For example, this movement is likely to receive millions of federal dollars to support its religious agenda through Mr. Bush's "faith-based initiative." Already the Religious Right's inane crusade for sexual abstinence is official American policy around the globe.

Fundamentalist-like trends are evident in other denominations as well, for example, renewed emphasis on the Bible in the United Methodist Church, intensified insistence on institutional loyalty in Roman Catholicism, backlash against women priests and bishops and against the gay bishop, Gene Robinson, in the Episcopal and Anglican Churches, and the growth of cross-denominational movements such as Campus Crusade and Promise Keepers. So when the meaning of *Christian* is in question, Fundamentalism is an angle worth considering.

On the other hand, the mainline churches are often at odds with Fundamentalism. They take a more moderate stance on sex education in the schools, evolutionary theory and other scientific conclusions, the role of women in family and society, opposition to abortion, acceptance of lesbian and gay relationships, the rights of workers, the needs of the poor, openness to immigrants, and concern for the environment. Whereas Fundamentalism asserts that the United States is a "Christian" nation and aims to make it so, the mainline churches respect the relationships among a range of religions and secular agencies. Whereas Fundamentalists maintain a remarkable clarity about who is a sinner and who is not, the mainline churches acknowledge the complexity of ethical matters and respect differences in conscience among people of goodwill.

Can Fundamentalist teaching and the teachings of other churches really both be Christian? The answer I give here is a firm No. This answer is a two-edged sword. It not only disqualifies Biblical Fundamentalism's core belief as incompatible with Christianity. In clarifying the essence of Christianity, it also calls all the churches to purify themselves of fundamentalist-like elements. This answer calls all who claim the name *Christian* to new fidelity to their heritage.

A MATTER OF THEOLOGY

Biblical Fundamentalism touts superior morality as the hallmark of its "Christianity," but ethics is not ultimately telling. Not only Fundamentalists but all Christians hold love for others and concern for the common good as basic values. Indeed, in their own way, Judaism, Buddhism, Hinduism, and Islam all foster compassion. Christianity has no monopoly on honest and virtuous living. Therefore, no ethical commitments ultimately distinguish Fundamentalists from Christians or Christianity from other religions.

Not even acknowledgment of Jesus as an important religious leader is distinctive of Christianity. Although not all would see Jesus as God or call him "Lord and Savior," what spiritually attuned person would object to following him or deny that his way is saving?

Focus on ethics or on Jesus will not do. A deeper analysis is needed. It must attend to underlying assumptions, to differing theologies. In the present case the key theological issue is Fundamentalism's approach to the Bible. The principal line of division among the many Christian churches is no longer the line between Catholics and Protestants. Differences between these groups have begun to blur. Today, more and more obviously, the split appears to be between the groups who claim to read the Bible literally and those who allow a "historical-critical" reading of the Bible. The key issue is differing ways of interpreting the Bible.

The literal reading insists that the meaning of a text is what anyone reading it today—and often only in the King James Version—would understand the text to say. In contrast, the historical-critical method insists that the primary meaning of a text is what it originally meant and that current implications of the text must depend on the original meaning.

Most mainline Christian churches today—Catholic, Lutheran, Presbyterian, Anglican, Methodist—officially accept a historical-critical reading of the Bible, and these churches share significant consensus on their interpretations of the texts. In contrast, insistence on a supposed literal reading is a divergent position. Fundamentalist literalism appears to be the alternative stance or, in traditional terms, a heresy.

I do not direct this judgment about Biblical Fundamentalism against individual believers. Without question, good people exist in the Fundamentalist movement, people doing, as best they can, what they believe to be right.

Nor do I want to belittle the powerful spiritual experience and the needed discipline that Fundamentalism has brought to many people. Religious conversion that brings wholesome meaning and purpose to life must always be respected. Still, people convert to many beliefs, so in itself a religious-conversion experience is no guarantee of Christianity.

Nor do I criticize here the goals that motivate the Fundamentalist movement. I agree that contemporary society is sick in many ways. In the face of an ever more fragmented society, somehow we do need to restore honesty, justice, love, and mercy as guiding virtues. Of course, what this restoration means in practice is highly debatable. I doubt that my ideal society would look similar to that of the Fundamentalists.

Nor am I judging the tactics by which different groups might hope to achieve those goals. My concern here is theological, not political.

My intention is only this: to analyze the theoretical core of the Fundamentalist movement—its belief about the Bible—and to compare it with long-standing Christian tradition. Mine is a theological enterprise. Its conclusions pertain to Biblical Fundamentalism as a creed, not necessarily to Fundamentalism as a lived religion.

Every religion shows a significant difference between what is officially professed and what is actually believed and lived. No doubt, the Christian tradition influences Fundamentalist believers more than their official position acknowledges, and, in fact, the Bible is not the sole source of their faith. However, my analysis here concerns only the core tenet of Fundamentalism: its supposed unswerving reliance on the Bible.

LITERAL INTERPRETATION
AND RELIANCE ON THE BIBLE ALONE

Fundamentalism includes a wide swath of "Bible religions." Many of them reject the name *Fundamentalist,* but they all tend toward fundamentalism to some degree. Often they reject the name only for political reasons, because it now has a negative connotation, but they are fundamentalist in all their doings. Here I take Biblical Fundamentalism to mean that approach to religion that claims to rest on the Bible as its sole foundation and insists that the Bible is free from error ("inerrant"), is inspired verbally by God, and is to be read literally.

The last item is the critical one: literal interpretation of the Bible. Only it distinguishes the Fundamentalist churches from the Christian churches. Reliance on the Bible alone might appear to be another distinguishing characteristic, but it is not. The option for a literal interpretation of the Bible already excludes openness to anything outside the Bible—such as centuries of Christian experience, insight, and teaching. Literal interpretation and reliance on the Bible alone go hand in hand. Both express one and the same underlying attitude: a disregard for history.

The historical-critical approach to the Bible acknowledges that ancient Israel and the early church produced the biblical texts. Accordingly, this approach sanely insists that these texts cannot be correctly understood apart from the historical experiences of Israel and the early church. That is to say, in the very formation of the biblical texts, the ongoing experience of the People of God has been integral to Christianity from the beginning. Attending to that experience, the historical-critical approach takes the early history of Christianity very seriously.

In contrast, the principle of literal interpretation implies that somehow the Bible was handed to the church ready-made, as it were. So the experience of the church during its formative period or at any period in history becomes irrelevant for determining what Christianity is and ought to be. Only the written word in the Bible, as it now stands, counts.

Considerations such as these are at the heart of the matter. One's approach to biblical interpretation is the focal issue. The Bible-alone issue merely repeats the literal-interpretation issue in another form. They are two sides of the same coin.

Likewise, belief in verbal inspiration and biblical inerrancy is not central. Many commentators point to belief in biblical inerrancy as the defining feature of Fundamentalism, but it is not. As Jerry Falwell explains, "To Fundamentalists, the inerrancy of Scripture is ultimately linked to the legitimacy and authority of the Bible." Similarly, according to James Barr, commitment to "the traditional Christian message based squarely on the Bible" is what ultimately drives Fundamentalism. These statements show that Fundamentalism is religion based on the Bible as it reads, period. We are again back to literal interpretation of the Bible.

Besides, the Christian churches would not want to deny the inspiration and inerrancy of the Scriptures, so they do not really differ from Fundamentalism on these points. Of course, the Christian churches do differ from Fundamentalism and among themselves about the nature of inspiration and inerrancy.

For example, at the Second Vatican Council in 1965, Roman Catholicism solemnly reaffirmed its belief that the Scriptures are "written under the inspiration of the Holy Spirit," so "they have God as their author," and the Bible teaches "firmly, faithfully, and without error that truth that God wanted put into the sacred writings for the sake of our salvation." Here is a clear insistence on verbal inspiration and inerrancy.

However, the Catholic understanding of these matters is quite different from the Fundamentalist. Catholicism would apply a historical-critical analysis to determine what exactly God meant to teach through the Bible, whereas Fundamentalism would look to the literal word. Thus, for example, for Catholicism the Genesis accounts of creation is not in conflict with contemporary scientific accounts— simply because Catholicism, unlike Fundamentalism, does not take the biblical account to be a literal geological or biological statement. The Bible teaches without error that God is the Creator of the world, and without conflict, the sciences explain how God's creation functions and unfolds.

So the disagreement is not about the inerrancy of the Bible. Rather, disagreement is about determining what the Bible inerrantly teaches. The issue is interpretation of the Bible. The problem with Fundamentalism is its insistence on a literal reading.

TAKING HISTORY SERIOUSLY

I propose three theological arguments that support the same conclusion: that Fundamentalism is not Christian. The first argument deals with the historical nature of Judaism and Christianity.

Judaism and Christianity are historical religions. That is, they are based on actual past occurrences; they claim to revolve around historical facts. These religions are not just a set of nice ideas, not just a philosophy of life.

Throughout the Hebrew and the Christian Testaments, this belief is clear: God is at work in history. Abraham's choice as father of a nation, Israel's release from Egypt in the Exodus, the fall of Jerusalem and the captives' later return to Jerusalem, all are understood to be the work of God. Christianity takes this belief to its limit: In Jesus Christ, God actually lived and died among us and rose from the dead unto our salvation. According to the Jewish and Christian understanding of the matter, we encounter God in human history.

The Bible, then, is the record of encounters with God in history. Inspired by God and inerrant in the message it conveys, the Bible is our means of learning about how God works among us. Belief in God's action in the past implies that God is still active in our own history. Fundamentalism would agree up to this point.

However, if we take seriously this belief in God's work in history, certain implications follow. Above all, we cannot know God without knowing the history of God's saving deeds. To understand God's work at any particular time and, thus, to understand what was written about God in any biblical passage, we must understand the historical situation that the passage expresses and out of which it emerged. We cannot really understand God's real action in real history as recounted in a real historical document, the Bible, unless we know the history of that time, the historical authors who wrote the document, their purpose in writing, the language they used, the literary form of the texts, the cultural presuppositions the authors had, the questions the authors were addressing, and so on.

In brief, we must first determine what the biblical text intended to convey in its own time and place before we can understand what the Bible teaches as God's action in that particular instance, and only by understanding God's modus operandi in the biblical instances are we then able to discern God's action in our own case. All this is to say, only a historical-critical reading of the Bible provides an understanding of God's Word that is consistent with a historical religion.

The alternative approach, a literal reading of the Bible, does not work. If I can understand the meaning of a biblical text without understanding its historical context or the cultural nuances of its language, then the historical and cultural circumstances must be irrelevant. If they are, you cannot claim that God really spoke in human history.

The literal approach makes the biblical text float above history, but history is essential to Christianity. Fundamentalism turns Christianity into an eternal fable, but Christianity is really about particular people and specific places and unique events.

Fundamentalists might object that they do not ignore history but attend to all the history that the Bible itself reports. However, restricting attention to the Bible itself is not attending to its formation and cultural context. Rather, such practice sequesters the Bible from the historical influences that shaped it. Such practice presumes that only what is written in the Bible is real or worth noting. Therefore, such practice is a denial of history; it imagines a Bible that is untouched by any history.

"GOD'S WORD" AS POLITICAL IDEOLOGY

The same point can be made in another way. My second argument shows that the literal reading of the Bible turns religion into a totalitarian regime centered on a rigid set of ideas that are immune to question and shut off from any possible deeper understanding. Such religion leaves no room for growth, change, development, or progress. Such static religion forbids that God can do new things as history advances. Such religion puts restrictions on even the Lord of history. Such religion imposes an end to history; it cancels history from the equation. So such religion cannot be Christian.

In one sense it is obvious that Biblical Fundamentalism does acknowledge God's action in history: God is involved in history *today* and precisely through the Fundamentalist movement itself. In going political, Fundamentalism reversed its founding emphasis on the relationship of the individual soul with God, and few religious movements in recent history have been as politically active as late twentieth- and early twenty-first-century Fundamentalism. However, the end result of Fundamentalist politics is a human program for social reform, not necessarily divine involvement in history.

To suppose that the Bible can be correctly understood apart from its historical and cultural context is to suppose that the Bible is some eternal formulation come down pristine and pure directly from heaven. Then historical and cultural considerations about the formation of the Bible are irrelevant. Only one form of divine involvement in history remains: God's supposed inspiration of the Bible reader today.

However, on this basis, anyone can claim divine authority for any personal interpretation, and the text can be said to mean whatever anyone feeling inspired takes it to mean. Of course, the inspirational use of the Scriptures has long standing in the Christian tradition, and such use of the Bible is more or less innocuous—as long as it is limited to private devotion. However, when used to determine a publicly proclaimed biblical message, this approach is dangerous. It includes no objective criteria to determine what God's Word in any particular biblical passage actually is. Then, supposedly, my opinion is God's opinion! My personal predilections automatically get a divine stamp of approval. Applied consistently, this approach would result in rampant relativism—the notion that anything goes—which is one of the very threats Fundamentalism was to oppose.

Of course, in practice, personal interpretation of the Bible carries little weight. Groups of believers usually hold some consensus about what the texts mean for them. Individual preference is not the ultimate criterion. Little room for individuality exists in Fundamentalism.

But then, what determines the consensus? It usually depends on some preacher. So the Bible comes to mean whatever any persuasive preacher takes it to mean. The result is the same, but now one individual controls a multitude. Such religion easily gets kooky. The Branch Davidians of Waco, Texas, provide a sad case in point, which even Fundamentalists decried. Another example is Pat Robertson's blaming lesbians, gays, abortionists, and feminists for natural disasters, or his public call for the assassination of a foreign head of state. Indeed, widespread Fundamentalist welcome of the fighting between Israel and the Palestinian state—because, supposedly, an apocalypse must occur in the "Holy Land" before Christ reigns in peace—is not only kooky but downright deranged and dangerous.

Still, one could insist that a whole generation holding the same opinion could not be wrong. Perhaps not, but then again, how does one judge? Whole societies have been wrong in the past. The massacring Crusades in Europe and the Holy Land were wrong. The Reformation's Wars of Religion were wrong. The Inquisition's tortures in Spain were wrong. American slavery was wrong. Nazi Germany was wrong. The destruction of the World Trade Center was wrong.

Times change. In a new situation the same biblical texts read literally take on a different meaning. "Give to Caesar what is Caesar's" has very different implications depending on who happens to be Caesar at any point in history.

Then must the former generation, who responded to the texts otherwise, be judged wrong, and is the new generation now right? Or does one just forget about other generations and their interpretations of the biblical texts? Does one ignore all history and simply claim that one's own generation is certainly in direct communication with God?

If so, we are again lost in complete relativism. The text means whatever people of any age decide it means, and in no way can the interpretation be judged. Rather than challenging each generation to question itself and grow more godlike, the biblical Word now merely supports the status quo—the status quo of the powers that be in that particular age.

Despite the warnings of both Jesus (Matthew 23:1-27; Luke 11:39-52) and Paul (2 Corinthians 3:6), a dead letter that kills supplants the transforming spirit of God's Word that gives life. The Bible becomes a book of political ideology, and a totalitarian regime reigns in the name of God.

To be oblivious to the demands of truth and justice in a changing world is not even humanly acceptable. All the more so, then, it cannot be of God or be Christian. But precisely such oblivion is the logical implication of Fundamentalism's basic principle. How, then, could Fundamentalism be Christian?

THE ESSENCE OF CHRISTIANITY

The suggestion is that Biblical Fundamentalism's principle of literal interpretation of the Scriptures is incompatible with the basic Jewish and Christian insistence on human history as the arena of

God's self-revelation to humankind. Before presenting my third argument, in this section I take a detour. I want to recall how essential historicity is to Christianity. To make the point, I will rely on the early Christian councils, which originally defined classical Christian orthodoxy. Of course, nowadays not everybody holds firmly to those ancient councils. As I said, it is difficult to say anymore what *Christian* really means. Thus, those who are uneasy with early Christian conciliar decrees might propose a different rendition. Nonetheless, I build my case on the ancient Christian councils, and I propose the following account.

The essence of Christianity is its insistence on the possibility of some union of the human and the divine, that is to say, some coincidence between the historical and the eternal. Now, in contrast, many would say that the essence of Christianity is love. In fact, these two suggestions fit together. Christianity is essentially about love because, above all, the God of Christianity is a God of love. God's love is evident within the Divine Trinity itself in the outpouring of self that results in the Father, Son, and Holy Spirit. God's love is evident, further, in God's plan to share even divine life with humankind and to incorporate humankind into the inner-trinitarian life of God. There is no reason under the sun that human beings, mere creatures, should ever become one with God, yet this very prospect is at the heart of Christian belief. As John 3:16 phrased the matter, "God so loved the world that he gave his only Son that all . . . might have eternal life." Therefore, to say that the essence of Christianity regards the union of humanity and divinity is not to deny that the essence of Christianity is love; rather, it is only to specify how God's overwhelming love unfolds, namely, by calling humans to love in kind—thus, John 17:21 has Jesus pray "that they may all be one. As you, Father, are in me and I am in you, may they also be one in us." In Christianity, universal love and human deification coincide; they are different aspects of one and the same idea.

The marvel that Christianity proclaims is that God and humankind could become one. Christianity accounts for this possibility through its unique belief in the divine Son, Jesus Christ, and in the Holy Spirit. Trinitarian theology is essential to the Christian understanding of how human beings could ever share in divine life. (Chapter 10 presents more detail on classical trinitarian theology.) Human deification is inextricably trinitarian. However, it is not only trinitarian; it is also inextricably historical—because it is about human beings. Any depreciation of the historical also upsets the delicate balance in question here. These issues lie at the heart of Christianity.

According to the Christian understanding, God the Eternally-Begotten surrendered all divine prerogatives and became human, similar to us in all things but sin. His was a real human life, lived out through personal free choices day by day amid the uncertainty of human history, just as is any of our lives. Chapter 9 discusses Jesus' human experience.

But because of who he was, the Eternally-Begotten of God, and because of his fidelity even unto death, Jesus was raised from the dead. In his human state he now shared in the divine glory that was his as divine before the world began. He, a human being, was deified. That is, his created human spirit was raised to its fullest possible ideal fulfillment: With a human mind he now understood everything about everything, and with a human heart he now loved everything that is lovable. *As human,* Jesus now shared in qualities proper only to God.

Then, through the saving mission of the Holy Spirit, other humans may follow that same path to deification, which Jesus opened for us and in his own case introduced as an accomplished fact into human history. Now others may become deified as Jesus was and, thus, share the life of the Eternal Parent.

Through such an understanding of Jesus, Christian belief explains the possibility of human deification. Without blurring the difference between humanity and divinity, Christianity presents a coherent account of human participation in divine qualities. Christianity envisages a marriage between historical human reality and eternal divine life. A surface comparison with other world religions suggests that this vision is distinctive to Christianity.

In contrast, Buddhism is not even theist. On the other hand, though in practice Buddhism is stunningly down-to-earth, its formal teaching has little appreciation for historical reality. For Buddhism the world is not real; it is illusion.

Judaism is theist, and it does value history as God's good creation, yet Judaism so exalts the Lord God of history that it would never countenance a union of the historical human with the transcendent—if also immanent—divine.

Islam, influenced by the Jewish tradition, also affirms the value of historical reality and, influenced by Christianity, believes in a heavenly paradise. But Islam rejects the Christian Trinity, so the Muslim paradise is a rapturous state of sensuous beauty and pleasure; it is not a state of participation in divinity. One attains that paradise by strict submission to Allah, as known through the teachings of Mohammed in the Koran. Islam does not believe in human deification.

Finally, Hinduism does conceive the deification of human beings, but this is no great achievement, for Hinduism is unclear about the difference between the human soul and divinity in the first place. The classic maxims of Hinduism make this very point: "That thou art," that is, you are Ultimate Reality; and "atman is Brahman," that is, the human soul is God. The Hindu state of divine fulfillment is simply the recovery of what one has been all along, and one recovers that state precisely by freeing oneself from involvement in this world. Hinduism, similar to Buddhism to which it is related, depreciates this world and obscures the reality of history.

So with Judaism, Christianity affirms the reality of divinity, the reality of historical humanity, and the inviolable difference between the two. But in addition, Christianity holds three distinctive, essential, and interlocking doctrines: a trinitarian God, the redemptive mission of the Son (Incarnation and Redemption), and the sanctifying mission of the Holy Spirit (Grace). With these doctrines only Christianity provides a coherent account of the union of the human and the divine: Human deification, the consummate expression of God's love, is the essence of Christianity.

Viewed against this sketch of world religions, Biblical Fundamentalism is similar to Islam. Also a religion of the book, Fundamentalism leads one to its paradise, heaven, by faithful adherence to the divine prophet, Jesus, and his teaching as recorded in the Bible. Again, Fundamentalism is like Hinduism in that it does allow participation in divine life but precisely by downplaying the reality of history. Finally, of course, the distinctiveness of Fundamentalism is that, similar to Christianity, it claims Jesus Christ as its central and founding figure.

However, if what I have presented is correct, Biblical Fundamentalism can hardly be Christian. In claiming revelation from God unconditioned by history, Fundamentalism releases the tension between the historical/human and the eternal/divine. Thus, Fundamentalism surrenders the essence of Christianity. Fundamentalism breaks the connection between the human and the divine.

Hinduism and Buddhism grew out of common roots, Christianity grew out of Judaism, and Islam emerged in contrast to both Judaism and Christianity. I argue that Biblical Fundamentalism is now branching off from Christianity to constitute still another separate religion. Fundamentalism is not Christian.

A LESSON FROM THE COUNCIL OF NICAEA

Again assuming classical Christian doctrine as the norm, I offer a third argument to confirm my conclusion about Biblical Fundamentalism. The divinity of Jesus Christ is one of the fundamentals of Christianity. A religion that cannot maintain the divinity of Jesus cannot be Christian. However, Fundamentalism, limited to its own principles, cannot maintain the divinity of Jesus, so Fundamentalism cannot be Christian.

Consider this argument in detail. The divinity of Jesus was first clarified at the Council of Nicaea in 325 CE, as noted in Chapter 9. Arius, a priest of Alexandria, had been teaching that Jesus, the Word and Son of God, was a creature, not God. Arius allowed that the Word was the greatest of creatures and the first of creatures. He even allowed that the Word was created before all time and was God's instrument in the creation and salvation of the world. Because of his preeminent status, the Word, Jesus Christ, is called Son of God, Word of the Father, Firstborn, Lord, and all the rest, but, in fact, the Son is not God, but a creature.

Under the leadership of Athanasius, the Council of Nicaea responded to Arius's teaching and condemned it. The council's teaching is enshrined in what is now called the Nicene Creed, a statement of faith still proclaimed in the Christian churches. The intent of the council was to clarify, once and for all, that the one Lord, Jesus Christ, is "God from God, Light from Light, true God from true God, begotten [of the Father] [but not a creature], [one in substance with] the Father." This conciliar statement is a direct response to Arius: Though generated from the Father, the Son is not a creature but is of the same substance as the Father, God even as the Father is God.

Two issues are relevant here. First, this clarification about Jesus' divinity emerged some 225 years after the close of the biblical era. Until Nicaea no precise account of Jesus' divine status existed, simply because the question had never yet been raised. Arius's contribution to Christian history was to pose the question in a way that was precise and unavoidable: What is the Word, God or a creature? Arius's question provoked a major crisis in the church, and even Nicaea's decree sparked a debate that lasted for half a century and nearly destroyed the church.

Evidently, before Nicaea Jesus' divinity was not as clear as people imagine. Evidently, on the basis of the Bible alone Jesus' status as divine leaves room for debate. In fact, Arius was able to account for all the biblical passages, in the Hebrew and Christian Testaments, that were usually applied to Jesus. He delighted in proving his position from the Scriptures. Therefore, on the basis of the Bible alone, Arianism is a defensible position.

It follows that Fundamentalism, which claims to rely only on the Scriptures, cannot maintain the divinity of Jesus. For the Scriptures can be read to teach either that Jesus was merely a supreme creature or that Jesus was, indeed, divine. However, which he is cannot be discerned on the basis of the Scriptures alone. The bishops at the Council of Nicaea knew this fact. By the time the Council of Nicaea was over, the whole Christian world knew it.

Now enters the second point. Some of the bishops at Nicaea argued that the council's teaching should be made only in terms already used in the Bible. The Bible, they said, was sufficient to express Christian belief. These bishops did not carry the day.

Others argued that if only biblical terms were used, Arius's argument could not be answered. Arius posed his question in terms that the Bible never used. Biblical terms could not address his question, and if his question were not addressed, Christianity would be undone. So the council chose a technical, nonbiblical term to counter Arius's teaching: *homoousios,* the term translated "one in substance." The intent was that the Only-Begotten is divine even as the Eternal Parent is divine.

The implication is blatant. The same event that first secured Christian belief in the divinity of Jesus is the very event that also proves the impossibility of basing Christianity on the Scriptures alone.

Of course, not everyone holds firmly to the Nicene Creed. Some Christians today do not believe literally that Jesus was God. However, whether Jesus really was God is not the issue here. In *The Transcended Christian* I explain my personal take on this question. I believe that whether Jesus was literally God or not should make no difference *in practice*. The requirement of wholesome human living, the meaning of love, compassion, and justice in this world, does not depend on Jesus' being God. So in practice, the question of Jesus' divinity is moot. The question is not worth arguing over. What matters is that we live as best we know how, and that "best" should be the same for believers and nonbelievers alike. As I argued in the first half of this book, even belief in God is not essential to good living and profound spirituality. We are to do our best and let God take care of the rest. It is not up to us to understand the intricacies of the Trinity and the Incarnation and Redemption. Nor should we spend our lives spinning our wheels in debate over other metaphysical questions—about which, as I explain in my upcoming *Spirituality for a Secular Society*, we could never have a secure answer anyway. There is no way of proving or disproving religious claims about metaphysical matters—including the assertions of the Nicene Creed.

My argument here does not depend on whether Jesus was really God. The important point is that Fundamentalism insists that Jesus was. Others may question this belief in the divinity of Jesus, but Fundamentalism stands on it. Moreover, Fundamentalism insists that this belief is essential to Christianity. I am simply pointing out that, on the basis of the Bible alone, Fundamentalism cannot sustain this belief. In the face of the Council of Nicaea, Biblical Fundamentalism should have to admit either that it is not Christian or that it does not adhere strictly to the Bible alone.

On the one hand, if Fundamentalism wants to continue affirming the divinity of Jesus, it must admit it is reading the New Testament in light of the subsequent Council of Nicaea. In this case Fundamentalism will also have to admit that it is abandoning its claim to simple appeal to the Bible alone.

By the same token, with the rest of Christianity, Fundamentalism will have affirmed that, in addition to the Bible, postbiblical Christian tradition is determinative of Christianity. Fundamentalism will have accepted historicity as essential to Christianity, and Fundamentalism will have clarified its Christian identity.

On the other hand, if Fundamentalism wants to continue insisting that it rests strictly and solely on the Bible, it must admit that it cannot securely maintain the divinity of Jesus Christ and that, as a movement, it is a failure—because the divinity of Jesus is one of the "fundamentals" that the movement originally proposed to maintain.

On the basis of its literal reliance on the Bible alone, Fundamentalism is unable to sustain its claim that Jesus is divine. Undoubtedly, it will continue making that claim, nonetheless. It must then admit the opposite and equally devastating shortcoming: It cannot present a truly human Jesus.

Reading the Scriptures "literally"—that is, on the unacknowledged presupposition of Nicaea—and strapped especially by the Gospel of John, which presents an otherworldly Jesus, Fundamentalism presents a Jesus who is more a superman than a real human being, a celestial visitor living among us but hardly one of us. A Jesus who knows in detail the full course of his life and of the whole world and who can invoke divine power to extricate himself from any situation at will is hardly, as Hebrews 2:17 puts it, "like us in all things." He is freed from the limitations of humanity and avoids the vicissitudes of history.

Fundamentalism has become the willing but unwitting curator of a problem that had plagued Christian orthodoxy until recently. Now, relying on historical-critical method, the Christian churches can understand the Gospels, including John, not as factual reports on the historical Jesus himself, but, rather, as evocative expressions of Christian faith about Jesus. Beneath such expressions of faith, Christian scholars can uncover the truly human Jesus while at the same time preserving Christian faith about Jesus' divinity and showing reasonable grounds for such faith. I treated this matter in detail in my *The Same Jesus: A Contemporary Christology,* and Chapter 9 of this book includes some of that detail.

In contrast, Fundamentalism is left with an unsustainable claim of Jesus' divinity and with an unhuman Jesus, as well. Strict Fundamentalism does not seem able to preserve the essential core of Christianity.

The connection between Arianism and Biblical Fundamentalism is profound. One of Arius's chief concerns was to preserve the transcendence of God. That is to say, Arius did not believe God could or should really become involved in the created world. Thus, Arius denied the divinity of the Only-Begotten-of-God, insisting that God created and saved the world through the mediation of a creature, Jesus Christ.

Similarly, Fundamentalism's refusal to admit the historicity of the Bible preserves its God from being really involved in human history. In addition, by a weird twist of ideas that without acknowledged basis presupposes the divinity of Jesus, that same depreciation of historicity this time keeps Jesus from being a real human being. Here the error is not Arianism, but Docetism or, at best, a form of Monophysitism, both ancient Christian heresies.

At this point—and surely for the nontheologian—these analyses may appear to be a tangle of ideas, all running off in different directions. In fact, this tangle of ideas merely reflects the incoherent core of Fundamentalist teachings and addresses some of them in their ever-shifting focus. One of the ways Biblical Fundamentalism maintains its mesmerizing control over people is to keep them always guessing. There is always another biblical passage to consult, always another Bible class to take, always a new preacher to hear, always another angle to consider, and always another reason for guilt and self-doubt—all geared to keeping people from ever trusting their own best judgment. Taking Luther and Calvin to their extreme conclusions, Bible religions place no trust in "depraved humanity"; they have no regard for historical beings. Thus, logical coherence and reasonableness are not hallmarks of Fundamentalism.

Indeed, if one is sure of possessing God's literal word of truth, it makes good sense not to be concerned about making good sense. With Tertullian one can exclaim, "I believe because it is absurd." But concern about reasonableness raises still another area of discussion, the relationship of faith and reason. Revealingly, this new concern is essentially related to the possible coincidence of the human and the divine: Can what we know through our human minds ever square with the truth that God knows? Can human understanding ever be true even in the eyes of God? Can human science ever have anything to contribute to religion? Fundamentalism would say, "No. Our human judgment is too corrupted by sin to ever lead us to the truth." In so responding, Fundamentalism denies the human possibility of knowing anything apart from blind faith. Write off all human science! Abandon all scholarship! Away with all human achievement! However, this terrifying prospect is not the explicit concern of this chapter. Chapter 14 does discuss the possibility of reasonable religious faith.

IMPLICATIONS FOR ALL OF CHRISTIANITY

My analysis is complete, and my conclusion is clear: The theological core of Biblical Fundamentalism is incompatible with Christianity; literalist Bible religion is simply not Christian. I still need to spell out some far-reaching implications.

I have pushed emphasis on history to the limit here. Such emphasis in Christianity is new, a mere nineteenth-century development. In fact, Fundamentalism arose precisely to counter this emphasis. Nonetheless, this recency does not invalidate this emphasis. Doctrine does develop. My theological analysis of the Fundamentalist principle highlights a heretofore underappreciated aspect of Christianity: historicity. This aspect lies at the core.

No appeal to ethical standards ultimately distinguishes Christianity from other religions. The difference is theological. The difference is belief in the coincidence of the eternal/divine and the historical/human. Christianity presents an account of this coincidence that leaves both elements integral. It is precisely the new emphasis on historicity that preserves the integrity of the human element. The effect of such emphasis is seen in recent accounts of a very human historical Jesus (as elaborated in Chapter 9), in the current emergence of incarnational or holistic Christian spirituality, in the opening of Christianity to the truth embodied in other world religions, and in my analysis of Biblical Fundamentalism.

Thus, from this discussion, first possible only in the late twentieth century, a renewed understanding of the essence of Christianity emerges—and none too soon: Sharing a shrinking planet with other great religions, Christianity cannot afford to remain unclear about its distinctive identity. Moreover, increasingly faced with the challenging findings of the natural and social sciences, for the sake of world peace, Christianity needs to champion the coincidence of the human and divine. In a word, the essence of Christianity is, seen from the divine side, deification, or seen from the human side, incarnationalism. Humanity is destined to share in divinity just as, in Christ, God shared in humanity. Elucidation of this matter represents a present-day advance in Christian self-understanding.

Because keen historical awareness is recent, strains of fundamentalist mentality continue to survive within all the Christian churches—for example, in ahistorical dogmatism or papism in Roman Catholicism, in overemphasis on the Bible in Protestant churches, in the search for security in popular piety, and in ethical rigidity on sexual matters in all the Christian communions. Nonetheless, Fundamentalism cannot claim, on that basis, still to be Christian.

As history progresses, the meaning of Christianity gets clarified. Then the Christian tradition leaves behind formerly accepted views now recognized as inadequate. If strains of fundamentalist thinking do survive within the Christian churches, none of the churches claims immunity to history as a basic premise, but Fundamentalism does. Whatever fundamentalist mentality remains in the Christian churches is an accident of history, not a deliberate choice. It is precisely the explicit claim to ahistoricism, its deliberate choice to ignore history, that renders Biblical Fundamentalism incompatible with Christianity.

By the same token, however, it is now also clear that wherever any form of history-denying fundamentalism occurs, even within a Christian communion, it cannot be Christian. The current advance in Christian self-understanding challenges all the churches and calls for a painful purification of the religion. So, as suggested previously, the line of division no longer falls between Protestant and Catholic but cuts through the churches and lies between historical-minded Christianity and ahistorical fundamentalism.

One is not Christian simply by belonging to a religious organization that somehow traces its roots back to Jesus or merely by accepting the Bible, the Hebrew and the Christian Testaments, as God's Word or even by proclaiming Jesus as Lord.

Belief in the real Jesus and in the real Bible, historical realities, entails belief also in God's involvement in real history through the Holy Spirit. So beyond conversion to Jesus, God, Bible, and Church, Christianity calls for further conversion—conversion to ever ongoing conversion, conversion to open-ended growth and unexpected outcomes, conversion that lets God be truly active and creative in history. Christian belief in human deification requires commitment to the unending transformation of the human situation into forms ever more worthy of God. From this point of view, Chapter 12's advocacy of gay marriage appears to be thoroughly and genuinely Christian.

Rejection of the historicity that is essential to Christianity disqualifies Biblical Fundamentalism as truly Christian. To a large extent this same rejection can also explain why Fundamentalism often does not stand with the Christian communions on many political or ethical issues.

Though such political and ethical considerations are not ultimately telling, they often do reflect the essential difference between Biblical Fundamentalism and Christianity. They reveal in Fundamentalism an ahistorical idealism that fails to take seriously the intricacies, vicissitudes, and inherent messiness of human life. Thus, people may often be right in pointing to those political and ethical differences as setting Fundamentalists apart, and Fundamentalism may often be right in claiming distinction in these practical matters. However, Fundamentalism is wrong in claiming that such distinction makes it Christian. Precisely the opposite is the case.

It is now perfectly clear—as it has always been somehow understood—that historicity is an essential facet of Christianity. This understanding disqualifies Fundamentalism's claim to be Christian. By the same token, this understanding specifies the meaning of the name *Christian* applied to any of the churches. *Christian* implies ongoing movement toward a state of affairs that is worthy of both God and humanity, for ultimately the two must coincide. Committed to the divine-human one, Jesus Christ, and presuming the inspiration of the Holy Spirit, *Christianity* means commitment to the ever unfolding expression of the divine within the worldly realm unto a fulfillment wherein God is all in all.

I arrived at that conclusion by delving deeply into Christianity. However, the ultimate fulfillment that Christianity projects is similar to what other religions, in their own way, would also envisage. True Christianity is not at odds with other religions or with the human race. As the next chapter explains, true Christianity opens onto a truly global community. Of course, this global community and ultimate spiritual fulfillment include lesbian, gay, bisexual, transgender, and intersex people and their relationships—despite what people such as Senator Rick Santorum might happen to think.

Chapter 14

The Bible, Homosexuality, and Christianity

What does the Bible teach? To tell the truth, it depends on what people happen to make of it. People get what they want out of the Bible. Different people have different interpretations. Add questions of sexual ethics and the discussion becomes even more complicated, for sex is emotionally charged, and emotions cloud thinking. Thus, what part the Scriptures play in determining sexual ethics is a complex matter, indeed.

Homosexuality provides a test case, because opinions about biblical teaching on homosexuality are so highly debated. For example, Romans 1:26-27 reads,

> Their women exchanged natural intercourse for unnatural, and in the same way also the men, giving up natural intercourse with women, were consumed with passion for one another. Men committed shameless acts with men and received in their own persons the due penalty for their error.

On first reading, this text appears to be rather straightforward and damning. In *What the Bible Really Says About Homosexuality,* I explained how mistranslations and oversight of context contribute to this impression. Actually, understood in its own historical situation, this text, part of a larger argument, is not condemning of same-sex behaviors at all. Rather, it is a rhetorical ploy, an attempt by Paul to gain the sympathy of the Jewish Christians in Rome by seeming to side

This chapter was originally published with documentation in *Pastoral Psychology,* 1999, volume 47, number 4, pages 261-271, under the title "Scripture, Sexual Ethics, and the Nature of Christianity," and abridged and reprinted in *Open Hands,* Chris Glaser, ed., 2000, volume 15, number 3, pages 20-23. Reprinted with permission.

with their anti-Gentile prejudices. However, not everyone accepts this affirming interpretation. There exists a whole array of elaborately reasoned opinions about this text, and they range from absolutely negative to fully positive.

This diversity of opinions is precisely the problem. It disqualifies the Bible from the discussion, for the biblical teaching appears obviously ambiguous; there is no agreement on its meaning. But if the biblical teaching must be disqualified, what is Christianity without its reliance on the Scriptures? The Scriptures must be relevant in some way, and, as I will argue, they are. However, when that way is specified, it differs from long-standing practice, and reliance on it transforms the very meaning of Christianity.

At stake in the Christian debate over homosexuality is the nature of Christianity itself. Both the Fundamentalists and the mainline Christians would likely agree with this statement. However, and most revealing, they will also likely differ on sexual ethics.

Apart from differing ethical opinions, the broad implications of this debate are the most important. What does it mean that people who all sincerely reverence the Bible cannot agree on what the Bible teaches? This matter is the real topic. This chapter will address that topic by

- spelling out the array of opinions in the case of homosexuality and the Bible,
- providing a deeper analysis of the role of the Scriptures in ethical decision making, and finally,
- pointing out the broad implications of this matter for a new vision of Christianity.

Certainly, not all will agree with my analysis. Still, the questions it raises are poignantly pertinent to anyone concerned about the Bible, Christianity, and religion in contemporary society.

AN ARRAY OF ETHICAL OPINIONS

There exists an array of opinions on what the Bible teaches about homosexuality.

Outright Condemnation Across the Board

On the conservative pole stand Evangelical Christianity and Biblical Fundamentalism. Though sometimes having very different religious emphases, when homosexuality is the topic, these two groups rely on what is basically a literal reading of the Bible—as I noted in Chapter 13. In Romans 1, the literal reading sees Paul condemning lesbian and gay sex as unnatural, degrading, and shameless, an affront to the very order of God's creation.

One of the most common mistakes in interpreting this passage is to run together the verses on sex (26-27) and the verses that follow (28-32). The literal reading makes this mistake. As a result, same-sex behaviors get associated with a long list of egregious offenses: evil, covetousness, malice, envy, murder, strife, and so on, which even have a death penalty attached. The conclusion of the literal reading is that the Bible condemned gay sex in ancient times and the condemnation remains as strong today as ever.

Different Meanings of Homosexuality

In contrast, across mainline denominations, contemporary biblical scholarship uses a more critical method of interpretation. It insists on reading Paul's words in the context of his own time and place. As a result, this "historical-critical method" comes to a more permissive ethical conclusion. Yet even then, a variety of opinions exist.

Some, such as Victor Furnish and Bernadette Brooten, believe that Paul did, indeed, condemn same-sex acts. However, they point out, his reasons for condemning them do not hold today because his understanding of same-sex acts was simply not what we mean by homosexuality today. Paul and the people of his day were concerned about external sexual behaviors, whereas we are concerned about internal sexual orientation. We understand homosexuality to be a component of the personality, biologically determined, beyond personal choice, fixed in early childhood, and linked not just to sex acts, but to a person's very capacity for bonding and affection. Taking into consideration the findings of today's medicine, psychology, and sociology, Furnish and Brooten conclude that the Bible's teaching never addressed today's questions, so current ethical answers must be based on something other than the Scriptures.

Neutrality Regarding Homosexuality

Still relying on a critical reading of the historical evidence, but coming to an even more liberal conclusion, L. William Countryman has argued that Romans 1 did not even condemn the same-sex behaviors of Paul's day. Rather, Paul saw sexual practices as a matter of "cleanness" or "ritual purity"—in the sense that the Jewish Law understood the matter. This is the interpretation that I propose in *What the Bible Really Says About Homosexuality* and that I summarized in the second paragraph of this chapter and in the following paragraphs.

In Romans 1:24, Paul announced the topic of his discussion of sexual behavior: *akatharsia,* impurity. This topic stands in contrast to the topic of that long list of sins in verses 28-32: *ta me kathekonta.* This latter phrase, translated "things not to be done," is a technical term from Stoic philosophy and clearly refers to unethical acts. Paul intended to contrast impurity with sin.

Moreover, Paul used another technical Stoic term, *para physin.* It is usually translated "unnatural," but this translation must be mistaken because in Romans 11:24 Paul uses the very same term to refer to acts of God. It makes no sense to say that God acted unnaturally because God created nature and made it what it is. Therefore, this term should be translated as "atypical." In fact, Paul was using the term *para physin* in its popular sense, not in its technical, philosophical Stoic sense. So similar to the other two descriptors in the passage on same-sex acts, *degrading* and *shameless,* the term *atypical* implies no ethical condemnation. Rather, Paul painted a picture of social disapproval and disdain. He was talking about ritual impurity, Jewish uncleanness, not immorality or wickedness.

Paul deliberately opened his letter to the Romans with a contrast between ritual impurity and wickedness. His purpose was to make one of the main points of his letter: The purity requirements of the Old Law have become irrelevant in Christ, and Jewish and Gentile converts should not splinter the Christian community by bickering over matters of custom and culture. Unless they are otherwise wrong, sexual practices in themselves are ethically neutral.

B. Barbara Hall provides further support for this interpretation. Coming from a completely different direction and apparently unaware of Countryman's interpretation of Romans 1, she concluded, as well, that Paul would not be concerned about differences in sexual orientation today.

According to Hall, Paul's vision of Christianity was revolutionary. Galatians 6:11-16 and 2 Corinthians 5:16-21 present a picture of a new order in Christ. In this new order, all social divisions and cultural categories become irrelevant. Galatians 3:28 gives a specific list and shows how radical Paul's thought actually was: "There is no longer Jew or Greek, there is no longer slave or free, there is no longer male and female, for all of you are one in Christ." Furthermore, 1 Corinthians 7 illustrates that in Paul's mind no one right way exists for Christians to live out their sexuality. Paul is open to all the options of his day. What matters for Paul is not one's specific lifestyle, but the Christian virtue one expresses through it.

Thus, a solid argument can be made that Paul did not even condemn the same-sex behaviors of his own day. Granted this interpretation, the Scriptures themselves would certainly allow loving gay and lesbian relationships today.

Affirmation of Same-Sex Relationships

Finally, pushing this conclusion a step further, an even more liberal reading of the Bible's teaching on homosexuality can be made: Not only does the Bible not condemn same-sex behaviors per se, but it actually supports them in some instances. Three clear cases are apropos.

First, in *Jonathan Loved David,* Thomas Horner argued persuasively that these two Old Testament heroes were sexual partners. Described in 1 Samuel, their relationship fits the model of noble military lovers. Such relationships were common and well-known throughout the ancient Middle East.

Second, Matthew 8:5-13 and Luke 7:1-10 recount Jesus' healing of a Roman centurion's servant boy. Scripture scholar James Miller and others have suggested that the centurion and the servant were lovers and, by healing the servant, Jesus restored their relationship. A number of textual considerations suggest that an important emotional bond existed between the centurion and his servant boy: the provocative alternation between two Greek terms for servant, *pais* and *doulos,* in those passages; the consistent quotation of the centurion's reference to the sick servant as *pais;* and Luke's comment that the servant boy was *entimos* (dear, valuable) to the presumably wealthy centurion. In addition, *pais*—literally *boy*, but also able to mean *servant* or even *son*—was sometimes used to mean *male lover*. Because Jesus said nothing about the relationship, we cannot outright conclude that, by not condemning this relationship, Jesus certainly approved of it: We don't know what Jesus was thinking. Still, in light of the often heard claim that homosexuality is the paradigm of human opposition to God's plan for creation, it is peculiar that Jesus never spoke out against same-sex behaviors, especially when he was face-to-face with the Roman centurion.

Third, in an explosive book, *The Man Jesus Loved,* the reputable biblical scholar Theodore Jennings mounts an extended argument that Jesus himself was actually gay and that the beloved disciple of John's Gospel was Jesus' lover. To support this provocative conclusion, Jennings examines not only the texts that relate to the beloved disciple but also the story of the centurion's servant boy and the texts that show Jesus' rather negative attitude toward the traditional family: Not mother and brothers, but those who do the will of God, are family to Jesus. Jennings suggests that Jesus' relatives and disciples knew he was gay and that, despite the efforts of the early Church to downplay this "dangerous memory" about Jesus, a list of clues remains in the Gospels. Piecing those clues together, Jennings suggests not only that Jesus was very open to homosexuality but also that he himself was in an intimate, and probably sexual, relationship with the beloved disciple. Thus, it can be argued that the Bible actually endorses homosexual love.

The Dilemma in Basing Ethics on the Bible

There is an array of opinions about the Bible's ethical teaching on gay sex:

- Either the Bible condemns it outright and totally or
- the Bible condemns same-sex acts but not in terms that apply to homosexuality as we know it today or
- the Bible does not condemn same-sex acts at all but sees them as ethically neutral in themselves or, finally,
- the Bible actually endorses same-sex love.

Not only is there a range of opinions about what the Bible teaches about homosexuality, but the same is true about other ethical questions such as divorce, the status of women in marriage and society, or the acceptable way to raise and discipline children. Besides, on numerous current questions—such as genetic engineering, cloning, nuclear energy, computer technology, environmental responsibility—it is hardly to be expected that the ancient texts of the Bible express any opinion at all. Thus, when we look to the Bible for answers about ethical questions, no clear and simple answers are to be found.

In light of this situation, the only honest response seems to be to disqualify the Bible as a sourcebook on ethics or morality. If the biblical teaching is so ambiguous that consensus on its teaching is impossible to achieve, the teaching cannot be helpful. We must disregard the Bible. We must answer our ethical questions on some other basis.

This is a disturbing conclusion for Christians. Where does Christianity stand if the Scriptures are irrelevant to Christian living?

A DEEPER ANALYSIS

The teaching of the Bible is not to blame for that disturbing conclusion. Actually, the principles of interpretation that were brought to bear on the Bible explain the differing opinions. Therefore, attention needs to turn to interpretation.

The Impact of Historical Awareness

The line of demarcation in the previous array of opinions fell between the literal and the historical-critical approaches. Only the literal approach resulted in the absolute condemnation of homosexual relationships. In one way or another, the critical approach always allowed room for acceptance. Therefore, not the Scriptures, but the mind that one brings to them, is what determined the ethical conclusions. This point needs to be emphasized.

Our human minds are both a blessing and a burden. Self-aware and capable of reflection, we have become historically, psychologically, and hermeneutically sophisticated. This is to say, we now take for granted the need to get behind mere words. We routinely ask, "What is their context?" "How are they used in this case?" "What is the concern of the speaker?" "What is his or her real intent?" And, thus, we cannot but ask, "What do the words really mean?"

We are aware that the meaning is the key and that, similar to a smile or a nod, the same words can carry very different meanings in different situations. In all things human, the human subject is the bottom line. We create our own worlds. We make our own interpretations. And more and more, we all know this fact.

Today, no one can hide from the awareness that the base of life has shifted. No longer do authority, convention, cultural inheritance, or tradition restrict individuals and societies. Rather, we routinely appropriate and adjust inherited teachings, applying them to our own situation according to our own best judgment. We realize that such a process of inheritance and adaptation was actually also behind the very traditions that we are now adapting.

We do the best we can with what we have, and we realize that our ancestors did the very same thing. If "God spoke to them," God did so in the same way that "God speaks to us"—not in miraculous utterances of American English words and full-blown sentences, but through the quiet insights of our hearts as we honestly and openly ponder the questions of life. If we have an advantage over our ancestors in this matter, the advantage is only that we have a longer history of prior examples on which to rely. But we, just as they, must still work things out as best we can. We are more aware of this process than any previous generation ever was. The very fact that I can make these statements outright and unapologetically is astounding, in itself. This state of affairs is typical of our contemporary historical awareness.

The Danger of Relativism

A religion that relies on texts—such as the Bible—must admit that the ground has shifted. As Bernard Lonergan suggests, the thinking mind, not the text or the inherited religious teaching, is now rock bottom. Some take this realization to mean that anything goes, that we can make things be whatever we want: "Imagine it hard enough, and it will happen." To this striking position they apply the name *postmodernism*. The suggestion is that we have entered a new era—and, indeed, we have. What remains to be seen, however, is how this new era will go down in history. One rendition is that the certainties of the past and even the hope for certainty have given way to thorough-going relativism. Nothing is absolute. Nothing is sacred. There is no right and wrong. All depends on what you want to make of things.

People concerned about ethics rightly shudder at that position. It is grossly mistaken and dangerous. The difference between truth and falsehood is real. The difference between good and evil is real. Even those who say that everything is relative must accept this fact, for they, themselves, indulge in truth claims. Their claim that firm truths do not and cannot exist is a statement about what is supposedly the truth. They do not walk their talk.

Besides, if our own creative minds are the critical factor in our construction of a meaningful world, our construction also depends on factors that are independent of ourselves. For example, the density of matter remains. Gravity continues to make things fall. Emotions eventually show themselves. Hatred is inevitably self-destructive. Falsehood forebodes an unstable future. In fact, we cannot make things into whatever we would like. Unavoidable regularities exist in the universe. Natural limits exist to what we can make of things.

The Mind of the Bible

With regard to the Bible, its verses do say something; its words and sentences do impose limits on what anyone could claim the Bible teaches. Although determination of the biblical teaching depends on the human mind, the Bible also has a mind of its own.

The approach of a former era—intent on texts, formulations, truth statements—was to locate the biblical mind in its stipulations, its direct teachings. That approach was narrow and has proved naive and simplistic. Looking more deeply, current understanding locates the biblical mind in its attitudes. It is not the *what,* but the *how* of the Bible, that turns out to be most important—not what the Bible says, but how it arrives at what it says.

Overall, the Bible fosters a spirit of wonder, praise, humility, thanksgiving, faithfulness, personal integrity, honesty, justice, welcome, concern, compassion, forgiveness, change of heart, reconciliation. These notions express the mind of the Bible, and their validity is everlasting. Only "the devil" could question their ongoing relevance to ethical decision making and life in general.

When the focus is on attitudes, the biblical teaching remains completely relevant to human living. The Scriptures still have an important role to play when we make ethical decisions—because the biblical mind informs our own minds and, thus, influences whatever we do.

The same point can be made in more technical terms. If we return to the Greek, Roman, and medieval concern for *aretaic ethics*—that is, ethics built on virtue, excellence, and character formation—the Scriptures remain fully relevant. The Scriptures teach us to be honest, loving, and kind, and this unchanging lesson applies everywhere and always. However, if our intent is the modern preoccupation with *deontic ethics*—that is, ethics built on rules that would spell out in legal fashion every act that is to be performed or avoided: Do this, don't do that—the scriptural teaching becomes moot, for it is debated. In this case, no agreement has been made on what the Bible actually teaches. The array of opinions about biblical teaching on homosexuality provided an example.

INTIMATIONS FOR A NEW CHRISTIANITY

It is the mind of the Bible, not its outright requirements, that is perennially valid. Far-reaching implications can be drawn from this insight. Follow it through to its logical conclusion and a new vision of Christianity takes form. We are truly entering a new era.

The Bible and Critical Thinking

First, the biblical mind actually corresponds to the mind of the critical thinker. Biblical wonder, questioning, dedication, honesty, personal integrity, and commitment to truth are the very qualities that come to fruition in current critical thinking. The Bible does not teach us to be unthinking dolts, believing without thinking, obeying without understanding. The Bible teaches us to be responsible, honest, and concerned, and to be this way we need to apply our minds and search our hearts. Indeed, the biblical attitude, along with the contribution of the Greeks, is behind Western civilization's achievement of modern science. And in the humanities, this scientific mentality is the heart of historical-critical method.

Thus, when you attend to the attitude of the Bible and not to its specific pronouncements, the historical-critical method turns out to enjoy biblical approval, and the literalism of Biblical Fundamentalism appears to be unbiblical. Although the Fundamentalists have virtually taken over the name *Christian,* their position is hardly biblical or Christian at all, as I argued in Chapter 13. By the same token, the more liberal ethical conclusion regarding homosexuality turns out to be true to biblical teaching: The Bible does not condemn homosexuality as we understand it today.

Biblical and Naturalistic Ethics

A second implication is that the biblical mind also corresponds with the mind of naturalistic ethics. The Bible fosters an unreserved commitment to good and the ongoing pursuit of justice and love in every situation. These are the same attitudes that motivate any person of goodwill who seeks to know the right thing to do.

As I suggested in Chapter 7, ethical people attend to all the evidence, look to personal experience, consult the experts of the day, apply their best reasoning, and collaborate with other honest seekers. Thus, ethical people arrive at ethical decisions. In doing so they are also implementing the mind of the Bible. They are embodying the holy attitude that the Bible enshrines. Whether they conceive the matter in these terms or not, they are acting "as God would want," they are doing "what Jesus would do," they are being "led by the Holy Spirit" in their present situation. Heard with both a secular and religious ear, the biblical teaching on ethics can be summarized in the words of Saint Augustine, "Love, and do what you like."

The Melding of Scripture and Tradition

Third, attention to the mind of the Bible brings insight into the relationship between Scripture and Tradition. Scripture, of course, refers to the Bible, and Tradition refers to the teaching of the church throughout the centuries. Differences about the importance of these two were central to the split between Catholics and Protestants in the sixteenth century.

As for Scripture: if the biblical attitude, not the biblical prescriptions, is what matters, the Bible is not to be read as a cookbook for

Christian living. The Bible was not intended to provide ready-made answers to our ethical questions. Rather, the Bible is a record of how godly people live. Our task is to learn a lesson from their example and to apply the lesson in our own lives.

This way of approaching the Scriptures presupposes that the Bible emerged from within the Christian community. The Bible did not descend pristine and pure directly from heaven. It was not transcribed by an entranced secretary responding to divine dictation. Rather, the Bible is the historical record of people's experience of God. To be sure, according to Christian belief, the Bible is the record of a privileged era. However, in that era the early Christians were facing their ethical questions just as Christians are today. The same process of ethical decision making operates throughout.

Recognition of this consistent process blurs the distinction between Scripture and Tradition. If Tradition means the ongoing teaching of the churches, then the Scriptures are a part of this Tradition. However, because of the Scriptures' privileged position, they inform whatever else comes later. They inform future decisions precisely by enshrining the attitude that keeps the ongoing Tradition on track.

Thus, the old Protestant-Catholic debate over Scripture versus Tradition dissolves, and the opposing sides fall together: Scripture is part of Tradition, and ongoing Tradition depends on Scripture. No opposition or possible choice between Scripture and Tradition exists. The historical-critical method and the mind of the Bible bring Catholic and Protestant Christianity back into unity. At the same time, the nature of Christianity, at least where ethics are concerned, is clarified. In the process, as I argued in Chapter 13, the literalism of Biblical Fundamentalism shows itself to have departed from the Christian religion. Mountains crumble. Valleys are filled. Monumental shifts are occurring. We are living through epochal change.

Evidently, the Christian approach to ethics is complex. The Scriptures play a role, but they are only one part of a bigger picture. The Methodist "quadrilateral" usefully depicts that whole picture: Christian decision making appeals to four things: (1) Scripture, (2) tradition, (3) reason, and (4) experience.

This four-sided approach is the very picture that I am painting here, and in varying configurations is the same approach that the other Christian churches besides the Methodist also hold. Appreciable consensus exists on these matters across denominations. More and more this consensus defines the Christian way, and Biblical Fundamentalism appears more and more clearly not to be Christian at all.

As for lesbian and gay relationships, the broad picture seems to include them. Evidence continues to mount on all sides. Genes certainly have something to do with sexual orientation, and so do other biological factors. The four facets of the quadrilateral work together as follows: As (3) the findings of medical and social science and (4) the experience of gay Christians accumulate, (1) the critical reading of the Scriptures, affirmative of lesbians and gays, gains more and more credibility and (2) the ongoing teaching of the churches, Tradition, gravitate toward a new balance. All the pieces—Scripture, Tradition, reason, and experience—converge to interlock and confirm one another. With increasing openness to gay and lesbian relationships, Christianity is taking another step forward on its life-giving mission through history.

AN ECUMENICAL CHRISTIANITY

The fourth and final implication of emphasis on the biblical attitude is this: The biblical mind is open to all religions and peoples. Insofar as the biblical mind corresponds with the mind of critical thinking and with the mind of naturalistic ethics, the biblical mind also corresponds with that of authentic humanism. The openness, questioning, honesty, and goodwill that the Bible requires are the very same qualities that, according to Bernard Lonergan, define genuine humanity in any of its cultural expressions. So the humanity we share in common—and share in common with Jesus—is the fundamental bond among us all, not our religious faith.

However, the emphasis is on *authentic* humanism and *genuine* humanity—because an alternative is possible. We can deform and misshape ourselves. Said in religious terms: We can sin. Still, despite our wrongdoing, the human spirit in all of us, fortified by the Holy Spirit, is geared toward what is right, true, and good. Said in religious terms: the human spirit is geared toward God. So again with Saint Augustine, we could pray, "Lord, you have made us for yourself, and our hearts are restless till they rest in you." This statement holds true whether a person believes in God or not, for this statement is not about religious faith, but about the human heart. Thus, genuine humanity, not necessarily belief in God or Christ, is the critical factor in the new ecumenical Christianity.

A Christianity that attends to the mind of the Bible rather than to its specific ethical prescriptions is a Christianity that is open to a global society. Such Christianity remains relevant in the third millennium. Such Christianity affirms and embraces any person of goodwill. All this is said without any prejudice to the distinctive Christian beliefs about God, Jesus, the Holy Spirit, and the Christian church. Although these Christian specifics do color the expression of the authentic humanism represented in the biblical mind, they do not reshape it in such a way as to require the exclusion of non-Christians from human communion. True Christianity is ecumenical Christianity because it includes authentic humanism, and the inclusion of authentic humanism entails the embrace of all peoples; gays and lesbians are not the only people that a new Christianity would embrace. This conclusion takes on importance when compared to outlandish statements by Biblical Fundamentalists: the condemnation of a minister who prayed at an ecumenical service after the September 11, 2001, tragedy; and the assertion that Hindus, Muslims, and even Jews are all doomed to hell.

CONCLUSION

This ethical discussion about homosexuality in the Bible has led to a vision of a new Christianity. Indeed, the very nature of Christianity is at stake in the current debate over gay and lesbian love. Claims about biblical teaching on homosexuality are linked with people's positions on how to interpret the Bible, and the positions on biblical interpretation are linked with differing conceptions of Christianity. In this chapter, I envisage a Christianity that is ecumenical in the broadest sense—open through our common humanity to all goodwilled and wholesome-living peoples, even while retaining the specifics of Christian belief for those who are Christian.

On the basis of this logic—as suggested here and argued in Chapter 13—Biblical Fundamentalism has abandoned authentic Christianity and is not Christian. Nonetheless, by turning condemnation of homosexuality into a litmus test of Christianity, Fundamentalism does reveal a correct intuition. The Fundamentalists fear the loss of Christianity, and this fear is certainly justified. The times are changing quickly, and all religion is facing serious threat. But Fundamentalism is mistaken and superficial to identify homosexuality as the threat.

My analysis suggests that the loss of Christianity will occur only if everyone adopts the literalism of Biblical Fundamentalism. Then the life-giving spirit of Christianity would have been squashed—even as Paul wrote to the Corinthians: "The letter kills, but the spirit gives life." Apart from a Fundamentalist strangulation of Christianity, not the loss of Christianity, but its transformation is at stake. It is the pain of the transformation of Christianity that Fundamentalists and Christians alike are feeling. Changing attitudes toward homosexuality are merely one expression of the deeper process of transformation.

Still, the Fundamentalist alarm is a useful reminder that mammoth shifts are underway and the churches do need to be careful about how far they allow things to shift. Surely, it is myopic to tie these shifts simplistically to homosexuality and other culturally conditioned biblical prescriptions. But if people insist on doing so, nonetheless, a disconcerting but unavoidable question arises: Does Christianity, itself, stand or fall with lesbians and gays? In light of the present analysis, the answer appears to be, Yes.

Chapter 15

Gay Bashing and 9/11 Terrorism: Religious Perversion

Solidarity Sunday is an annual, national event celebrated on the first Sunday of October. It expresses support for gay, lesbian, bisexual, and transgender people in the face of the violence they so often suffer. In light of recent national events, the 2001 celebration took on particular meaning.

The focus of Solidarity Sunday is delicate. This event raises a touchy topic. Generally, people are uncomfortable about homosexuality. Ignorance—and the ensuing chain of prejudice, fear, anger, hatred, and violence—still often surround this topic. Yet Solidarity Sunday asks so little: It does not require support of gay people's adopting children, gay and lesbian marriage, gay relationships, gay and lesbian sex, gay social establishments, or even gay people's right to housing and employment. It presumes only the right of lesbian, gay, bisexual, and transgender people to exist, to be free from attack, to be safe from violence. But homosexuality is so emotional a topic that even this minimum is difficult to secure, difficult to codify into law, difficult sometimes to experience even in a democratic society celebrated for promising all the right to life, liberty, and the pursuit of happiness.

Sad to say, the most powerful force that keeps antigay prejudice alive is religion. To be sure, many religious groups have made important progress on this matter. Officially, however, the majority of religious bodies continue to oppose sexual diversity, although, as best as

---

This chapter was originally delivered as an address for the Solidarity Sunday celebration, October 7, 2001, at the Church of Reconciliation, San Antonio, Texas, and published in *DignityUSA Journal*, 2002, volume 34, issue 1, pages 15-18, under the title "Life Rich Enough to Share: Religion, Gay Bashing, Terrorism, and Solidarity Sunday."

religious studies, history, and science researchers can determine, nature built such diversity into the human species, or, said otherwise, God created it among us. The more conservative and outspoken religions wage a deliberate—and lucrative—misinformation campaign against lesbian and gay people. For example, the Reverends Jerry Falwell and Pat Robertson laid the blame on gays and lesbians, among others, for the terrorist attacks on the World Trade Center and the Pentagon. The ongoing Fundamentalist vilification of gay people erupted in an outlandish and outrageous use of religion. There can be no doubt that preaching from conservative pulpits is a major factor in the antigay violence that we see in our world.

Violence against gays and lesbians and the terrorist attacks are intertwined. The celebration of Solidarity Sunday in 2001 and ever after takes place in the shadow of September 11.

THE RELIGIOUS ROOT OF VIOLENCE

It is important to notice the parallel between antigay violence and the terrorist attacks, for premeditated violence of any kind grows from the same root. That root is the unswerving commitment of true believers to their particular and well-defined worldviews, and these worldviews are most often couched in religious terms. Supposedly, God puts the ultimate stamp of approval on these petrified beliefs, so, following these beliefs, people think themselves exempt from the requirements of humanity, reason, and compassion.

To be honest about the matter, religious belief is always a veneer on life, a superstructure that holds life's uncertainties together, a bright, clean, and smooth wrapping that covers over life's messiness, a dazzling floodlight of imaginative insight that blinds us to the dark shadows of life. Of course, at its best religion does know deep spiritual concerns, and the proper role of religion is precisely to grapple with the unknowns we must all face: illness, injury, heartbreak, disillusionment, betrayal, loss, weariness, aging, and inevitable death.

However, religious grapplings with the depths often get distorted as deep issues bubble up to the smooth surface of publicly shared and officially approved beliefs. Then beliefs become rigid and grow ever more distant from lived life. Eventually the beliefs take on a life of their own, and they impose their own narrowly rational form onto life itself. Then, rather than expressing the mysteries and marvels of life at its depth, the beliefs squash life and force it into a prefabricated box. Religious belief, iron-hard, sterile, and brittle, becomes a haunting monster of our own creation; a well-intentioned contribution to life becomes a murderous Frankenstein's monster turned back in hostility against us.

THE STRANGLED SOUL OF RELIGION

Clutching at the security of supposedly infallible beliefs, we strangle the soul of true religion: wonder, marvel, question, quest. We lose sight of the elusive Force that pervades all things, the Power at work behind the unfolding of the universe, the heaving and shifting channel that ineluctably leads toward the good, the graciousness and compassion that show in ever ongoing life, whose hope springs eternal. We may call "This Thing" Brahman, God, Buddha Nature, Tao, Allah, Grandfather, Goddess, or Eternal Spirit. These names do not mean the same thing, but in their own ways they all point in the same direction.

Regardless of how we haltingly name This Thing, we lose sight of It when all-too-easy religious beliefs pretend to tell us "everything we ever needed to know" about life. Religion, you see, is a human creation, so it can lose sight of the Power behind the universe and instead worship an idol, mere human dogma.

All too often, even in religion, the sense for the truly sacred gets lost. Sterile religious formulas cover over the disconcerting unknowns of human life. Deeply seated fears prevent any attempt to break beneath the surface and plumb the uncharted depths of the soul and of world process. Desperate self-protectiveness, blind to the Big Mystery, cannot tolerate any mystery or any difference in other people.

Then religious belief becomes a justification for violence. Whether the rationalization is that Allah is on our side against an American monster or that the Lord Jesus is on our side against perverted homosexuals, the underlying phenomenon is one and the same. Perverted religion supports and even endorses violence.

SHAKEN FROM DOGMATIC SLUMBER

So the events of September 11, 2001, speak to Solidarity Sunday, and the message is instructive. Evidently, we pitiable human beings often need violence on a massive scale to shock us, to stop us in our tracks, to wake us from our walking sleep, to make us ponder anew the meaning of life.

The cruel crucifixion of innocent Jesus provoked a spiritual renewal that became Christianity. The heartless beating and murder of Matthew Shepard in 1998 made people face the atrocity of gay bashing. But we forget so easily! The murders of thirty-seven gay and lesbian people in the first ten months of 2001 hardly made the news; there has been no public outrage.

But two planes crashed into the Twin Towers of the World Trade Center, a third, into the Pentagon, and a fourth, in a Pennsylvania field, and the psyche of America was shaken, and much of its daily life came to an agonizing halt. Finally something got the attention of our workaholic, fast-moving, superficial, materialistic, money-driven American society.

The aftereffects of the tragedy were sobering in themselves. People stopped going to the malls; they wanted to spend time with their families. The cinemas were empty. Sports events were cancelled. Sales dipped to record lows. People did not want to travel—not only because of fear of further terrorist attacks but also simply because they wanted to stay at home. Work suddenly took on a lower priority as people began asking themselves, "For what am I working so long and so hard when I don't even have time or energy left to enjoy the people and the things I love?" The powerful poignancy of the fragility of life and the ultimately unavoidable insecurity of being human began to bond us with loved ones and even with strangers. People took time to greet one another, to pause and talk with one another, to be patient in checkout lines or in downtown traffic snarls. Suddenly life was more humane.

THE POSITIVE EFFECTS OF THE TRAGEDY

The insanity of the terrorist attack exposed the insanity of our own way of life. To this extent, perhaps the attacks achieved their intended purpose. What was bad for the economy and an affront to our national pride was good for the soul. For a while we sought a healthier balance and settled for a less American way of life.

The positive effects of this tragedy should not go unnoticed, for they hold a clue to the achievement of peace on earth. Collectively, as a people, we slowed down. We appreciated each moment more than we used to. We realized how precious and delicate life is. Again we came to appreciate human touch, caring, companionship, love. We gathered together to sing and to read poetry. We used art and performance to express the anguished groanings of our souls. We, macho America, were not embarrassed to shed tears. We turned from the artificiality of our plastic and chrome world to seek out beauty, simple and true beauty, and we remembered its healing power.

These shifts in focus elicited the deeper currents of human hearts. Firsthand, we touched the spiritual, which lay encrusted beneath our religions and politics. We touched the spiritual, and, lo and behold, the lines of social division began to blur. Religion did not matter; we are all brothers and sisters, children of a common Source. Color of skin did not matter; we have all died and all helped the injured and dying. From the highest levels of government, we heard outright protests against prejudice, and national leaders went out of their way to insist that we all respect one another. Astonishingly, for a while even sexual orientation did not matter because gay people were also killed in the attacks and rescue efforts, and gay people were cited among the public heroes—notably, Father Mychal Judge, the Catholic chaplain to the New York Fire Department and supporter of many gay and lesbian causes who died ministering at the Twin Towers, and Mark Bingham, who was a leader in thwarting the terrorists on United Airlines flight 93 and bringing down the plane in Pennsylvania before it could reach Washington, DC.

These shifts in focus opened us up to deeper inner experience. Our routines fell away, and our rigid worldviews broke open. We came in touch with the mysterious, poignant, and rich sources of life and death buried in our hearts and communities. We touched, actually touched, that Force that works through all things—even as in every good religious service or solemn public commemoration, the beauty and majesty of the celebration teases us open, and we touch the Power of the universe at work among us again. The pageant, the dance, the ritual, the candles and lights, the bells and gongs, the flowers, the song— the beauty and anguish of religious ceremony allow us to actually know what life at its depths is about. Once tapping this source, once learning its taste, we can return to it whenever we choose. We can live our lives out of life's own depth. We can transform our way of life.

TOWARD A GLOBAL COMMUNITY

It is so important for us to recognize the creative Energy of the Universe that surges beneath the crust of everyday living. For we, our society, our world, all of us, we are at a breaking point. We have stumbled across a crack in the cosmic egg. Our world is shattering; the old ways do not work anymore.

The strategies we employed to hold our world together are outdated. Our very religions, for example, need to be overhauled. They do not address contemporary questions. On many fronts—sexuality is only the most obvious—our religions are out of touch. Likewise, our now standard political practices—government by and for the moneyed, systematic obfuscation of the issues, manipulation of public opinion, legalized subversion of democratic process, reliance on wealth and weaponry, stubborn insistence on having it our way, disregard for other peoples and their cultures and traditions: all obvious in the current crisis and "War Against Terrorism"—cannot sustain a new world order, let alone preserve democracy in our own country.

We have entered a new millennium. We are structuring a new world. For the first time in human history, we are verily engaged in forming a global community, and we cannot avoid doing so. No one religion, no single form of government, and, of course, no military power will ever be able to unite the human race. As Pope Paul VI succinctly phrased the matter in his address to the United Nations, "If you want peace, work for justice."

Only that which respects every human being can unite the human family. Only that which is common to all humanity can be the basis for human solidarity. Only tapping the spiritual potential that lies in the human heart will allow all humans to see themselves in all others. Only living more regularly in the spiritual moment will allow us to achieve the solidarity that our commemorations proclaim and that the human race needs.

To the extent that particular religions or governments are genuine and valid, they will support this view. To the extent that they do not support this view, they cannot be genuine, they are not worthy of humanity, they do not express the "ways of God," and they are not "under God." Nothing can be of God that is oblivious to the spiritual reality in each of our hearts, about which I am speaking.

RESURGENCE OF THE SPIRITUAL

Our hearts are broken and our spirits heavy as we face a fragmented world and long for solidarity. Our aching need is to find a place of peace where our souls can be refreshed. Our need is to find life so rich that we spontaneously overflow in generosity to all others. Our need is to experience our very selves as so rich that we feel no need to protect ourselves against feared losses and no need to lash out in defensiveness against others.

In quiet moments and in sacred places, we touch the eternal—as we may often do in our daily living and loving. We access the spiritual core from which all fullness flows. Through beauty and quiet and human fellowship, boundaries fall away, and we know ourselves to be one. Let us cherish this sacred solidarity and commit ourselves to it worldwide.

Appendix

A Statement of Spirituality

Through the ages, concern with religion, spirituality, and the meaning of life has fascinated people who today would be called gay or recognized as homosexual. Highly revered in many cultures, they were among the originators of myth and religion. Their outsider's perspective naturally gave them valuable insight. Today, though outcasts of religion, homosexual people could not but continue to nurture their spiritual sensitivity. Forced to break new ground on their own in a world of change and diversity, they have struggled to discern the true meaning of spirituality.

Accordingly, on May 1, 2004, at Garrison Institute in Garrison, NY, USA, a small work group of participants in the first Gay Spirituality Summit (see www.gayspiritculture.org) prepared this Statement of Spirituality. Revised to address the input of many, it is offered for discussion to help clarify the nature of spirituality in the gay community and beyond.

Spirituality is the outworking of the human capacity for self-transcendence, variously called consciousness, Buddha Nature, atman, true soul, higher self, or human spirit. Spirituality shows itself in increasingly aware and deliberately chosen participation in the positive unfolding of the universe. Beliefs and behaviors that are hurtful and destructive shut down this unfolding; those that are helpful and upbuilding further it.

Apart from any otherworldly implications that it might have, spirituality pertains to life on this Earth, and the measure of spirituality is compassion, love, truth, gratitude, growth, and goodwilled give-and-take among human beings. In the final analysis, spirituality is as spirituality does.

Spirituality has no truck with the hateful, destructive, intolerant, and divisive. Nonetheless, loving attention to negative tendencies, forces, occurrences, and persons fosters the personal and collective healing and integration that allow the human spirit to flow freely and to bring something positive from the negative.

The forces that govern spirituality, however they are conceived, are built into and work through the human spirit. Ongoing cultivation of the spirit—in communion with fellow seekers and through spiritual practice, psychological healing, bodywork, virtuous living, and ecological concern—brings on expanded awareness that flows into genuine harmony with all people, all living creatures, all inanimate things, and all life forces, for spirituality is ultimately concerned with the unity of all things. Profound sensitivity to this awareness and harmony makes for what the religions have called mindfulness, enlightenment, holiness, mysticism, soulful living, expanded consciousness.

Although they are not identical, spirituality is certainly related to religion. Religion is at the service of spirituality. The role of religion is to express and foster spirituality, and it does so in a rainbow of cultural variations. These might include belief in God (by whatever name or conception), revelations, doctrines, religious myths, sacred texts, rituals, prayers, meditations, trances, and ideas about afterlife, former lives, and metaphysical entities. All these religious matters have legitimacy insofar as they support spiritual sensitivity, elicit transcendental awareness, and, thus, contribute to the positive unfolding of the universe.

"My religion is kindness," says the current Dalai Lama. And Jesus said, "By their fruits you will know them." Therein lies wisdom about true spirituality.

Thus, loving kindness is the measure of goodness or sanctity or holiness or spirituality. The rules of ancient societies or the trends of public opinion do not determine the moral worth of homosexuality or of anything else. In the final analysis, what matters is the loving kindness that real, live people—homosexual or otherwise—show to one another and to their neighbors, the positive contributions that people make to one another and to their societies. Such is the spiritual path.

Original committee:
Cami Delgado
Kip Dollar
Daniel Helminiak
Toby Johnson

Index

Order a copy of this book with this form or online at:
http://www.haworthpress.com/store/product.asp?sku=5480

SEX AND THE SACRED
Gay Identity and Spiritual Growth

_____ in hardbound at $39.95 (ISBN-13: 978-1-56023-341-1; ISBN-10: 1-56023-341-9)

_____ in softbound at $16.95 (ISBN-13: 978-1-56023-342-8; ISBN-10: 1-56023-342-7)

Or order online and use special offer code HEC25 in the shopping cart.

COST OF BOOKS_____

POSTAGE & HANDLING_____
(US: $4.00 for first book & $1.50
for each additional book)
(Outside US: $5.00 for first book
& $2.00 for each additional book)

SUBTOTAL_____

IN CANADA: ADD 7% GST_____

STATE TAX_____
(NJ, NY, OH, MN, CA, IL, IN, PA, & SD
residents, add appropriate local sales tax)

FINAL TOTAL_____
(If paying in Canadian funds,
convert using the current
exchange rate, UNESCO
coupons welcome)

☐ BILL ME LATER: (Bill-me option is good on
US/Canada/Mexico orders only; not good to
jobbers, wholesalers, or subscription agencies.)

☐ Check here if billing address is different from
shipping address and attach purchase order and
billing address information.

Signature_____

☐ PAYMENT ENCLOSED: $_____

☐ PLEASE CHARGE TO MY CREDIT CARD.

☐ Visa ☐ MasterCard ☐ AmEx ☐ Discover
☐ Diner's Club ☐ Eurocard ☐ JCB

Account # _____

Exp. Date_____

Signature_____

Prices in US dollars and subject to change without notice.

NAME_____

INSTITUTION_____

ADDRESS_____

CITY_____

STATE/ZIP_____

COUNTRY_____ COUNTY (NY residents only)_____

TEL_____ FAX_____

E-MAIL_____

May we use your e-mail address for confirmations and other types of information? ☐ Yes ☐ No
We appreciate receiving your e-mail address and fax number. Haworth would like to e-mail or fax special
discount offers to you, as a preferred customer. **We will never share, rent, or exchange your e-mail address
or fax number.** We regard such actions as an invasion of your privacy.

Order From Your Local Bookstore or Directly From

The Haworth Press, Inc.

10 Alice Street, Binghamton, New York 13904-1580 • USA
TELEPHONE: 1-800-HAWORTH (1-800-429-6784) / Outside US/Canada: (607) 722-5857
FAX: 1-800-895-0582 / Outside US/Canada: (607) 771-0012
E-mail to: orders@haworthpress.com

For orders outside US and Canada, you may wish to order through your local
sales representative, distributor, or bookseller.
For information, see http://haworthpress.com/distributors

(Discounts are available for individual orders in US and Canada only, not booksellers/distributors.)

PLEASE PHOTOCOPY THIS FORM FOR YOUR PERSONAL USE.
http://www.HaworthPress.com

BOF06